Population and Political Systems
in Tropical Africa

ROBERT F. STEVENSON

Population and Political Systems
in Tropical Africa

COLUMBIA UNIVERSITY PRESS
New York and London 1968

To Sally

PREFACE

THIS IS A STUDY of the relationship between population distribution and the evolution of the indigenous (precolonial) states of tropical Africa. Its aim is to demonstrate for Africa, as has already been abundantly demonstrated for other continents, that the complexity of the political institutions and the density of the population are related in a positive manner —that is, states are generally denser than nonstates. As such, this study is a response to the section in *African Political Systems* (Fortes and Evans-Pritchard, eds.) wherein the existence of such a relationship is specifically denied in conjunction with a series of empirical cases suggesting, if anything, that chiefless societies may be denser by far than primitive states. The *African Political Systems* formulation is not only very interesting, but it is to this date the single most authoritative statement of the matter to come out of anthropological field research in Africa. I have accordingly paid considerable attention to its analysis and criticism and have devoted a chapter each to the restudy of five of the six classic cases—Zulu, Ngwato, Bemba, Tallensi, and Bantu Kavirondo. Here I have been critical of the rigid synchronic functionalism of classic British Social Anthropology and have endeavored to add the diachronic dimension by recourse to the historical materials available. I have then proceeded to a more general survey of the problem based upon the work of the population geographers. Finally, I have used culture-historical materials for a reinterpretation of Ibo political organization, an important case in this debate. Thus, although this book is written from the standpoint of anthropology and primarily for anthropologists, it is my hope that there is within it also much that would interest geographers, historians, political scientists, and sociologists as well.

The basic research upon which the book is based was nearly all carried out between the early summer of 1963 and the early spring of 1965. This period saw united an interest in the evolution of state systems which derived from two of the earliest and most durable of influences upon my thinking, the teaching and writings of Julian Steward and the writings of V. Gordon Childe, and an interest in African studies more recently kindled by Elliott Skinner. My theoretical debt to Morton Fried is considerable, as the reading of the pages which follow should abundantly attest. Marvin Harris did much both to sharpen my theoretical insights and to encourage me to commence and continue with this work as a doctoral thesis in anthropology at Columbia University. As thesis chairman, Professor Harris was throughout a most sympathetic supporter and uncompromising critic of this work. To him, as well as to Elliott Skinner, I am deeply grateful for the many fruitful suggestions and constant trenchant criticisms that saved me from many a pitfall. If, despite all, I have slipped here and there, it is not because their guard was down. I feel a similar gratitude toward other members of the Columbia family. Robert Murphy, Andrew P. Vayda, Alexander Alland, Abraham Rosman, Sol Miller, and George Morren and the members of Professor Skinner's seminar on political systems were all most helpful with criticisms and suggestions. The award of a Richard Watson Gilder Fellowship for 1963–1964 made possible a year of uninterrupted research and writing. I am also more indebted than can ever be expressed here to the pioneering work of Professors Fortes and Evans-Pritchard and to Max Gluckman and the other authors of *African Political Systems*.

Finally, I should like to thank collectively all the many

whose contributions helped produce this book and individually express thanks to the following: Gus W. Grammas for statistical advice and assistance, Dr. William Warntz for advice on demographic problems, and to Mrs. Jessie Malinowska and Frederick Skinner who typed the manuscript. My wife Sally was not only patient and understanding through it all but helped immeasurably with typing, editing, and proofreading.

R.F.S.

September 1967

ACKNOWLEDGMENTS

ACKNOWLEDGMENTS are due to the following for permission to quote copyrighted material:

Aldine Publishing Company for material from *Horizons in Anthropology*, Sol. Tax, ed.; Edward Arnold Publishers Ltd. for material from *The Great Plateau of Northern Rhodesia* by C. Gouldsbury and H. Sheane; The Association of American Geographers for material from "Population Patterns in Tropical Africa" and "The Population Geography of Belgian Africa" by G. Trewartha and W. Zelinsky, reproduced from the *Annals* of the Association of American Geographers, 1954, vol. 44, by permission; Cambridge University Press for material and map from "Kazembe and the Portuguese" by Ian Cunnison, published in the *Journal of African History*, and for material from *The British Settlement of Natal* by A. Hattersley; The Clarendon Press, Oxford, for material from *Trade and Politics in the Niger Delta* by K. O. Dike, *The Tribes of the Ashanti Hinterland*, vol. 2, by R. S. Rattray, and *History of East Africa*, vol. 1, by R. Oliver and G. Mathew; Columbia University Press for material from "On the Evolution of Social Stratification and the State" by Morton Fried, published in *Culture in History: Essays in Honor of Paul Radin*, S. Diamond, ed.; Harvard University Press for material from *Portuguese Africa* by J. Duffy; W. Heffer for material from *Economic Development and Tribal Change—A Study of Immigrant Labour in Buganda* by Audrey Richards, for The East African Institute of Social Research; the Editor of the *Journal* of the Historical Society of Nigeria and the author for material from "The Present State of Ibo Studies" by S. Ottenberg; the Institute for Social Research, University of Zambia, and the authors for material from "Aspects of Bemba Chieftainship" *Rhodes-Livingstone Communications No. 2* by W. Brelsford and "Studies in African Land Usage in Northern Rhodesia," *Rhodes-Livingstone Papers No. 15* by W. Allen; International African Institute and the authors for material from *African Political Systems,* M. Fortes and E. E. Evans-Pritchard, eds., *The Tswana* by I. Schapera and *The Western Lacustrine Bantu* by B. Taylor; Longmans Green for material and map from *Olden Times in Zululand and Natal* by A. T. Bryant; Longmans, Green and John Wiley for material from *West Africa: A Study of the Environment and Man's Use of It* by R. J. Harrison Church; Manchester University Press for material from "Analysis of a Social Situation in Modern Zululand," *Rhodes-Livingstone Papers No. 28* by M. Gluckman; McGraw-Hill Book Company for material from *The Elements of Geography* by V. Finch, G. Trewartha, et al., and *Africa: Its People and Their Culture* by G. P. Murdock; Oxford University Press, Capetown, for material from *Politics in a Changing Society: A Political History of the Fort Jameson Ngoni* by J. A. Barnes and *The Bechuanaland Protectorate* by A. Sillery; Oxford University Press, London, for material from *The Web of Kinship among the Tallensi* by M. Fortes, *The Dynamics of Clanship among the Tallensi* by M. Fortes, *The Trading States of the Oil Rivers* by G. I. Jones, *An African Aristocracy: Rank among the Swazi* by Hilda Kuper, *Land, Labour and Diet in Northern Rhodesia* by A. Richards, *The Historian in Tropical Africa* by J. Vansina, R. Maury, and L. V. Thomas, and material and map from *The Bantu of North Kavirondo,* vols. 1 and 2, by Gunter Wagner; Penguin Books Ltd. for material from *A Short History of Africa* by R. Oliver and J. D. Fage; Frederick Praeger for material from *A Handbook of African Affairs,* The African-American Institute, Helen Kitchen, ed.; Random House for material from *A History of Africa South of the Sahara* by Donald Wiedner; Routledge and Kegan Paul for material from *Natives of the Northern Territories of the Gold Coast* by A. W. Cardinall; Routledge and Kegan Paul and Humanities Press for material from *Tribes without Rulers,* by J. Middleton and D. Tait; the Royal Geographical Society for material from "A Population Distribution Map of the Eastern Region of Nigeria" by J. H. Jennings, published in the *Geographical Journal* 23; I. Schapera for material from his *Native Land Tenure in the Bechuanaland Protectorate;* Shuter and Shooter Ltd. and the author for material from *The Social System of the Zulus* by E. J. Krige; Sidgwick and Jackson Ltd. for material from *Ibo Village Affairs* by M. Green; the Editors of the *Southwestern Journal of Anthropology* and the author for material from "Ecology of Central Asian Pastorialism" by L. Krader; the Editors of the *Southwestern Journal of Anthropology* and the author for material and map from "Ibo Oracles and Intergroup Relations" by S. Ottenberg; Twentieth Century Fund for material from *Tropical Africa,* vol. 1, by G. H. T. Kimble; University of Chicago Press for material from *Continuity and Change in African Cultures,* W. R. Bascom and M. J. Herskovits, eds.; and University of London Press for material from *The Republic of Sudan* by K. M. Barbour.

CONTENTS

I. Introduction 1

II. Functionalist Demography 10

III. Low-Density States I: The Zulu 27

IV. Low-Density States II: The Ngwato 53

V. Low-Density States III: The Bemba 88

VI. The Classical Segmentary Societies I: The
Nuer and the Tallensi 115

VII. The Classical Segmentary Societies II: The
Logoli 132

VIII. State Formation and the Population Pattern 160

IX. High Density and State Formation in Southeastern
Nigeria: The Ibo Problem 188

X. Conclusion 228

Notes 233

Bibliography 263

Index 294

CHAPTER I. Introduction

A CONSIDERABLE number of New World anthropologists have for some time noted a positive correlation between societies of higher population density and the presence of state organization. An exhaustive list would be tedious, but a partial sampling would include such names as Armillas, Carniero, Harris, Kroeber, Millon, Palerm, Sanders, Steward, White, and Wolfe. Though the theoretical interpretations often differ, the empirical conjunction has been noted in terms that are clear and explicit. These and others have, in their work, attested equally to the opposite proposition—that the lowest human population densities are found in societies at the lowest levels of socio-cultural integration (Steward 1955; Service 1962) — the band. I am not aware of any explicit attacks on these formulations in the American literature.[1]

One would further expect, when due allowance is made for special and disturbing factors, that a systematic survey, ranging societies according to Service's (1962) Levels of Socio-cultural Integration (band, tribe, chiefdom, state) would also yield a corresponding order of population densities.[2] This indeed is the result strikingly indicated by a survey of aboriginal South America in Steward and Faron's recent standard text. To quote their conclusions:

In comparative terms, the density of the Central Andes was about two hundred times that of the guanaco hunters, forty times that of the archipelagic shellfish gatherers, about twenty times that of the tropical forest farmers, and half again that of the Araucanians of

Chile and of the Circum-Caribbean chiefdoms. . . . The aboriginal population of continental South America is estimated to have been over 10 million, of which *more than one-third was in the Central Andes.* (1959:54, my italics) [3]

Driver's conclusions for aboriginal North America are markedly similar:

The size of the political unit is also correlated with population density (Map 6) although this relationship, too, is far from perfect. It was in Meso-America, with more people than in all the other culture areas combined, that the largest states developed. In the areas of sparsest population, the Arctic, Sub-Arctic, Great Basin, and Northeast Mexico, political integration was either absent or at the minimum. (1961:351) [4]

In Britain the work of the late V. Gordon Childe has been notable in lending support to the aforementioned generalizations. His summaries, contained in *Man Makes Himself* (1936) and *What Happened in History* (1942), present a dramatic panorama of sudden population advances following major technological revolutions. It should be noted that the "Urban Revolution," which is coincident with the second major population advance in human history, contains among its manifestations the first emergence of the state. Childe's surveys cover such broad areas of the Old World as Europe, Egypt, the Near East, India, and China,[5] in a time span extending from the Paleolithic through Roman imperial times.

As for modern tropical Asia, including China, India, the Tonking Delta,[6] northern Annam, and Indonesia, the French geographer Pierre Gourou sums up the matter thus:

the human peculiarity of hot, wet Asia lies in its densely peopled areas. The superabundant population in these is associated with good soil, advanced social and political organization, intensive rice cultivation, and sound agricultural methods; in a word with an advanced state of civilization. (1961:106) [7]

The correlation between higher density and state would seem then to have considerable empirical support—support which is

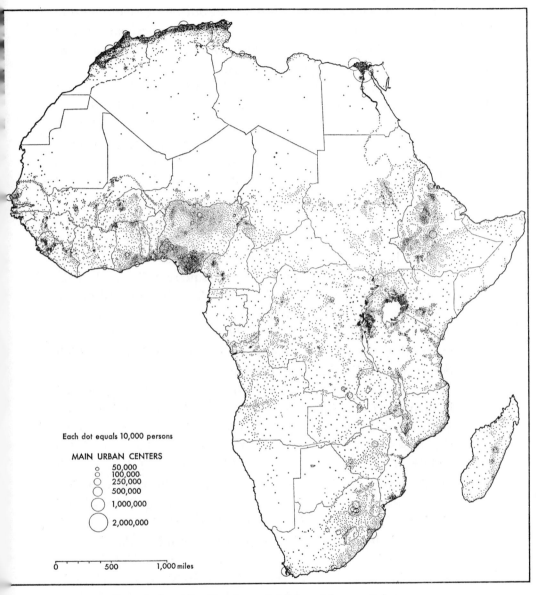

MAP I. Population distribution of Africa (circa 1960)
Courtesy University of Stellenbosch

Each dot equals 10,000 persons

MAIN URBAN CENTERS

50,000
100,000
250,000
500,000
1,000,000
2,000,000

0   500   1,000 miles

not only global in geographical spread but impressive in chronological span, and, support of such an order of acceptance as to have brought it from the preserve of the specialized account into the standard regional overviews.

In startling contrast to the foregoing, then, are the assertions of two of the leading spokesmen of British Social Anthropology. I am referring to the statements by Meyer Fortes and E. E. Evans-Pritchard contained in Section VI of the Introduction to *African Political Systems*. (Fortes 1940:7–8) Here, on the basis of six out of the eight societies studied in the book, we are told that "it would be incorrect to suppose that governmental institutions are found in those societies with greatest densities. The opposite seems to be equally likely judging by our material." This is buttressed by three states whose densities all cluster around the low figure of three per square mile, and three acephalous, segmentary societies whose densities range from 7 to 391 per square mile. In addition we are told that, "evidence from other African societies *could be* cited" (my italics) to prove that there is no necessary connection between high political centralization and high density.

One might have expected a major controversy to have ensued in the professional journals. Such was not the case. This was not (entirely at least) from lack of interest in demographic relationships to culture. Although the sources I have cited are mainly of more recent vintage, Childe's *Man Makes Himself* (1936) was in its third impression by 1939, the same year that marked the appearance of Kroeber's pioneering *Cultural and Natural Areas of Native North America*.[8] Steward (1936, 1937) had already published articles indicating similar interests and viewpoint. Nonetheless, reviewers of *African Political Systems* either passed over Section VI entirely or, like Hambly (1940:797), observed without further comment that it dealt with the influence of demography upon political structure. Herskovits only went so far as to assert that: "The relationship between the size and density of a given population and its political system, and the influence of the prevalent economic system on the type of political structure are analyzed in the light of data from these various tribes." (1941:466) Not an eyebrow was raised, no criticisms directed at the assertions made nor at the incongruity of the conclusions reached.

What is most sobering, however, is that these assertions have stood virtually unchallenged for nearly twenty-five years.[9] Eisenstadt's has been a lonely voice crying for the needed reappraisal.[10] In discussing density and political organization among the pastoralists of Inner Asia, Krader has noted:

Fortes and Evans-Pritchard have propounded a relation between political centralization and population size, but they have divorced political centralization from conceptions of density. While such is the case in the African societies they discuss, among the steppe pastoralists of Asia there is a three fold relation between complexity of political organization (upon which centralization is predicated there), population size and density. (1955:323)

Krader's acceptance of the evidence in *African Political Systems* is carefully qualified and limited to the actual six cases. Nonetheless, his statement dramatically indicates both the weight and extent of influence of the British school's position. Krader may or may not be obliquely implying that a wider sample might show different results. He at no point challenges the evidence itself or questions its value, and Africa is left as the upside-down continent.[11]

In the Introduction to the recent *Cultures and Societies of Africa*, the Ottenbergs have observed that African states "in most cases have a fairly high population density for Africa"— this without criticism of views in *African Political Systems*.[12] (1960:53) Most recently, Doctorow (1963:314) in explicit reference to Section VI has noted, again without further comment, that density is "specifically excluded from consideration." Yet it is precisely population density that Bartholomew and

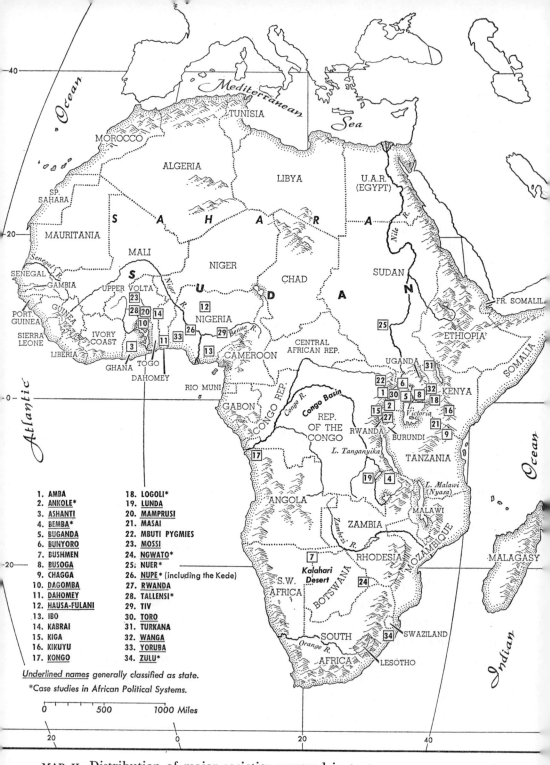

MAP II. Distribution of major societies surveyed in text

1. AMBA
2. ANKOLE*
3. ASHANTI
4. BEMBA*
5. BUGANDA
6. BUNYORO
7. BUSHMEN
8. BUSOGA
9. CHAGGA
10. DAGOMBA
11. DAHOMEY
12. HAUSA-FULANI
13. IBO
14. KABRAI
15. KIGA
16. KIKUYU
17. KONGO
18. LOGOLI*
19. LUNDA
20. MAMPRUSI
21. MASAI
22. MBUTI PYGMIES
23. MOSSI
24. NGWATO*
25. NUER*
26. NUPE* (including the Kede)
27. RWANDA
28. TALLENSI*
29. TIV
30. TORO
31. TURKANA
32. WANGA
33. YORUBA
34. ZULU*

Underlined names generally classified as state.

*Case studies in African Political Systems.

0   500   1000 Miles

Birdsell (1954:486, 488) have termed the "most critical single ecological datum."

As this last remark would indicate, this is by no means a minor problem area for a young science interested in developing valid generalizations. In fact, it is precisely at this crucial juncture—state formation and population density—that the principles of biological evolution and those of socio-cultural evolution intersect in an important manner and, contingent upon the *continued* validation of a positive correlation between state and higher population density, the state can be demonstrated to be an adaptive institution.[13] Despite its importance to theory this major lacuna has been left open almost as if modern anthropology were in the grips of a Navaho-like "fear of closure," [14] with the result that we are left with generalizations that are valid everywhere but in Africa. Is it possible that the general principles of socio-cultural evolution do not apply south of the Sahara?

The aim of this study, then, is to resolve the apparent contradiction by showing that the African data are compatible with the major generalizations already convincingly demonstrated for other ethnographic areas. In explicit terms, then, my thesis is:

The African data also demonstrate that population densities are generally higher at state than at nonstate levels.

This demonstration is to be achieved in the following stages:

(1) A detailed analysis and critique of the statements, sample, and individual cases adduced by Fortes and Evans-Pritchard. This will include a short preliminary chapter analyzing the structure and content of their argument as a whole and the nature and representativeness of the evidence. Since the evidence they actually present (as contrasted to the evidence they only imply) consists of a trio of low-density states paired against a trio of high-density acephalous societies, it will be convenient

to devote one chapter of detailed analysis to each case, with the exception of the Nuer (included in Chapter VI with the Tallensi).

(2) A general survey of the African data utilizing the demographic summaries and regional studies of the population geographers, which will indicate on a broad regional basis that the generalization is confirmed. Exceptions will be analyzed as encountered, but one complex exception of major significance will be held over for more detailed treatment in a separate chapter. This is the southeastern Nigerian region.

(3) An intensive analysis of this major exception. It involves a major subregion where some of the highest rural population densities in all sub-Saharan Africa have been reported—densities which in places approach those of Ruanda. At the same time, the societies (Ibo, Ibibio, Yakö) are conventionally classified as segmentary or as "acephalous, autonomous villages." (Eisenstadt 1950:209) This is probably a much better case for the Fortes and Evans-Pritchard position than any they themselves actually presented. For, under the stimulus of a considerable trade in palm oil, impressive densities had been induced in the palm-producing regions quite in advance of colonial penetration. As was to be expected, political development was also stimulated. Where political organization was most widespread geographically, extending intermittently even beyond the boundaries of the region itself, it tended to be restricted in scope to control of the vital markets and trade routes. These political developments as well as the volume of the trade have both been de-emphasized in the standard ethnographic accounts.[15] At the same time, the very nature of the trade itself tended to inhibit the development of more comprehensive political units. This will be dealt with in detail in a separate chapter—the last before the conclusion.

Finally, I should like to say a word about my overall approach. I am interested in the establishment of generalizations in anthropology and the discovery of regularities. My specific aim here is resolving, or helping to resolve, one particular problem. I am convinced, however, that any attempt to demonstrate the validity of the high density-state relationship for Africa without directly confronting *African Political Systems* would be inevitably suspect. This, of course, will necessarily involve certain criticisms of the methods employed by Fortes, Evans-Pritchard, and other representatives of the British School of Social Anthropology.

The positive material contained in the survey chapter and on Ibo should absolve me of charges of mere partisan infighting, though I feel that there is much of positive value that comes out of the more critical chapters as well. Of course, this survey chapter in itself is not completely separate from countering the position of *African Political Systems*. In a real sense it may be taken as a countermove to Fortes' and Evans-Pritchard's concluding remarks: that data from other African societies could be cited which would equally prove their case. This claim, it is to be noted, is neither supported by evidence nor backed by actual citation. Nonetheless, it must be convincingly countered if the attempt here is to carry weight. The logic of the approach will be more fully explained in that section.

It has been duly noted that there is impressive empirical evidence from other continental areas of a positive relationship between high population density and state formation.[16] I propose to demonstrate that the African data when meaningfully analyzed also supports rather than contradicts this relationship.[17]

CHAPTER II. Functionalist Demography

SECTION VI of the introduction to *African Political Systems* consists of two paragraphs jointly entitled "The Influence of Demography."

The first of these paragraphs deals with the relationship between the size of population in terms of total numbers and the presence or absence of centralized rule. This passage is not clearly formulated and it is difficult to determine whether the size of population in a single political unit, the size of population in "a society," or both is the intended empirical referent. The initial statement is clear enough but is almost a truism: "It is noteworthy that the political unit in the societies with a state organization is numerically larger than in those without a state organization." (Fortes 1940:7) Tallensi, Nuer, Zulu (c. 1870), Ngwato, and Bemba are cited as demonstrating this relationship. The authors then note that stateless political units "need not be very small" and conclude that "it is probably true that there is a limit to the size of a population that can hold together without some kind of centralized government." This last proposition has recently been dissected by Doctorow. (1963:314) Doctorow has observed the lack of clarity in "holding together" and has analyzed the statement in terms of three possible meanings of the phrase—(1) geographical contiguity, (2) "a society forming a single whole," and (3) political centralization (which logically is the same thing as talking about the size of population of a single political unit). Doctorow sees that the Dinka and Masai both contradict the

formulation if the first meaning is inferred, that the Dinka
again contradict it if the second meaning is taken, and that the
third meaning converts the entire proposition to a "trivial
statement if not a tautology." Doctorow's attack has the merits
of demolishing what could have been taken as a rather vague
and almost mystical causal hypothesis concerning the process of
state formation.

However, in another sense the attack is unfortunate for,
intuitively at least, Fortes and Evans-Pritchard seem to have
been on the track of an important relationship. That is, granting the rather vague definitions of "a society" or "a culture"
still currently in use, and using as units only those units usually
called "a society" or "a culture" by anthropologists who have
studied them, the total populations in state societies in Africa
would seem to be generally, though not invariably, larger than
the total populations of acephalous societies.[1] We have already
quoted Krader (1955:323) as having noted a threefold relation
between complexity of political organization, population size,
and density among Central Asian Pastoralists. As we shall see,
this same threefold relationship would seem to hold for Africa
as well.

It is the second paragraph in the same section that forms the
major focus of my argument, and it had best be quoted in
full:

Size of population should not be confused with density of population. There may be some relation between the degree of political
development and the size of population, but it would be incorrect
to suppose that governmental institutions are found in those
societies with greatest density. The opposite seems to be equally
likely, judging by our material. The density of the Zulu is 3.5, of
the Ngwato 2.5, of the Bemba 3.75 per square mile, while that of
the Nuer is higher and of the Tallensi and Logoli very much
higher. It might be supposed that the dense permanent settlements
of the Tallensi would necessarily lead to the development of a centralized form of government, whereas the wide dispersion of shifting

villages among the Bemba would be incompatible with centralized rule. The reverse is actually the case. In addition to the material collected in this book, evidence from other African societies could be cited to prove that a large population in a political unit and a high degree of political centralization do not necessarily go together with great density. (Fortes 1940:7–8)

The first point to be noted is that, although the phrase "state organization" began the entire section on demography, neither this phrase nor the word "state" appears in the paragraph on density. It seems reasonable to suppose that this is still what they are talking about and that for stylistic reasons they have substituted such expressions as "governmental institution," "centralized form of government," "centralized rule," and "high degree of political centralization." Nonetheless, as this point is really crucial to the entire discussion, it becomes here absolutely necessary to determine if a state is indeed what they are talking about. An important clue is provided by the antithesis drawn between Zulu, Ngwato, and Bemba on the one hand as against Nuer, Tallensi, and Logoli on the other. This corresponds exactly with the dichotomy between societies of Group A and Group B drawn in Section IV of the same Introduction under the heading "The Two Types of Political Systems Studied." Here both the classification and the grounds of classification are made clear:

One group, which we refer to as Group A, consists of those societies which have centralized authority, administrative machinery, and judicial institutions—in short, a government—and in which cleavages of wealth, privilege, and status correspond to the distribution of power and authority. This group comprises the Zulu, the Ngwato, the Bemba, the Banyankole, and the Kede. The other group, which we refer to as Group B, consists of those societies which lack centralized authority, administrative machinery, and constituted judicial institutions—in short which lack government —and in which there are no sharp divisions of rank, status, or wealth. This group comprises the Logoli, the Tallensi, and the Nuer. Those who consider that a state should be defined by the presence of governmental institutions will regard the first group as primitive states and the second group as stateless societies. (Fortes 1940:5)

It is noteworthy that the criteria for classification here employed include such socio-economic indicators as "cleavages" or "sharp divisions" of wealth, privilege, and status, which are generally grouped together under the term "social stratification." This is a crucial point. By including cleavages such as these, their definition for a state is brought reasonably close to that of Nadel (1951:188 fn) who lists as his third essential aspect, "a specialized privileged ruling group or class, separated in training, status, and recruitment from the body of the population" and Fried (1960:728–29) who sees the state as emerging only in stratified societies which are qualitatively distinct from ranking societies.

Unfortunately, neither the editors nor the other contributors to the volume always adhere to this full formulation, and in practice range from a certain hesitation and ambivalence to a near exclusion of the vital socio-economic criteria in favor of the purely formal "political centralization." This often leads to a confusion of chiefdoms (Fried's ranking society) with states— a distinction which, I would argue, should be carefully maintained, not blurred. Thus I would reserve the application of the term state to stratified societies only. Fried has offered a set of criteria for identifying states which, because it is cast in terms of primary and secondary functions, enables the investigator to penetrate the diversity of concrete institutional forms. Consequently, when I use the term state it is not in the same largely formal sense as that of the dichotomy of *African Political Systems* but rather in the terms of Fried's criteria. A full exposition of Fried's model can best be developed in conjunction with an application to a specific case. Therefore, I will reserve detailed discussion of these criteria to Chapter IV (pp. 80–82),[2] where they are applied to the Ngwato. Finally, Fortes and Evans-Pritchard seem somewhat reluctant to use the term "state." Nonetheless, in the passage quoted they are clearly proclaiming that when they use the phrase "presence of governmental institutions" or "centralized form of government" they intend to be talking about the same thing as those others who prefer to use the somewhat simpler and more straightforward term "state." Further, it is precisely in terms of "state vs. stateless" that the Group A–Group B dichotomy has been incorporated in the literature. It should be clear, then, that when they deny a correlation between high density and governmental institutions or between high density and political centralization, they are in actuality denying the important correlation between high density and state. This is the crux of the debate.

With this all-important point established—even at the risk of unduly belaboring it—we may proceed with an analysis of their arguments on density. Let us turn, then, to a closer scrutiny of the focal paragraph quoted at the beginning of this chapter (pp. 11–12). In the first place, the middle section of the paragraph is a rather special variant of the density argument which involves the dense permanent settlements of the Tallensi versus the dispersed shifting villages of the Bemba. Treatment of this is best reserved until we have had a chance to examine concretely each of these societies. This also simplifies matters here by leaving the argument in its most general form. Logically, the argument is reducible to the following alternative sets of propositions:

I. States are correlated with high population densities; stateless societies with low population densities.
II. States are correlated with low population densities; stateless societies with high population densities.

The paragraph begins by denying that (I) is true and asserts that (II) "seems to be equally likely." Six cases are brought forward, all of which empirically attest to the truth of (II).

Now, since all of the evidence actually brought forth supports
(II) and (II) alone, one might be led to suppose that this is the
position the editors are actually asserting. Our analysis shows
that this is not really the case. Their contention is that proposition sets (I) and (II) are both equally likely. Nonetheless, the
validity of (I) as a generalization is just as seriously challenged.
This point must be both clarified and underscored. The appearance of the word "necessarily" in the last line of the
paragraph might make it appear that all that they are arguing is
that there is no inevitable, necessary, or direct relationship
between state organization and population density. The concept of necessity, however, is only expressed in the terminal
sentence of the paragraph and there in terms of a rather more
complex relationship between (1) size of population in a single
political unit, (2) a high degree of centralization, and (3)
population density. I shall analyze this statement presently, but
in terms of what Fortes and Evans-Pritchard are actually saying,
it must be maintained that what is at stake is not merely the
question of an invariant relationship but their denial that any
relationship exists at all. Thus, ". . . it would be incorrect to
suppose the governmental institutions are found in those societies with greatest density. The opposite seems to be equally
likely, judging by our material." (Fortes 1940:7) [3] A statement
like this can have only one meaning—the matter is declared to
be completely indeterminate. It is precisely in this sense that
Doctorow (1963:314) and Krader (1955:323) have taken it.
Furthermore, the claim is made in the same Introduction that
these cases are typical of a large number of others and that
". . . the eight societies described will not only give the stu-
dent a bird's-eye view of the basic principles of African political
organization, but will also enable him to draw a few, perhaps
elementary, conclusions of a general and theoretical kind."
(Fortes 1940:4) Here a statement is not only being made about
six individual cases but about tropical Africa in general.

Finally, the last sentence of this paragraph merits special consideration: "In addition to the material collected in this book, evidence from other African societies could be cited to prove that a large population in a political unit and a high degree of political centralization do not *necessarily* go together with great density." (Fortes 1940:8, italics mine) In the first place, no cases are cited or even mentioned in support of this claim. As such, it is a statement of confidence but not a demonstration. In the second place, at this point the editors are clearly talking about invariant relationships, but the context has been extended from one concerning population density and state formation to that of a threefold relationship between

(1) A large population in a single political unit.
(2) A high degree of political centralization.
(3) Great density.

Now, I would contend that (1) and (2) together generally involve (3). Furthermore, (1) and (3) together would by definition entail political centralization, although the degree of political centralization could be considered problematical. Certainly these conditions would tend to *favor* high political centralization though not necessarily entail it. But (2) and (3) taken together would not necessarily entail (1) except in a very relative sense. The empirical example of this would be a rather small though highly dense state such as a city-state.

If each of these three components be taken separately, the degree to which they might be said to imply the other two is less clear. For instance, (1) would necessarily and by definition entail political centralization, though not necessarily a "high degree" of political centralization. Here it is important to distinguish between purely formal centralization (for example, monocephaly) and actual de facto centralization along a continuum ranging from acephalous societies to totalitarian models.[4] Furthermore, the level of development of communications and transportation technology, as well as environment (rivers, swamps, mountain barriers, and others), intersect in a complex fashion and importantly condition the capacity of the state to extend a truly centralized control over a large population. Given equally effective communications and transport in terms of both technological and environmental factors, it would seem that the more highly centralized states would also be densely populated. Certainly, nucleation at both district and national administrative centers is implied. The foregoing analysis would also indicate that (2) would necessarily imply either (1) or (3) and usually both. The truly problematical relationship and the one which is questioned by evidence from Ifugao, New Guinea, and other areas is whether (3) high density necessarily entails (2) political centralization. Fortes and Evans-Pritchard have formulated this as a "high degree of political centralization," but the cases mentioned all involve political systems which are described as stateless.

Obviously the problem of high density in the absence of state organization must be settled before refinements can be introduced on the degree of centralization. Given the evidence and being well aware that the relationship between state organization and density is indirect, reciprocal, and complex, I am not prepared to argue an invariant relationship between population density and state formation. The general evidence we have cited in the introductory chapter as well as the survey of Africa to follow both demonstrate a rather pronounced general conjunction of these two factors, and that is specifically what is denied by Fortes and Evans-Pritchard when the section on demography is taken as a whole. This is the heart of the matter and I have only taken up this detailed analysis of their last statement in order to clarify just what has and what has not been said. In short, I am solely and exclusively interested in discussing their assertion that African data indicate that in Africa at least there is no relationship at all between population density and state. Let me repeat, I shall attempt to show that there is a highly probable though indirect relationship between population density and state organization. I shall not attempt to show either a direct causal nor an invariant connection. I do not postulate that all states will have higher population densities than all nonstate societies. Empirically, the evidence is against this, not only from areas such as New Guinea, the Philippines, and northwestern aboriginal Mexico (Armillas 1961:264), but there are apparent exceptional cases from Africa as well. The point is that these exceptions are minor in nature when compared to the very broad global support for a general correlation between population density and state formation.

Some of the special features of the argument set forth by Fortes and Evans-Pritchard should now be mentioned. Their evidence consists mainly of a trio of low-density states (2.5 to 3.75 persons per square mile) in antithesis to three segmentary, acephalous, and nonstate societies of increasingly higher density, ranging from the Nuer with a density of 7 up to Logoli with the very high density of 391 per square mile. It is to this sample, its meaning and relevance, that we shall address ourselves at some length.

A most important consideration in the assessment of any sample is the question of typicality. Certainly, much of the strength of the agreement put forth by *African Political Systems* depends upon the degree of typicality and the range of systems covered. There is no question but that the editors claim a high degree of typicality for their sample. On the first page of the Introduction they assert: "As the sketch-map on p. 2 shows, the eight systems described are widely distributed in the continent. Most of the forms described are variants of a pattern of political organization found among contiguous or neighboring societies so that this book covers by implication, a very large part of Africa." (Fortes 1940:1) Viewed soberly, this would seem to be a rather serious overstatement. In the first place, all food-gathering bands have been omitted by definition in the construction of the Type B category. Furthermore, subsequent criticisms by Brown (1951), Eisenstadt (1959), and Smith (1956), as well as remarks in *Tribes Without Rulers* (Middleton 1958) have seriously questioned the number of types covered in the "middle range."

The sampling of state systems may equally be criticized. In the first place, the sketch map on page 2 also shows that all three of the states offered in the formulations concerning density are concentrated in the southeastern section of Africa. In the second, not one of the recognized *major* state systems of Africa, such as Hausa-Fulani, Buganda, Bornu, Ruanda, and others, are cited. In fact, as a comparison of the two passages already quoted from Section IV and Section VI will show, two states, Kede and Banyankole, although mentioned in Section IV, are not included in the important discussion in Section VI. Nor is any reason given for their exclusion. I would concur that, because Kede is a subsystem within a state system, its omission is justified, but there is no reason why broader demographic data from Nupe as a whole might not have been utilized. Certainly data from the Ankole District of Uganda, with density of 45 per square mile in 1931, could at least have been mentioned,[5] although this would necessarily have upset the neatness of the "reverse case" presentation. The sample, then, is not even truly representative of the studies actually included in the book.

Murdock's criticism of British Africanists as being exclusively "Anglo-Africanists" is, by now, well known. (Murdock 1951:467) In the present instance, however, this is not particularly a meaningful criticism. Actually, a quite reasonable representation of the range of African political systems could have been gathered entirely from the British colonial area. At the least, data from two important and geographically separate areas of significant indigenous state formation—the Interlacustrine region and the Western Sudan—could have been included.

This, I should hasten to make clear, is not the same thing as to demand that *African Political Systems* should have contained detailed studies and comparisons of all these systems. As a pioneering collection of empirical studies of particular political systems and an overview comparison of these, it had, necessarily, to rely upon the current research interests of its contributors. Their selection of problems and societies to study was, of course, not determined by the ideal requirements of the book, which came later. The editors, then, are in no way to be blamed or accused for including or excluding this or that society from the volume. Such stringency would not necessarily lead to the wholesale burning of books, but it would lead perforce to the condemnation of many symposia both before and since. Given the practical exigencies of publishing and the stringencies of the anthropologist's career, the volume was certainly an eminently reasonable undertaking. Furthermore, it was recognizably a pioneer effort in a hitherto neglected field of anthropology. As such it made a significant contribution to knowledge. All that is to the good. Nonetheless, the editors did essay a rather serious exploration into the relation of political organization and demography and they did claim a certain typicality for the societies studied. When it is further considered that demographic information of the same quality (or better) than what they used in their formulations was readily available for wider comparison, I feel it is fair to point out their responsibility. Finally (and although Fortes and Evans-Pritchard are certainly to be credited with this, they should not be held responsible), the book has become very much a classic in political anthropology,[6] and it has become the starting point of all subsequent significant debates. The well-deserved prestige of the editors has only added to the force of their generalizations. The result has been to lead to either one or the other of two (both equally undesirable) conclusions in the minds of the readers. These are that either the African data upset all generalizations that there

is a relationship between population density and state formation, or, that Africa is in some way unique in the political and
demographic processes. In either or both cases, I feel a reappraisal is long overdue.[7]

I feel that such a reappraisal, in order to be convincing and
fair, must begin by confronting *African Political Systems*. Here
I will use a diachronic approach, utilizing whatever historical
material from the precolonial period is available, as here, far
more than in the question of typicality, lies the essential flaw in
the method of *African Political Systems*. Fortes and Evans-
Pritchard have endeavored to employ in a strictly synchronic
context empirical data from the colonial period [8] and from areas
where the colonial state was conspicuously present, in order to
test generalizations concerning the formation processes of indigenous states. Implicit in this approach is the assumption that
the ratios between colonial period densities of *formerly* [9]
"acephalous" societies and former indigenous states are in some
way a true reflection of precolonial ratios. This, of course, is an
empirical question never established in their presentation.
Then, after analyzing these cases in full historical depth, I will
endeavor to see just what reasonable inferences can be drawn
from the present synchronic distribution of Africa's indigenous
population [10] and in the process analyze some rather important
and apparently exceptional cases not mentioned by Fortes and
Evans-Pritchard.

At this point I feel it is important to clarify what is here
meant by "density," as several specifically different types of
density have been developed by geographers and demographers
and are in current use. So far, concentration has been upon the
simple man-land ratio, known as arithmetic density [11] or simple
average population density. I will continue to use this as my
primary frame of reference when using the term "density" in
the ensuing pages, as (1) this is the type of density figure reported by ethnographers (when, indeed, they report any den-

sity figure at all); (2) this is usually the only density figure readily extractable from colonial reports and censuses; [12] and (3) this is the type of figure used in the continental surveys already mentioned in my Introduction as well as in the formulations concerning density and also in the figures adduced in *African Political Systems*. Here a cautionary note must be sounded. An average density figure for Egypt based upon its political boundaries is essentially meaningless when it is realized that the population is heavily concentrated in a thin ribbon along the Nile. A similar, though not as extreme, situation will be found to hold for the Ngwato (Chapter IV). In such cases I shall supplement analysis of average density with consideration of important nucleations within it, including, where important, the concentration of population in large nucleated settlements (Ngwato, Chapter IV). This aspect of density has been judiciouly noted by the geographers: "It appears, then that the idea of density is almost inextricably tied up with that of distribution. Only where people are dispersed rather widely and evenly over an area is the figure for average arithmetic density alone highly significant." (Finch 1957:524) The same authors then note that arithmetic density is usually not a very satisfactory measure of *real* density or pressure upon the land. If a figure which stood for the *productive capacity* of the land were substituted for the simple area in the denominator, the *economic density,* which is a better indicator of *real* density, would be obtained. This figure is not easily arrived at, as the technological system used to exploit the environment, as well as the selection of micro-environments exploited, enters most importantly into its calculation, even for subsistence economies. It has been impossible to use any index of economic density in a study such as this, where historical studies are important sources of evidence. In these historical studies information for the calculation of economic density is lacking entirely, and data for the assessment of even average density at times leave much to be desired. It is also to be noted that in most of the societies studied the matter has been further complicated by the important position of trade. Again, to essay a broad comparison of contemporary distributions in relation to state formation, figures of economic density cannot be used, as such information is simply not available on a continent-wide basis.

Another type of density mentioned by Finch, Trewartha, et al. is *physiological density,* or the ratio of population to land under cultivation. Here, although detailed studies in individual cases may have approximated the desired figure, the data are simply not available for broad comparisons. Dispersion of plots, irregularity of shape, and the prevalence of mixed and succession crops have tended to inhibit the production of reliable estimates except in a limited number of cases. When to this difficulty is added the necessity for calculating pasture areas, areas utilized for the gathering of wild flora and fauna which in most if not all indigenous African societies importantly contributed to the food supply, it can be seen that the data are not yet available to use such a figure for broad comparisons. In fact, many official estimates of areas under cultivation are projections based upon simple population enumerations, estimates of acreages cleared (of dubious value in shifting cultivation), extrapolations from assumed per capita consumption, or simple intelligent guesses. (Johnston 1958:56) *Agricultural density,* or the number of agricultural people per square mile of cultivated land, is, of course, subject to the same strictures, which are strictures of practicability given the existent data, certainly not strictures concerning conceptual value. In fact, anthropologists should be urged to confront this problem at least in terms of reasonable sample areas within the societies they study.

Finch, Trewartha, et al. continue by noting that:

The problem of comparing population density and productive capacity of land becomes further complicated in those regions where men do not live directly from the soil. There is no *simple* way of expressing the potential capacity of areas for supporting population in a complex industrial and commercial civilization. . . . So difficult is it to evaluate the general economic density for the various regions of the world that comparative data are as yet not available. (Finch 1957:525–26)

The authors then conclude: "Admittedly arithmetic density is far from being a satisfactory index of actual population pressure upon the resource base, but its use is made necessary since figures for more refined ratios are not at present available for much of the earth." (Finch 1957:527) It should be noted that in the Ibo region and the Niger Delta city-states the investigator is confronted by an area where trade and commerce were highly developed well in advance of colonial rule. In fact, most of the state systems I shall discuss were highly dependent upon regional and long-distance trade.

I am inevitably, then, forced back upon arithmetic or average density, at least for the present. Even were data available on which to construct and compare broadly the other types of density, simple man-to-land ratios are not without sociological significance in terms of influence upon interaction patterns. Here, as Krader (already quoted, p. 5) has noted, concentrations or nucleations within average density patterns would seem to have greater political significance and, I would add, sociological (in the sense of interaction) significance as well. Still, until data are sufficient to bring in the other types of density (particularly physiological and economic), I would argue that it is necessary to include average density as mediating between productivity and political integrational indices. With these simple arithmetic averages, pronounced nucleations in the distributional pattern should be observed wherever possible. It will be seen how important this is to assessing the Ngwato and other Tswana groups, as well as the Ngoni and Zulu. Furthermore, as I shall later elaborate (Chapter VII), great care must

be taken in comparing the average density of a society whose
total area is very small to the average density of a society of
much greater area, as, in effect, one may well be comparing a
nucleation or peak in the first case to an average in another.
This is certainly true when one is using data from contemporary (and several historic) African societies where there is a
decided involvement in commercial, trade, and market networks.

Before turning to the task at hand, which is an assessment of
the empirical evidence, I feel I should say a few cautionary
words concerning theory. I am not here engaged in the development or elaboration of a theoretical model concerning the relationship between population density and state formation. What
is at stake here is whether empirically any such relationship is
indicated. However, in discussing this problem I have too often
found that others readily assume that I am proposing a single
direct and unicausal relationship between population density
and the emergence of the state or, less frequently, that I am
proposing a unicausal model in which the state *causes* density.
Actually I feel that the matter is far more complex and that the
relationship between state and population density is both indirect and reciprocal and mediated importantly by such other
factors as productivity in the subsistence sector and, for the
overwhelming majority of indigenous African states, the development of both regional and long-distance trade.

Summaries of studies presented at the Fourth International
African Seminar (1961) have made this last point abundantly
clear.

Trade relations in Africa were not limited to purely commercial exchanges between overseas countries, for there were
economic ties between cultural regions, as in West Africa where
there were major routes on both a north-south axis continuing the
trans-Saharan routes and on an east-west axis in the forest zone, or
in parts of Africa where a trans-continental route had existed since

the eighteenth century. African trade has long been stimulated by contacts between distinct ecological regions and different and complementary cultures. (Vansina 1964:85)

Our empirical studies will show that such exchanges both stimulated and made possible higher population densities. The seminar summary then proceeded to note the other important relationship, that between trade and state formation.

The development of long-distance trade seems to have been related to political development. For while political centralization may not have been indispensable for trade to develop and flourish, the development of trade itself in some areas favoured the creation of centralized political systems. And these in turn contributed in large measure to the further development of trade by providing organization and security for markets and caravans. A close link between long-distance trade and state organization must then be assumed in many states. (Vansina 1964:85) [13]

Against this background, then, we may turn to an examination of the sample of *African Political Systems*.

IT HAS already been noted that the three states of Fortes' and Evans-Pritchard's density sample are all from the southeastern portion of the African continent. What is more important to our discussion here is that two of them, the Zulu and the Ngwato, were both products of the same general set of historic circumstances—the increasing penetration of the southern end of the continent by Boer and Briton in competition, compressing and rolling back the frontier of the southwards-expanding Bantu. The squeeze was first reflected in the early nineteenth century by rapidly accelerating political centralization and militarism in Zululand. Severe shocks went out in waves from these disturbances, and groups like the Kololo and the Matabele were sent raiding across the Transvaal, Bechuanaland, and up into Southern Rhodesia. These in turn raided and dislocated Tswana groups, including the Ngwato, profoundly influencing the developments there. Finally British and Boer competition (with the additional threat of German entrance into this competition) can be said to have played a crucial role in the creation of a British protectorate, and as a result a state, in Bechuanaland and hence in the Ngwato Reserve.

The Bemba, further to the north in northeastern Rhodesia, were not directly affected by these same events, although eventually they had to face the Ngoni, a Zulu offshoot whose predatory trajectory carried them far to the north. Rather, Bemba development was indirectly affected by Portuguese penetration into the Zambesi watershed and the build-up of

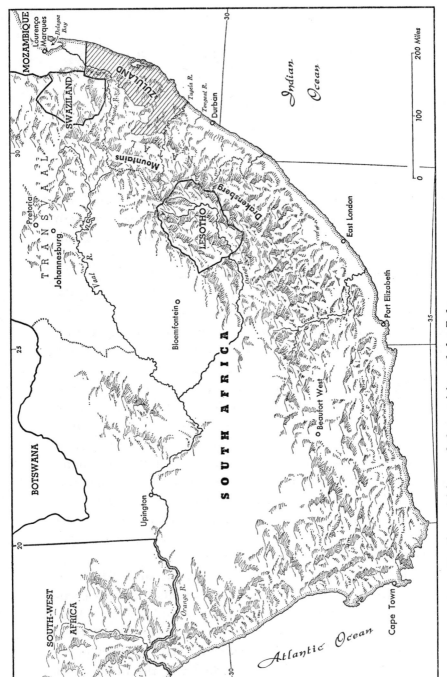

MAP III. Southern Africa and the position of the Zulu
Zululand boundaries, after A. T. Bryant, *Olden Times in Zululand and Natal*,
Longmans, Green and Co., 1929

trading networks in that region and more directly, at least from the middle nineteenth century on, by contact with the Arabs and a flourishing trade in ivory and slaves in return for cloth and guns.

As the development of these three societies cannot be understood apart from this historical context it will be necessary to delineate it at some length. It will be convenient, however, to treat in this short prologue only that part of the historical background leading to what might be termed the "Zululand explosion" and take up specific events affecting the other two societies in the appropriate chapters.

Diaz first rounded the Cape of Good Hope in 1488, to be followed in 1497 by Da Gama on his way to India.[1] No permanent European settlement was established, however, until 1652 when what was to become Cape Town was founded. The economic necessity underlying this event consisted in the requirements of the Dutch East India Company for a supply station for Java-bound vessels. The station on St. Helena was unsatisfactory to the East Indiamen as it lay outside the track of ships seeking the best winds and was also technically within the sphere of the Dutch West India Company. Consequently, after a shipwrecked crew had successfully passed the winter of 1647–1648 in South Africa, the company directors decided to move the station to the mainland.

The company had intended a rather concentrated colony, compact for effective defense and administration and prosperous, with an ample surplus to supply ships. However, partly to escape the irksome regulations and control of company government and largely because it was simply more profitable, settlers initiated the process to become famous as "trekking"— moving further and further into the hinterland along the frontier. Here the capital needed to establish a substantial ranch was minimal, cattle could be driven relatively long distances to market, the demand was steady, and the returns uniformly high. (Wiedner 1964:118–19)

The general direction of this movement was in the shape of a fan extending from northeast to due east of Capetown. Seventy or eighty miles was the maximum distance agricultural products could be transported, but cattle could be driven longer distances and marketed at a profit. Further, the general ecology favored cattle over gardening. Profitable ranching required rather large open areas, which tended to push the frontier outward. Nonetheless, there was a maximum distance beyond which cattle could not be effectively and profitably driven to market. This served as a regulator and check on Boer migrations. Wiedner has noted that whereas in 1700 all Europeans were within 55 miles of the Cape, by 1750 some were 225 miles away and by 1775 a few had reached the Fish River almost 500 miles away. During the next half century, however, the frontier did not move. The inland Karoo Plateau, too arid for anything but grazing, remained the focus of Boer economic activity in this period. "The main restriction on Boer expansion had been the distance from the Capetown markets. It had not been profitable to expand beyond the Fish River, or as far as the Orange in the interior, because cattle would not survive the long drive to Capetown." (Wiedner 1964:136) After 1823 when new supply centers grew up around Albany Bay, a vast new area was opened for profitable expansion. It is noteworthy that from this time on the Boers began settling as far inland as the Orange River.

The expansion of the Boer frontier to the Fish River is of historic significance for another more important reason. For here they were brought into lasting contact with the southward-moving Xosa. "The encounter was momentous because it brought two powerful, advancing frontiers into conflict with one another. Subsequent history is dominated by the manner in which they reacted to, and ultimately overlapped, one another."

(Wiedner 1964:124) From the outset there was friction and conflict. The Boers branded their cattle and grazed them on the open range. To the Xosa, who concentrated their herds in kraals, this was an open invitation. The Boers leveled charges of cattle "stealing" at the Xosa, and raids and counter-raids ensued. There was also some flow of traded cattle from Xosa to Boer. This tended to increase the meat supply at Capetown and bring still more Boers into the area. The entry of the British into the South African situation served to complicate matters further. Britain had taken Capetown in 1795 as part of the wars with the French. Her position on the Cape was confirmed by the Congress of Vienna in 1815. Around 1812 the British endeavored to stabilize the Fish River frontier by the erection of forts and the establishment of agricultural colonies in the area. This intensified rather than solved the problem. Ecologically, agriculture could not supplant cattle-raising in this relatively arid zone. British actions and regulations further irked the Boers and further stimulated the Boer advance, as did the establishment of new ports to the east of Capetown. Through the first quarter of the nineteenth century Xosa pressure also increased markedly along this frontier.

Population growth increased the demand for land, but the immediate causes of conflict lay deeper in Bantu society. Like many southern Bantu tribes, the Xosa tended to divide into separate subtribes upon the death of a chieftain. Such a break, into East and West Xosa, had caused the West Xosa to migrate toward the Fish River in 1775. Thereafter, there was no more vacant land, so the tribe could not divide. Instead, tension built up within Xosa society and contributed to the increase in frontier raiding. (Wiedner 1964:133)

But though the pressure was constantly mounting against the Fish River frontier, the explosion, when it came, came not here but some five hundred miles further to the north. It is to this area, Zululand, then that we shall next turn, and against the background of the broad historic events we have here discussed, consider the formation of the first of the low-density states—the Zulu.

It is both overly complicated and unnecessary to attempt to trace Bantu migrations into Zululand and Natal from their very beginnings, and contemporary authorities still disagree as to exact origins and dates. We are certainly on safe ground if we begin, as Barnes does, with the Nguni chiefdoms of the seventeenth and early eighteenth centuries. These "were according to all accounts, comparatively small. There were many of them and they were unstable." (Barnes 1954:7) [2] The social structure consisted of exogamous agnatic lineages whose members were graded by primogeniture and the ranking of wives. There was a dominant lineage in each chiefdom to which the chief belonged. Around this dominant lineage were clustered other lineage segments and most lineages had segments in a number of chiefdoms. There was fairly constant fissioning because of succession disputes and other quarrels, and segments often transferred allegiance from one chief to another or formed new independent chiefdoms. Residential settlements were small. Most contained the descendents of a living man with their wives and children. Chiefs' homesteads were larger and contained other members of the dominant lineage as well as genealogically unrelated dependents. Agnatic kinsmen, heads of other lineages, and sometimes unrelated men were placed as *indunas* over districts or given specific administrative, judicial, or military duties. For war and hunting there were loosely organized divisions based upon chiefly homesteads. There were also small age sets composed of youths circumcised together. (Barnes 1954:5) There was constant raiding and fighting among these small chiefdoms, but, according to Bryant (1929) and Shepstone (1875), warfare was largely ceremonial in nature.[3] It is interesting to note that these political units are never termed "states." They contain in embryo, however, all the elements that characterized the wider formations which were to emerge so suddenly and dramatically.[4]

Then, in the late eighteenth century, the system seemed to approach a crucial threshold:

As the population increased the process of migration over unoccupied land became impossible, and tribes were in closer and more continuous relationship. In clan histories this trend becomes noticeable about 1775, and for the next thirty years newly formed tribes percolated into unoccupied land between the lands of other tribes, and even ousted possessing tribes. Gradually some tribes were able to dominate their neighbours. (Gluckman 1958:30)

Barnes also sees the year 1775 as an important threshold: "After about 1775 the pattern of political alignment began to alter and larger states appeared. By 1810 three kingdoms, the Mthethwa, Ndwandwe, and Qwabe, dominated the rest." (Barnes 1954:7) It will be remembered that this was also the year of the establishment of the Fish River frontier, and along this frontier the so-called Kaffir Wars were to begin in 1779.

There is general agreement that the reorganization of the traditional and smaller age sets into age regiments, cutting across the entire chiefdom, and their pronounced centralization under the chief began in the Mthethwa under Dingiswayo sometime around 1808. With Dingiswayo also apparently began the attack pattern of encircling and enveloping "horns," which is derived from traditional hunting practices.

At this time Shaka, the most famous of all the Zulu rulers and the one popularly credited with founding the Zulu state, was only a vassal of Dingiswayo. Shaka, for his part, further improved military techniques by substituting the short stabbing assegai for the longer throwing assegai, thus placing emphasis on close hand-to-hand fighting by massed regiments. Shaka also intensified the pattern of warfare, exterminating all adult males and capturing women, children, and cattle. Villages and fields were ransacked and burned. Dingiswayo is described on the other hand as being not so much bent upon extermination as upon pillage of grain bins and cattle and the placement of defeated groups under tribute. This, of course, would be consistent with his trading operations as detailed by Fynn. (Stuart 1950) The expansion of the Mthethwa chiefdom by massed raid and plunder set in motion a series of shocks, collisions, and repercussions among the neighboring people. "Tribal migrations began, with fighting between those who desired to escape him and those through whose land they had to pass in order to do so." (Gibson 1903:14)

Disturbance and disruption radiated in accelerating and expanding waves, finally ejecting some groups like massive particles from a giant cyclotron and hurtling them on long, destructive trajectories far to the north and northwest, a process described by one writer as "migratory brigandage." (Barnes 1954:6) Basically, this was a twofold process. On the one hand, groups tended to amalgamate in polar opposition to other combinations of groups, while on the other, fissioning occurred within these polar groups, leading to new aggregations and new oppositions. The main opponents of the Mthethwa were the Ndwandwe, who, under their paramount, Zwide, occupied the Pongola River region near the borders of present-day Swaziland in the north. During this conflict Shaka rose steadily as an important commander and vassal under Dingiswayo, through whose influence he was able to secure the succession to the Zulu chiefship when it became vacant. Up to this time the Zulu had been a rather insignificant Nguni clan. Now Shaka began to strike out somewhat on his own, while still acknowledging the overlordship of Dingiswayo. He further intensified the pattern of destructive warfare by initiating a policy of following the enemy home, killing the chief and as many males as possible, and returning with the cattle and women. Surviving males were drafted into the Zulu regiments.

Shaka's wars were therefore fiercer and more destructive than anything the Bantu had previously known. Whole tribes fled before him, creating havoc wherever they went, in their turn becoming marauders, and dislocating tribes in regions many hundreds of miles away from Zululand from where the original impetus came. (Krige 1936:11)

Then the Ndwandwe seized and killed Dingiswayo and routed the leaderless Mthethwa. Zwide now turned his attention to Shaka and the rising Zulu power, but Shaka discreetly kept his distance. He defeated the Qwabe, who were three times as numerous as the Zulu, and then annexed the entire Mthethwa chiefdom by the device of installing his own candidate in the position left vacant by Dingiswayo's death. Finally Shaka was strong enough to mount a major expedition to destroy the headquarters kraal of Zwide. The Ndwandwe were completely broken and the greater part driven across the Pongola. The breakup of the Ndwandwe had far-reaching consequences. "Small clans, hitherto under Ndwandwe control, were now thrown upon their own resources." (Krige 1936:12) Soshangane (Manukisi), a classificatory younger brother of Zwide, moved coastwards into the Delagoa Bay area, raiding the Thonga. Zwangendaba of the Jele clan, which was subject to Zwide, departed somewhat in advance of Soshangane but went north where he remained for some time along the right bank of the lower Limpopo, from which position he attacked both the Thonga and the Portuguese. (Krige 1936:12–13)[5] Mzilikazi (Moselekatse in Sotho), head of the Kumalo clan of Ndwandwe, temporarily submitted to Shaka. Then, after a dispute concerning the possession of raided cattle, the Kumalo clan moved in 1820 into the Transvaal and then to Hurutseland, where they raided the surrounding Tswana and Sotho. The group snowballed with the incorporation of captives and the arrival of other Nguni fugitives from Zululand, forming in the process the Ndebele (Matabele) nation. Defeated by the Boer Voortrekkers under Hendrik Potgeiter in 1836, and under attack by Zulu impis (regiments) sent by Shaka's successor, Dingane, the Ndebele crossed the Limpopo into Southern Rhodesia where, after some further wanderings, they finally stratified themselves over the indigenous population on the High Veld near modern Bulawayo (Hughes 1956:6–7)

While these groups were cutting a swath of destruction to the north and west, Shaka, by this time uncontested in Zululand, turned his attention to Natal. "Between 1820 and 1823 Shaka's armies, aided by wasting hordes of Chunu, Thembu and other tribes fleeing before him, swept Natal clean." (Krige 1936:13) To the south, groups were sent crushing against the Pondo and Xosa, while to the west, across the Drakensberg Mountains, marauders such as the Makololo under Sebitwane and the Batlokoa under the woman regent, Mantatisi, were unleashed. "This period is referred to by the Basotho as the Lifiqane, a word denoting a state of migration—not the ordinary movements of peoples, but the struggles of wandering tribes accompanied by their families, flocks and herds." (Krige 1936:14) People in the area were reduced to living on roots, grass-seed, and other humans. Cultivation ceased and the game vanished from the region. One composite refugee group which formed around Moshesh in the inaccessible rocky recesses of Basutoland emerged as the Basuto nation. Sebitwane and the Makololo turned north, smashed through the Tswana, and established themselves in the Zambesi Valley, where they attacked the Barotse and then stratified themselves over the conquered group, producing the Kololo. (Krige 1936:13) [6]

There were also related and generally parallel events occurring throughout this entire period in Swaziland, which borders Zululand on the northwest and lies almost due west of Delagoa

Bay. The modern Swazi are descendants of the Dlamini, who for over two hundred years had dwelt in the area of Lourenço Marques and had established close and peaceful ties there with the Tembe, a Thonga group. Then under Ngwane II (d. 1780) they suddenly left and crossed the Lubombo range to settle in what is now southeastern Swaziland. Ngwane's son, Ndungunye, and grandson, Sobhuza I, were contemporaries of both Dingiswayo and Zwide. Kuper informs us that at least some Dlamini were paying tribute to the Mthethwa chief when a dispute over fertile garden lands along the Pongola brought the Dlamini to the point of conflict with the Ndwandwe. Sobhuza characteristically avoided an open clash and led his followers, composed mainly of Dlamini but with other accretions, north into central Swaziland. There they imposed their domination over the indigenous Nguni and Sotho of the area.

Groups that submitted humbly, implicitly acknowledged their inferior strength. They gave occasional tribute in food and service, and were permitted, as long as they remained loyal, to retain their hereditary chiefs, their land and a limited autonomy. Those who resisted were defeated and plundered; the men were usually slain and the women and children were assimilated by marriage and adoption into the nation. (Kuper 1947:14)

Sobhuza's policy was to avoid clashes with groups of vastly superior strength and on the other hand to form strategic alliances with the dominant chiefs. Thus he took a daughter of Zwide as his main wife. From this union was born Mswati, the greatest of the Swazi fighting chiefs, who, under the influence of his mother, "borrowed" much of the Mthethwa–Zulu military organization. (Kuper 1947:15) [7] Two of Sobhuza's daughters were sent to Zululand to be wives of Shaka.

As to Shaka himself, "having driven out all his enemies and laid waste to the greater part of Natal," he is described as largely living a barracks existence at kwaBulawayo, his headquarters kraal. (Krige 1936:14) From this time [8] to his death, the major expeditions were few and far between and against distant tribes. It is perhaps ironic, then, that about the same time (1825–1835) Soshangane and Zwangendaba were both operating in the Delagoa Bay area, raiding the Thonga and their cattle and alternately harassing the Portuguese and selling them their captives as slaves. (Bryant 1929:459) Further research and analysis of trade in this period may indeed reveal that Shaka, the conquerer, had only succeeded in neutralizing himself for further profitable trade. Although Isaacs (Hermann 1936) encountered a Portuguese cattle trader at Shaka's kraal, this scarcely indicates a major commerce. What Zulu trade there was after this time, and, from Isaacs' diary it does not seem to be of great consequence, was with the British party which was more or less living in their midst. These traders began under Fynn and Farewell to establish a small settlement at the Bay of Natal under a paper grant issued by Shaka. This settlement grew slowly and later became the modern city of Durban. (Hattersley 1950:13)

Attempted explanations of the Zulu phenomenon can be conveniently classified into those that stress the influence of (1) the creative military geniuses of Dingiswayo and Shaka; (2) acculturation; (3) population density; and (4) a combination of population density and social structure. From an anthropological standpoint, the first type is deficient in that it fails to explain the number of leaders and societies of this class that rapidly rose and spread in this area and period. The second, in its most extreme form, is seen in Shepstone's suggestion of a refugee though perceptive Dingiswayo haunting the parade grounds of the Cape. This has been rightly dismissed by Bryant as sheer fiction.[9] There still remains a plausible but by no means demonstrated role for acculturation in terms of trade and other contacts with the Portuguese. Hilda Kuper offers an interpretation that combines population density with considerations of acculturation.

Throughout Southern Africa in the late eighteenth century nations were rising rapidly to power under ambitious rulers. The land

needs of an increasing peasant population made it more difficult for
independent groups to roam about without coming into conflict
over garden lands and pasture. Moreover, Europeans had established mastery in parts of the south and east of South Africa; fugitives and spies brought back reports of military domination; and
the area available for Bantu habitation was diminishing. (1947:13)

It is, of course, difficult to support a population density explanation with a density figure as low as 3.5 per square mile.
Gluckman seems to realize this full well. In his article in *African Political Systems* he only tentatively advanced a population
density argument. "By 1775 the motives for war changed, possibly owing to pressure of population. Certain tribes conquered
their neighbors and small kingdoms emerged." (1940:25) Then,
in a more recent account, he explicitly confronts this problem
and offers an explanation of the fourth type I mentioned. Referring to the same process as above, he says:

These results are not to be ascribed to the simple increase in
numbers of the population. The population of Zululand was not
dense until recently, and its present density is partly due to the
expropriation of Zululand by Whites. . . . As far as one can
understand the process from the almost contemporary records,
under the distribution of population then prevailing it became
more difficult for tribes to divide and dissident sections to escape to
independence; as the Nguni cultural stress on seniority of descent
and the relatively great inheritance of the main heir caused strong
tensions in the tribes, chiefs began to press their dominion not only
on their subordinate tribal sections, but also on their neighbours.
(1958:31)

I personally feel that it is difficult to support even this modified
density explanation on the basis of a figure of 3.5, but before
pursuing this part of the argument, it is appropriate to inquire
into the basis and validity of the figure itself.

The editors of *African Political Systems* do not indicate the
source or basis for this figure. However, Professor Max Gluckman, who wrote the article on the Zulu for the volume, has
kindly supplied me with information which greatly clarifies the
matter. Professor Gluckman informs me that he added 10,000 to

an estimate of 200,000 of the Zulu population circa 1850. This latter estimate, in turn, was that of a Norwegian missionary. As a divisor, Gluckman used an area of "Zulu influence" extending 300 miles from north to south and 200 miles inland. This was intended to be an estimate of the "density of population at the time when the kingdom reached stability in the reign of King Mpande." [10] The resulting density is the 3.5 figure used by the editors in the Introduction.

One must certainly respect the difficulties faced in formulating an estimate of this type, for the earlier estimates of Zulu population and area have been almost as multiple and varied as the estimators themselves. Nonetheless, I believe that 3.5 is not a meaningful figure in terms of the problem we are analyzing. In the first place, as I shall argue shortly, I feel that systems of the Zulu type are inherently unstable and that the situation in the 1850s was conditioned largely by the English and Boer presence. It must be remembered that 1850 is *after* the Boers had reduced the Zulu to the position of a puppet state and had themselves formally organized the Natal Republic (1839) and after the British occupation and annexation of Natal (1843). (Wiedner 1964:146–47; Krige 1936:21) In fact, from 1838 on the Zulu had been confined by treaty to the region north of the Tugela River. (Gluckman 1958:36)

This brings up the question of area, and I think here it can be shown that, granting Gluckman's population estimate of 210,000 for 1850, the actual density of Zululand then was not 3.5. Bryant's map (1929 following p. 697) shows a 1929 Zululand area of approximately 9,000 square miles. The *Encyclopaedia Britannica* (1963 edition) gives an area of 10,362 square miles for Zululand, noting that this includes Amatongaland, Zaambauland, and the Ingwavuma District, which was not part of the former Zulu domain. The southern boundary in either case is the Tugela River. Allowing for the possibility that Zulu territory in the 1850s may well have overlapped these boundaries in places, but further considering Gluckman's observation that northern Zululand had been largely depopulated in the wars of the Shaka period, I would consider 10,000 square miles a reasonable divisor and one whose very roundness would underscore the general imprecision of any estimate. This would give a density of 21.[11]

At this point we must confront a major flaw in the approach of *African Political Systems* and that is the inadmissible confusion of two time levels. Gluckman has offered an estimate for 1850 for the Zulu and this is placed by the editors in combination with figures from the 1930s for all of the other societies involved. Despite the supposed greater reliability of actual census figures (and we shall have reason to question this reliability later on), I feel Gluckman is, in the nature of the case, on the track of a more important type of information than that used in the other cases. Ultimately, what is needed to test the generalizations on the relationship between state formation and population density is reliable data from the period in which indigenous states and indigenous acephalous societies were functioning as such; for example, historical information or archaeological estimates or both. In the absence of such information, data from the present can perhaps be used cautiously and within narrow limits to draw inferences concerning the past. But when this is done all the data should be from as close to one single time horizon as possible if the comparisons are to have any validity; for example, the average density of Ankole was 45 in 1931 (Kuczynski 1948,2:252) and 90 in 1959. (Taylor 1962:96) Ideally, figures should all be from 1960, or 1950, or 1930, depending on which census material is generally the most reliable. It is considered, however, that errors resulting from the use of statistics which vary as much as a decade in time are no greater than those involved when the data are all from a single time horizon. The margin of error in the actual population counts themselves is that large. (Trewartha 1954a:137) But this use of a strictly

synchronic approach to draw inferences about a diachronic process is subject to severe limitations and is justified only in the
absence of other information. Such an attempt is controverted
by lumping data from two widely separate time spans, such as
1850 and 1931. As we shall see in Chapter VII, Logoli densities
have climbed from an estimated 50 to 70 in 1898 to a figure
probably in excess of 400 in 1931. Tallensi densities have been
swelled by migrations across the border (Chapter VI) ; on the
other hand, the evidence would indicate a Bemba decline
(Chapter V). I cite these figures here only to underscore my
contention that, whereas present ratios of densities could be
used to support historical estimates where these were found to
be rather imprecise, the two types of data cannot be mixed in-
discriminately. In effect, the editors of *African Political Systems,* in merging two time horizons, replace conjectural history [12] with collapsed history.

I do not, then, disagree so much with Gluckman's population
estimate—Bryant gave an identical figure as his estimate for
1885, only some three decades later (1929:81) —as I do with the
area used.[13] I do feel that in terms of the theoretical argument
that adduces a modified density theory to explain the Zulu phenomenon, we should want information or estimates of the pre-
Shakan period. And, as it is possible to regard the Shakan period
as a peak of Zulu development and expansion, even though admittedly unstable, we might inquire into estimates of density
for that period as well. In fact, as quantitative estimates for the
pre-Shakan period are usually extrapolations backward from
contemporary estimates by those who visited Shaka's court, the
two may conveniently be discussed together.

One of the best known, and certainly one of the most careful
attempts to estimate the pre-Shakan population of Zululand is
Bryant's. He estimates 78,000 for Zululand in 1816 (the date of
Shaka's accession to power) and 100,000 for the "much
larger" area of Natal, carefully separating the two totals. This

gives a grand total of 178,000. (Bryant 1929:81–82) I assume, from this context and from the fact that Bryant plotted his distribution of the pre-Shakan clans upon a map displaying the 1929 boundaries of Zululand and Natal, that these boundaries express the areal referent for the terms Zululand and Natal when used by Bryant.[14] Although a grid placed on Bryant's map yields an area of 9,000 square miles, the estimates are so imprecise that 10,000 square miles should reasonably serve our purpose. This yields an average density of 7.8, but to underscore the imprecision of this estimate I shall round the resulting density to 8 per square mile.

Before this figure is accepted unequivocally, its basis should be examined. Bryant takes 900, the complement of warriors (regiment) at Dingane's headquarters' kraal in 1835, to represent the average size of a Zulu regiment. He then assumes that there were fifteen such regiments at the time of Shaka. This gives a total of 13,500 warriors. Bryant finds that this checks reasonably closely with the 14,000 estimate by Lieutenant Farewell, who was at Shaka's headquarters in 1824. Bryant therefore accepts Farewell's count and subtracts from it 2,000 as representing those warriors probably recruited from other groups. This leaves 12,000. Bryant then assumes that the warriors (males between twenty and forty years old) comprise roughly one-eighth of the total Zulu population, and his estimated total for 1824 is consequently 96,000 (a density of approximately 10 per square mile). He then projects backward by what he assumes to be a normal growth of the population. This projection is checked in turn by projecting the same growth rate forward against official government estimates for the year 1898. This gives him his population figure of 78,000 for Zululand in 1816. The figure for Natal is on far shakier grounds and can only be considered a very rough estimate. It is derived simply from the Zululand estimate by assuming that Natal was (1) equally densely populated in occupied areas; (2) much larger in area;

and (3) characterized by large unpopulated sections. The result is an estimated population of 100,000 for Natal.[15]

We shall confine our analysis to the Zululand estimate. In the first place, estimates based upon the size and number of regiments should probably best be carefully eschewed. Ferguson, who wrote an analysis of the Zulu military system which appeared in *Harvard African Studies (Varia Africana)*, observed that both the size and number of regiments varied considerably. Size of regiments varied from 600 to 1,000 and Ferguson specifically pointed out that a headquarters regiment such as that used by Bryant could in no ways be regarded as typical. It was a special group gathered at the headquarters and consisted largely of village headmen brought there for purposes of political control. (Ferguson 1918:199) Nonetheless, Bryant's resulting total of 13,500 is the precise mean of the range of 12,000 to 15,000 accepted by Ferguson as the total military strength in Shaka's time. Ferguson, in a footnote (p. 199), gives a summation of the varying estimates for Zulu military strength at the time and names the various estimators. Grout gave a figure of 12,000 to 15,000; Isaacs, Kay and Shooter all gave estimates of 15,000; Arbousset indicated a range of 15,000 to 20,000; Fynn gave 50,000 but qualified this as including women and boys in the commissariat. Of later writers, Theal (1888, III:297) has given a range of 40,000 to 50,000. Hattersley (1950:12) accepts the high end of this as representing the probable strength of Zulu arms when Natal was invaded in 1820 or 1821. Given this range, 15,000 would seem an eminently cautious assessment.

There is next the question of the ratio of the military to the total population. Bryant's use of a factor of eight rests upon two assumptions. One is that the males in the age groups between 20 and 40 years constitute one-eighth of the Zulu population. This, in fact, corresponds rather closely with the percentage of this group in the modern population as given in the *Natal Regional Survey*. (Alsop 1952:29–36) Alsop also noted that this population profile still displayed the general characteristics of an "aboriginal" population. The second assumption is that the members of the military are the same as the members of this male age group, no more no less. This is open to some question. Here we must carefully keep separate what is said about the Shaka period and what is said about 1816.

Ferguson insists that the typical Zulu regiment consisted of two types of warriors—young warriors and veterans. The veterans may well have been over 40 years in age.[16] In addition "there were associated with each regiment children who had not yet entered the army." (Ferguson 1918:199) These would be well under 20 years of age because Ferguson also indicates that boys collect at the kraals to enlist when they are between 16 and 18 years old. (1918:200) These considerations would indicate that the military group constituted a larger percentage of the population. I believe that this would be more than counteracted by the Zulu policy of killing off the mature male warriors among their opponents and incorporating women and children. Prior to 1820 this process had been going on largely within the confines of modern Zululand. After 1820 large accretions to Zulu population came as the result of forced incorporations from Natal. "Clans had been either broken up and driven south or west beyond the confines of Natal, or compelled by Tshaka to take up residence north of the Tongaat River. Neither Kraals nor cattle remained. Natal in 1824 was almost completely depopulated." (Hattersley 1950:13) Given this process and the emphasis upon killing off the male warriors among those opposing, it would seem that a factor of eight is too low. By 1824 Zulu population had been swollen considerably in the twin categories of females and young boys. Recognizing full well the crudeness of the procedure, I shall use the factor 8 against a military figure of 15,000, divided by an area of 10,000 square miles to give an estimate which I feel represents an estimate of minimum average density for 1824. The population estimate is 120,000 and the

density is 12.[17] Given the tendency of systems of the Zulu type
to concentrate their populations within an area protected by a
depopulated "ring," the effective densities within the Zulu area
of occupation were undoubtedly much higher—perhaps as much
as 20 to 40 per square mile.[18]

With the Zulu pattern of wide depopulation externally and
drastic incorporation internally, the very process of state formation here precludes extrapolation backwards by natural or normal growth rates such as Bryant used. For the pre-Shakan
period we are, then, forced back on conjectural estimates. In
1875 Sir Theophilus Shepstone estimated the pre-1812 population of Natal at one million. As Zululand was not made a part
of Natal until 1897, he is presumably talking about an area
roughly 25,000 square miles in area.[19] This would give a density of about 40 for Natal. If one assumes that Bryant's estimates
of the ratio of Zululand to Natal densities (2/1) is essentially
correct, a density of 80 per square mile is the resultant figure for
Zululand.[20] This would seem to be rather on the high side.
Hattersley, more recently, after giving an estimation of 90,000
for the Zulu kingdom (Shakan period) goes on to note: "Prior
to the year 1810, though the pastoral highlands north of the
Mooi River carried no more than a sparse Bantu population,
density of settlement in the coastlands and eastern midlands
seems to have been as great as in the Zulu kingdom." (1950:8)
Hattersley then goes on to mention without further criticism
the estimates by Shepstone and Bryant that we have already discussed.

There are qualitative statements as well which indicate that
this area was rather densely populated in the early decades of
the nineteenth century. "Up to about the year 1812, then, and
for how many centuries before we cannot now tell, this country
was thickly populated by numerous tribes under independent
chiefs." (Shepstone 1875:192) And Theal, in his history of the
early period, has maintained: "When Tshaka commenced his

career, the lower terraces of the territory that is now the colony of Natal were the most densely people districts of South Africa. The soil was rich, the water plentiful, the climate such as the Bantu of the coast love." (Theal 1891:297) This of course would go against Gluckman's contention that Zululand was never densely populated until recently, but I feel that it is necessary to subscribe to a view such as that advanced by Theal if one is to support an explanation of the Zulu development such as those advanced by Kuper and Gluckman. Furthermore, I have deliberately searched the literature in the attempt to support an alternate theory based upon the influences of trade and acculturation and have been unable to find convincing evidence to support it. It is true that Fynn's diary (Stuart 1950:7) contains statements that Portuguese soldiers from Delagoa Bay assisted Dingiswayo in his initial seizure of power, but to my knowledge this is neither confirmed nor followed by any other sources. Even if true, it can scarcely explain the continuation, acceleration, and extent of the Zulu eruption. Nor, I think, can the trade between Dingiswayo and Delagoa Bay, first reported by Fynn and apparently accepted as fact by such later writers as Bryant, Gibson, and Krige, explain the rapid rise of the Zulu state. In this case the density theory as advanced by Gluckman would seem to have the greatest explanatory cogency of any yet advanced. Here, however, Gluckman is faced by somewhat of a contradiction if he attempts at once to maintain this explanation and to insist that Zululand was never dense until the present.[21] If the conception of a large area of Zulu "influence" be abandoned, however, this contradiction will largely disappear. I believe it has already been demonstrated that this area, as a divisor, does not yield a realistic population density estimate for any of the periods considered.

Actually, the conception that the Zulu controlled a vast area has a rather respectable antiquity, going back to Shepstone's paper of 1875 at least. Speaking of Shaka, Shepstone said:

His genius overbore all opposition, and he died within the territory which now constitutes this colony, on the 23rd September, 1828, undisputed sovereign of all South-Eastern Africa, from the St. John's River on the south to the King George's River on the north; including a large portion of what now forms the Orange Free State, and the Transvaal Republic, as well as the tribe and territory of his old master and patron, Dingiswayo. (1875:196)

Writing in 1958, Gluckman observed:

When he died in 1828, by superior strategy and weapons he had made himself master of 80,000 square miles of land, and his armies were invading into distant territories. After a half-century of slowly expanding small states, in some five years the decisive change to a state embracing a large area took place. (1958:31)

By placing a grid on a standard map I have ascertained that an area of 80,000 square miles would stretch westwards from the coast to include large stretches of the Orange Free State, Basutoland, the Transvaal, and Swaziland. Such an area might be encompassed by a rectangle drawn through the furthest points of penetration of several, temporally quite separate, expeditions by Zulu armies (and even this is difficult unless the movements of groups like the Matabele, who actually fled from Zulu influence are included). In any event this is quite a different matter from effective control of an area by a political unit. A more sober assessment is given by Hattersley. Speaking of the southward invasion of 1820–1821, he reports that one by one the tribes south of the Tugela were attacked and overpowered and that remnants found refuge in the foothills of the Drakensberg while hordes of fugitives were sent careening toward the Cape frontier. "From Zululand further waves of upheaval overspread the inland plateau of South Africa, extending the area of desolation to the neighbourhood of the northern Transvaal." (Hattersley 1950:12) But, "Beyond the Berg, the work of destruction, set in motion by his impis, was actually wrought by others." (Hattersley 1950:12) Hattersley describes Shaka as controlling, at the peak of his power, "the destinies of the entire population from Delagoa Bay southward to the Pondo frontier," but we know that in northern Zululand the population had mostly disappeared, and the same seems largely true of Natal. The southward drive had been an overextension, and by 1824 the southern frontier of Zululand was the Tongaat. In the area to the south "Neither kraals nor cattle remained. Natal in 1824 was almost completely depopulated." (Hattersley 1950:13) Bryant has reported that in 1828, immediately following the assassination of Shaka by his brother and successor, Dingane, the latter immediately withdrew from Natal north into Zululand proper.

He had scarcely done so, when fearing lest his Natal subjects, relieved of his restraining presence, might conceive the idea of union and so rebellion, he ordered all forthwith to remove the kraals, for better surveillance, to the country northward of the Tongaat river. Still suspicious, he soon afterwards ordained that they should vacate the coastal district of Natal altogether, in all those parts lying between the Tongaat and Tukela rivers, and so be placed out of the reach of any temptation to throw off their allegiance and join the White men then congregating about Durban. (1929:388)

As Zulu arms pulled back out and moved northward, displaced clans began moving back into Natal. Given these fluctuations, it is difficult to establish anything like boundaries for the Zulu state during this period. However, in light of the pronounced depopulation in both north and south, 10,000 square miles does not seem too small.

We must conclude, then, that there is no support for a figure of 3.5 as a density for the Zulu kingdom; even pre-Shaka period estimates would seem to be at least around 10 per square mile. For the period of 1850, which Gluckman feels is a time of stability, an estimate of 20 per square mile (minimum 14) seems reasonable. For the Shaka period, which was one of warfare, rapid expansion, and then equally rapid contraction, 12 per square mile can be taken as a minimum. It is indeed probable that the density within the area actually occupied was considerably higher. The modern density of "tribal areas" in Zululand has been given by Schapera (1956:35) as 46 per square mile. As such, then, the Zulu case does not actually contradict the generalization that states will have higher population densities than nonstates. As we shall see, there is only one genuinely acephalous society (among the six presented) whose historic density exceeded the historic density of the Zulu or whose present density, for that matter, exceeds that of the present Zulu. That is the Logoli, and analysis will show that it was along the borderline of both an advancing frontier of high density and coupled state formation. Internally it was showing signs of entering into the same process. Furthermore, we are confronted by a rather short time span in which the Zulu erupted and expanded under Shaka and by 1828 were contracting again. Within a decade they were being confined and contained by first the Boers and then the British. It may be that both the time span and the scantiness of accurate data preclude an adequate analysis of full potential for systems of this type.

It might be helpful to take a glance at the Fort Jameson Ngoni, who, like the Zulu, stemmed from original Nguni clans in Zululand and whose formation was part of the same process as that of the Zulu, with the difference that the Ngoni were sent careening out to the north and were not contained by the intervention of colonial powers until 1898. In a real sense, then, the Ngoni may reveal more markedly the typical life trajectory of such a system as well as its relation to population and resources. Barnes, who has studied them intensively both from field and historical documentary studies, describes then in this fashion:

The Ngoni State . . . was born suddenly, moved about from one part of Africa to another, and recruited most of its members from outside itself. . . . This history of the Ngoni from 1821 down to 1898 is essentially the history of an armed nation on the march. (Barnes 1954:1) During the period of migration the Ngoni flourished. They were successful brigands on the march. Yet they were brigands in a poor land, and despite their military successes their economy remained one of subsistence cultivation, even though others did some of the cultivation for them. They were well-organized for war and their enemies were not, but both they and their enemies were poor people relying on shifting cultivation with a poor technology and with access to only moderately valuable natural resources. (1954:63)

The traditional Ngoni pattern was to enter an area and settle it, driving off the inhabitants and incorporating captives. Through further raiding, they depopulated a large ring [22] around the area of their settlements and continued raiding the peoples beyond this zone for captives, cattle, and other resources. Within the area occupied the Ngoni used up the land resources faster than they could be replenished and, when the area was exhausted, moved on. The result was a long migratory trajectory. On the basis of the reports of early travelers and administrators, Barnes has estimated that, within the area actually occupied by the Ngoni, population density ranged from 100 to 375 per square mile. This is an impressive density, higher than the nineteenth-century density of any of the societies cited in *African Political Systems.*

Highly unreliable as these figures are, it is clear that the density of population was considerably greater before the conquest than it is now, when it averages 68 persons to the square mile. Even the present-day figure is nearly three times the destiny which the land can sustain in perpetuity. (Barnes 1954:104)

In short, these are largely predatory systems that have a markedly different relationship to resources and to population than do the larger, more stable state systems characteristic of the Sudan or the Lacustrine area. This is a matter of degree, of course (all states engage in military expeditions involving plunder and looting), and when the dependence upon plundered resources (both labor and food) is so great as it is in systems of the Zulu and Ngoni type we would seem to have markedly different results. Such systems are inherently transitory and evanescent, their rate of liquidating resources far higher than the capacity of areas occupied to supply them. Either they must keep moving (as did the Ngoni) or successfully stratify themselves over sedentary populations capable of support (Kololo and perhaps the Matabele are cases in point). The only other alternative would seem to be collapse. I should suggest that as generalizations concerning the relationship between population densities and state formation are further perfected, and better typologies of state systems and types are advanced, systems of the Zulu and Ngoni type be kept carefully to one side as operating under rather special and necessarily transitory conditions. In other words, this type of state provides a dubious case, even with adequate data for the testing of generalizations which involve the relationship between resources, population, and complexity of political development. As generalizations in this area are perfected and approach more closely to the "law statements" of other sciences, it is very likely that the "initial conditions" of these laws will specify the exclusion of such "evanescent states." All of this is in the way of a rather important postscript to my argument, though a postscript nonetheless. The population figures and areas themselves, as far as they may be reasonably ascertained and analyzed, support rather than contradict my contention that states are generally higher in density than nonstates.[23]

CHAPTER IV. Low-Density States II: The Ngwato

THE NEXT state we shall consider has the lowest average density of any of the societies studied in *African Political Systems*. As such it would seem to give rather strong credence to the editors' contention that "the opposite" (that is, an inverse relationship between population density and state formation) is "equally likely." This state is that of the Ngwato, one of the Tswana tribes of the Bechuanaland Protectorate,* and the average density is given as 2.5. We shall examine this case from two standpoints: (1) the relevance of this (1936) population density to aboriginal conditions, and (2) the question as to just when, where, and under what conditions the term "state" can be meaningfully applied to their political system. As to the first question, it will be seen that the 2.5 density is based upon Reserve boundaries and tends to mask an important sociological reality of Tswana existence, the concentration in large settlements (10,000 to 15,000 in aboriginal times and even higher today). Although there are no estimates available for pre-Protectorate average densities in areas utilized, inferences will be drawn combining data from present land-use patterns with what is known or can be reasonably conjectured concerning the past. Indications are that densities may have been as high as 20 per square mile as far as land under cultivation is concerned. The maintenance of distant cattle posts poses problems that are essentially unresolvable without more complete data. The second problem is more complex and demands a threefold analysis

* As of September 30, 1966, the Republic of Botswana.

of the Ngwato state as delineated by Schapera in *African Politi-cal Systems,* the state (?) as it existed in the nineteenth century, and the pre-nineteenth-century state. We shall turn to this problem first, but it will be convenient in so doing to consider problems of density as well.

The native peoples of the Bechuanaland Protectorate are for the most part members of the Tswana [1] (Western Sotho) cluster of Bantu-speaking peoples. They are primarily divided into eight separate tribes—Kwena, Ngwato, Ngwaketse, Tawana, Kgatla, Lete, Tlokwa, and Rolong, of which the Ngwato (commonly called BaMangwato) are both the largest and, historically speaking, the best known. Each tribe ". . . has its own name, occupies its own territorial reserve within which no European may own land, and, subject to the overriding authority of the British Administration, manages its own affairs under the direction of a chief *(kgosi, morena)*, who is indepen-dent of the rest." (Schapera 1940:56) Schapera's account in *African Political Systems* is based upon field investigation car-ried out in 1935 and is entitled, "The Political Organization of the Ngwato of Bechuanaland Protectorate." It is the last word in this title whose full meaning should first be pondered. Consequently, I believe that the first step in the present analysis should be to attempt to establish as closely as possible the empirical referent of the term "state" when applied to the Ngwato.

I shall rely, in the first instance, on the testimony of Schapera himself.

Bechuanaland Protectorate, together with Basutoland and Swazi-land, is under the general legislative and administrative control of a High Commissioner responsible to the Secretary of State for Do-minion Affairs in Great Britain. The Territory itself is directly governed by a Resident Commissioner, with headquarters at Mafek-ing. The Ngwato Reserve, one of the twelve administrative districts into which it is divided is under the immediate jurisdiction of a District Commissioner stationed at Serowe. He is assisted to maintain law and order, and to carry out his other duties by a small body of police and a few subordinate Europeans and Native officials. Some technical officers representing the medical, agricultural, and veterinary branches of the Administration also live and work in the Reserve. (Schapera 1940:65)

Schapera also states that the general purpose of the Administration is to preserve tribal laws and customs and the authority of the chiefs within limits imposed by the power and jurisdiction of the Crown and the requirements of "peace, order, and good government." However, the Administration early took away from the chiefs the right to make war or enter into independent political agreements. Cases involving culpable homicide or any case involving Europeans were placed under the jurisdiction of the European courts, and appeals were permitted from the decisions of the chiefs in all serious cases. The Administration also defined the boundaries of tribal territories and imposed an annual tax on all adult males.

for many years thereafter the manner in which the chief administered the tribe was not a matter of Government concern, except when it led to open trouble, and in most cases the tendency was to support him as far as possible in his dealings with his people. (Schapera 1940:66)

In 1919 provisions were made for hearing appeals in any kind of case, civil or criminal, by a special combined court presided over by the chief and the local District Commissioner acting jointly. In 1926 divorce proceedings between natives married according to European law were brought under the District Commissioner's jurisdiction. In 1927 the trials of alleged sorcerers were removed from the jurisdiction of tribal courts. Then, in 1934 "the powers of the chief were for the first time clearly defined" by the Native Administration Proclamation (No. 74 of 1934). This Proclamation:

makes succession to and tenure of the chieftainship subject to the approval of the Administration, which has the power to pass over

an unsuitable heir or suspend an incompetent or otherwise unsatisfactory chief, provides machinery whereby the tribe can depose a
chief, makes conspiracy against the chief a statutory offence, and
establishes a formal Tribal Council to assist him in the execution of
his duties. (Schapera 1940:66–67)

The Native Tribunals Proclamation (No. 75 of 1934) removed
the following types of cases from tribal jurisdiction: treason,
sedition, murder or its attempt, rape or its attempt, assault,
conspiracy against the chief, and numerous statutory offences.
This Proclamation further streamlined the tribal court system
and recognized only three grades of courts whose decisions were
binding, with appeal from the highest grade to the District
Commissioner's Court and, under special circumstances, to the
Special Court of the Protectorate. Rules governing procedure
were laid down, written records open to the inspection of the
District Commissioner were made mandatory, and the forms of
punishment severely curtailed. These Proclamations were opposed by Tshekedi, the Ngwato Regent, who, together with
Bathoen, Chief of the Ngwaketse, took legal action against the
High Commissioner in December 1935. The contention of the
two chiefs was that these Proclamations could not possess legal
force because they (1) exceeded the Commissioner's power to
alter Native laws and customs and (2) violated treaty rights
reserved to the tribes. The decision of the Special Court which
heard this case in July 1936 is informative.

The court found in favour of the High Commissioner, holding that,
while the Proclamations undoubtedly altered existing Native law
and custom, he had acted within his powers; while on the question
of treaty rights a ruling by the Secretary of State, that the power of
the Crown in Bechuanaland Protectorate 'is not limited by Treaty
or Agreement', was taken as conclusive. (Schapera 1940:68) [2]

It is quite clear, then, that we do indeed have a state in
operation here; it is equally clear that the state is British. The
African-American Institute's *A Handbook of African Affairs*

expresses this reality succinctly. Under "Bechuanaland Protectorate" it states:

Political Status: British protectorate since 1885; High Commission Territory since 1909.

Chief of State: Queen Elizabeth II, represented locally by Sir Hugh Stephenson, High Commissioner for Basutoland, the Bechuanaland Protectorate and Swaziland, with headquarters in Pretoria: in Bechuanaland by the Queen's Commissioner (formerly Resident Commissioner) R. P. Fawcus.

Head of Government: The Queen's Commissioner for Bechuanaland Protectorate, assisted by an Executive Council composed of the Queen's Commissioner exofficio, 5 officials (the Government Secretary, the Financial Secretary, the Legislative Secretary and two others appointed by the Queen's Commissioner), and 4 unofficial members (2 European and 2 African) appointed by the Queen's Commissioner from among the elected members of the Legislative Council. (Kitchen 1964:62)

In fact, the proposals for a "next stage in constitutional development" which would "transform Bechuanaland into a self-governing multi-racial state by 1964," although providing for a Prime Minister and Cabinet system, still "would leave responsibility for defense, external affairs, internal security, finance, public service, and certain other matters to the Queen's Commissioner." (Kitchen 1964:63)

It should be pointed out at this juncture that the type of state described so far cannot be introduced into an argument concerning the relationship between population density and indigenous state formation—not without rendering the entire discussion absurd. The state Schapera has described is pre-eminently a British imposed protectorate. By the same token, either as colonies or protectorates, all other societies studied in *African Political Systems* were under state control. If a protectorate is to be offered as an example of a state then what is being compared is no longer low-density states versus high-density acephalous societies but low-density states versus high-density states. I feel certain that this is not what the editors of *African Political Systems* intended. Implicit in their approach is the notion that the fact of colonial rule is to be put to one side and the traditional indigenous political systems compared one to the other. As will be seen, this creates rather serious difficulties when a strictly synchronic approach is used and history ignored. The approach further carries the implication that the density figures of the colonial period (decade of the 1930s when British social anthropologists were studying these societies) can be taken as directly representative of the indigenous situation. Furthermore, the validity of this implication can be challenged for each of the six cases they have used. Final judgment on this last point is best reserved until the cases have each been analyzed, and I shall here limit myself to a discussion of the Ngwato.

Since the argument is about indigenous states, the Ngwato cannot be introduced as evidence of a low-density state until it is demonstrated that they indeed had a state prior to the coming of the Protectorate and British Rule. Since Schapera's article in *African Political Systems* never clearly separates the indigenous system from the Protectorate, the task here involves recourse to Ngwato history. This history, in turn, can best be understood against the background of a brief description of the Bechuanaland environment.

Bechuanaland is included within the "Western Drought Lands" by Goodwin. (1937:38–41) It lies mainly within the Kalahari ecological region, the main desert extending from the upper Molopo River in the south to Lake Ngami in the north, and from the main railway line in the east to the border of South West Africa in the west. This is an arid area but not true desert, and it lies between 3,000 and 4,000 feet in altitude. It is an area of ephemeral rivers and is scored by old river beds. Many undrained depressions or pans supply brackish water after rain. There is evidence both that the water supply (surface water and size of rivers) was formerly greater and that

desertic sands were more extensive in earlier times. The Okavango Marshes, 100 miles long, form one of the few areas where
there is permanent open water. (Goodwin 1937:38–39; Sillery
1952:196–97)

With this background in mind, it is possible to turn to a discussion of what is known of first Tswana and then Ngwato history. In this survey I shall attempt to demonstrate that the
indigenous Ngwato political system was neither, strictly speaking, that of an acephalous society nor that of a state, at least during the period for which there is historical information. Further, it will be shown that the 2.5 per square mile density figure
of the modern reserves cannot be considered as giving a particularly realistic indication of indigenous densities.

Nothing like accurate history can be delineated for the
Tswana before the early nineteenth century:

But it seems certain that at the time of the Bantu migrations into
southern Africa, a group of people called Sotho, allied by ties of
language and by similarities in social organization, penetrated as
far as the Vaal River and beyond, and spread from the Kalahari to
what is now the Eastern Transvaal, forming a belt across that part
of southern Africa. It is to this group that the Tswana belong, as
well as the people of modern Basutoland and many smaller tribes.
(Sillery 1952:1)

The first wave in this movement was composed of ancestors of
the Kgalagadi, who settled in the region after either expelling
or absorbing the still earlier Bushmen. Next came the Rolong
and their offshoots, the Tlhaping and the Kaa, and finally, in
the last and greatest wave came those who later split to form the
other Tswana tribes as they are known today. This last movement can be tentatively dated as occurring in the fifteenth or
sixteenth centuries. (Sillery 1952:1)

The first Europeans to contact the southern Tswana were
Pieter Jan Trüter, Dr. William Somerville, and the missionary
Anderson and party who journeyed to the interior to procure

draught oxen. In 1801 they encountered the Tlhaping living along the Kuruman River, and their descriptions have been recorded by another contemporary traveler, John Barrow. (1806:56–57) They commented, in some astonishment, upon what has since become known as a distinctive Tswana settlement pattern, the tendency to group almost the entire tribe in one large, compact settlement. The underlying reasons for this pattern, quite different from that of other members of the Southern Bantu, have been variously given as the requirements of defense (Sillery 1952:28) and the requirements of reliable water sources. (Goodwin 1937:40; Schapera 1956:35)

The report of the Trüter-Somerville Expedition also included comments on the durable quality of Tswana housing, the many granaries, the large tracts of ground under cultivation, and the large population of the settlement:

The town in its circumference, was estimated to be fully as large as Cape Town including all the gardens of Table Valley; but from the irregularity of the streets, and the lowness of the buildings, it was impossible to ascertain, with any degree of accuracy, the number of houses; it was concluded, however, that they could not be less than three thousand, all nearly of the same size and construction and differing in nothing from that of the Chief except that his was a little larger than the others. The whole population, including men, women, and children, they considered to be from ten to fifteen thousand persons. Round numbers are rarely exact. The two commissioners, it seems, at the end of fifteen days, on comparing notes, found that the estimate of one was ten, of the other fifteen thousand. The truth may probably lie in the middle. (Barrow 1806:390–91)

The Tlhaping were visited again in 1805, this time by a German surgeon, Henry Lichtenstein, who was in the political service of the Cape government. In the two-volume account of his travels Lichtenstein left a rather good ethnographic "profile" of the culture. (1930:363–419) He estimated the numbers

of the tribe and size of the settlement at 5,000 (1930:373), but
was informed that at the time of the Somerville-Trüter visit the
Tlhaping had been living with the Rolong. Since then they had
split off, some two-thirds of the original settlement having gone
with the Rolong. This would tend to confirm the 15,000 figure
of the previous estimate. On the other hand, if size of the settlement can be said to be a factor contributing to fissioning, it
might also be inferred that the Rolong-Tlhaping had by that
time already surpassed the optimal and hence typical figure. In
practice this figure probably varied, depending upon such
ecological factors as the water supply and availability and
proximity of garden lands and pasture, as well as such factors in
the superorganic environment as threat of attack.[3]

Lichtenstein described the settlement as a labyrinth of alleys,
large places, and broad streets, with houses numbering between
five and six hundred. He also commented upon the "com-
modiousness and durability" of the houses, on the extent of the
cultivation of two kinds of beans, gourds, melons, and millet,
but noted that the primary wealth was in cattle. He also made
the following observation upon the power of the chief: "The
king of the Beetjuans has nearly uncircumscribed power, since
he can punish all offences according to his own pleasure, and no
one has any right to oppose his decisions. He seldom, however,
exercises his power, for there is no positive law of which the
king can be regarded as the executor." (1930:413–14)

The general picture left by Lichtenstein was, on the whole,
one of general peace, although there were some small quarrels
with neighboring groups. This peaceful state of affairs was soon
to be shattered rudely by the repercussions of events in far off
Zululand. Apart from casual references to the power of the
chief, there is no real evidence that Tswana society was in any
sense organized into a state at this early period.[4] Now I shall
continue the story down to the time of the Protectorate by

dealing specifically with the Ngwato. The history of the Ngwato can, in general, be taken as rather typical of that of the other Tswana groups.

Tswana traditions record that some centuries ago, perhaps about the sixteenth century, a man called Masilo had two sons, Mohurutshe and Malope. Malope in turn had three sons, Kwena, Ngwato, and Ngwaketse. These last three are the traditional founders of the three major Tswana tribes of the Bechuanaland Protectorate. The Hurutshe, traditionally the senior branch, were so often attacked and dispersed that today they live in scattered groups among the major tribes. (Sillery 1952:xi) The history of these groups is one of constant fissioning and the formation of new groups. The Ngwato were presumably part of the following of Kwena when he split off from the Hurutshe, and the separation of the Ngwato from the Kwena probably did not take place until several generations after the death of Ngwato himself, in fact probably not until the time of Mathiba, chief of the Ngwato section in the last half of the eighteenth century. (Sillery 1952:115)

However, it would seem that while regarding themselves as a part of the Kwena, the Ngwato were actually living some distance apart long before the split. And after the split, Kwena chiefs often intervened in the internal affairs of the Ngwato. The actual causes of the split are not known; but, in the course of the conflict, the Ngwato were attacked by the Kwena, were seriously defeated by them, and fled to Shoshong where they found the Kaa and the Phaleng. The Phaleng had asked that the Ngwato be allowed to settle among them, but the Kaa were not so agreeable and were attacked by the Ngwato and driven back to the Kwena.[5] Shortly after its arrival at Shoshong the Ngwato tribe itself split.[6] A dispute broke out between Kgama I, son of Mathiba's first wife, and Tawana, son of the third wife. The upshot was that Tawana moved to Kedia on the Botletle River, thus founding the Tawana tribe in about 1795. He was followed by his father Mathiba, who had favored him throughout, but Mathiba later returned to the Kwena. Kgama I died of old age about 1817. During his chieftainship the town had been moved several times and at his death was at Serokolwane, near Serowe. Kgama I was succeeded by his son, Kgari, who moved the town to Serowe. Here the Ngwato were severely attacked by a force of Sebetwane's Fokeng.

At this time Kgari had under him a force of Kwena under Segokotlo and some Tlokwa under Lesage who were themselves refugees from Sebetwane. Kgari moved to the Kutswe Hills, was attacked again by Sebetwane, and so moved north hoping to recoup his losses by plundering the Shona. His forces successfully raided the Kalaka and took their grain, but the attack on the Shona proved disastrous. Kgari was killed, and the Ngwato were sent fleeing back to the Kutswe Hills. During the next decade the Ngwato were first overrun by Sebetwane's main army on its route north, then assisted by Sebetwane in further quarrels with the Kwena. This period saw Sedimo as regent, followed by Kgama II about 1835 and then Sekgoma, on whose accession (c. 1835) the Ngwato were a "sadly scattered and disorganized tribe owing to their military defeats." (Sillery 1952:118) Sekgoma set out with some success to build a strong and united tribe but soon was to feel the effects of another predatory chiefdom cutting its swath across the region. This was the Ndebele or Matabele, under Mzilikazi, who, in about 1838, were on their way north after their reverses in the Western Transvaal at the hands of the Boers. The Ngwato were driven out of the Kutswe Hills to Paje near Serowe and from there fled to Mosu (Mosung) near Makarikari. It was about this time that Sekgoma's son Kgama (III) was born somewhere along the banks of the Botletle River. As the Matabele moved on through, the Ngwato returned to Shoshong, upon the invitation of the Kaa and Talaote who had remained there. It was here that the Ngwato, under Sekgoma, were contacted by adventurous European traders and by missionaries like Moffat and Mackenzie.

There was continuing dissension within the tribe during this period. The mother of Kgama II had quarreled with Sekgoma (his half-brother) and had fled to the Kwena, taking her son Matsheng. The boy was subsequently captured by the Matabele and taken north with them, where he grew up as one of Mzilikazi's warriors. In 1854 Setshele, the chief of the Kwena who was allied by ties of marriage to the Ngwato, requested that the missionary Robert Moffat bring Matsheng back to the Ngwato, as he was the legitimate heir.[7] Moffat did nothing on this trip, but on his fourth journey in 1857 he persuaded Mzilikazi to release the young man. Assisted by Setshele and Sekgoma's cousin, Tshukudu, Matsheng was duly installed as Ngwato chief. Sekgoma and his son Kgama fled to the Kwena. Their exile was not of long duration, however. It is said that the Ngwato quickly tired of the Matabele-style discipline Matsheng tried to install, and soon Tshukudu (again with the assistance of Setshele) was moving for Sekgoma's return, which was effected in 1858.

In 1862 the missionaries Mackenzie and Price of the London Missionary Society came to work among the Ngwato. This missionary presence was to have considerable influence on the future development of the Ngwato. Sekgoma's two eldest sons, Kgama and Kgamane, became Christians and began to look down on the tribal customs to which their father still adhered. They refused to take part in tribal initiation and Kgama refused to enter into a polygynous marriage.[8]

In 1866 the conflict between father and sons became open warfare. Kgama and Kgamane fled for their lives to the neighboring hills, and for six weeks Shoshong was divided into two armed camps. A truce was arranged and Kgama returned after having secured sanctuary for Tshukudu among the Kwena. Tshukudu, however, was murdered at the order of Setshele. At his juncture, Matsheng returned, followed by those Ngwato who had fled with him in 1858. He had been summoned by Sekgoma, who by now had had second thoughts and conspired to rid himself of Matsheng, Kgama, and all his enemies by luring them into the kgotla (tribal assembly ground) and killing them there. Kgama discovered the plot and warned Matsheng. Sekgoma fled and Matsheng again became chief, but after five years was deposed again, this time at the instance of Kgama.

Needless to say, Setshele, who throughout these troubled times acted alternately as kingmaker and host to kings deposed, again took a hand. After Chief Gaseitsiwe of the Ngwaketse and Sekgoma himself had refused to have anything to do with the affair, Setshele sent an army to Shoshong with Kgama's brother, Kgamane. Kgama ousted Matsheng with the help of this force and without more ado was himself installed as chief. Matsheng became a wanderer, and his descendants now live inoffensively at Shashi. (Sillery 1952:121)

Kgama became chief in 1872 but did not have the power at this time to ensure continuance of his rule. Faced with a conspiracy from Kgamane in 1873, he called upon Sekgoma to return and resume the chiefship. Kgama then took his own followers and left Shoshong, first for Serowe and then finally north to the Botletle River. Returning to recover some cattle, he was ambushed by Sekgoma's forces but managed to escape. Then, in 1875, he returned with all his followers, cattle, and possessions and drove Sekgoma out for good. Kgama remained chief until his death in 1923, a period of forty-eight years.

I have traced the political history of the Ngwato during this period because I feel that it demonstrates the following important points:

(1) Although there is a definite institution of chiefship and rule of agnatic succession, Ngwato socio-political organization would apparently conform more closely to that of a chiefdom, as defined by Service (1962:143ff), than to that of a state. (Fried

1960:728) [9] Furthermore, the actual power of chiefs was severely limited by the ability of major segments to secede and
establish new political units. This is what Easton has called
segmentation of the support structure. (1959:246)

(2) Social stratification would seem to have been rather
minimal among the Tswana (Tlhaping) in Lichenstein's time.
He does mention a difference in the house size and the orna-
ments worn by the "poor," but these poor are not further
identified nor is a differential role in the economy indicated.
Specifically, there is no evidence that access of these people to
strategic resources was impeded. This last is important because
impeded access to strategic resources [10] for a subordinate group
versus unimpeded access for a superordinate group is the crucial
criterion of social stratification proposed by Fried (1960:721)
and utilized by the present author. Social stratification in itself
is viewed as an essential condition for a state and serves to
distinguish it from a chiefdom. Some tendencies toward stratification occurred during the wars of the nineteenth century.
Here, two complementary processes were visible: conquest of
weaker groups, and the clustering of refugees under the protection of stronger chiefs. I sketch this process in somewhat greater
detail for the Ngwato themselves.

Under Kgari and Sekgoma I, control had been extended over
Bushmen, Kgalagadi, Kaa, Phaleng, Tswapong, and Botletle
River peoples (Yeei and others). Also, because of the depredations of such groups as Mna-Ntatisi's Tlokwa warriors (Mana-
tees), Sebetwane's Fokeng (Kololo), and Mzilikazi's Matabele,
portions of other tribes and entire tribes themselves were set in
flight. The Ngwato, as a case in point, were joined by large
numbers of Kalanga and other people who fled from the
Matabele in Southern Rhodesia. The coming of the Boers and
of the various European adventurers, freebooters, and filibusters added to the dislocation of groups and the production of
refugee formation. The results of this process, persisting on into

the present, have been graphically illustrated by Schapera. Of the 101,481 comprising the 1936 population of the Ngwato Reserve

Only one-fifth belongs to the nuclear community, comprising the ruling dynasty and other descendants of the people who founded the tribe. . . . The remainder are bafaladi (foreigners, 'refugees') who became subject to the Ngwato chiefs at various times through conquest in war, voluntary submission, flight from an invading enemy, or secession from some other tribe. Most of them retain sufficient corporate life to be regarded as separate communities or groups of communities within the tribe. Some like the Kaa, Phaleng, Pedi, Tswapong, Kwena, Seleka, Khurutshe, Birwa, and the Kgalagadi, are themselves of Tswana origin, or come from the closely allied Northern Sotho cluster. Others are linguistically and culturally distinct. The Kalaka (who actually outnumber the Ngwato proper), Talaote, and Nabya belong to the Shona group of Southern Rhodesia, and the Rotse, Kuba, and Subia to the peoples of north-western Rhodesia; the Herero are refugees from South-West Africa, and the Sarwa are Bushmen with a large admixture of Bantu blood and culture. (1940:57)

During the period of the nineteenth century which preceded the Protectorate, these groups were either living under their own chiefs in a loose tributary relationship to the capital or on other occasions had been absorbed into the pre-existing ward organization of the Ngwato and were residing in their own wards in the capital with their own leaders as ward headmen. After the Protectorate there was further rationalization of the administration of these heterogeneous groupings based upon territorial districts.

As the coming of the Protectorate has other important implications for the argument, it would be well to return and again pick up the threads of the historical narrative at the point where they were left off—at the accession to office of Kgama III. It will shortly be seen that this event was to be followed within a decade by the coming of the Protectorate itself.

It has already been noted that Kgama III had been educated

and heavily influenced by the missionaries. In the words of Schapera:

Their great chief, Kgama III (c. 1837–1923), attained world-wide prominence as a zealous convert to Christianity, a fanatical prohibitionist of alcoholic liquor, and a strong supporter of British imperialism in central South Africa. He promoted in various ways the economic progress of his people, and keenly encouraged the spread of education. (1940:56)

In turn the missionaries endeavored to convince the British Government that its interests would best be served by extending a protectorate over Bechuanaland. By themselves these efforts would likely have availed little, but a wider logic of world history was favoring just such an eventuality.

For his part, Kgama III was confronted not only with the presence of missionaries in the Ngwato midst but traders, adventurers, freebooters, voortrekkers, and filibusters as well. It was apparently these last considerations in addition to concern for the effect upon his subjects of Europeans using liquor, and probably also fear of encroachment from Boers in the Transvaal, that led Kgama as early as 1876 to write a letter to the High Commissioner, Sir Henry Barkly, asking him under what conditions Her Majesty would receive his country and his people under her protection. In the same year Mr. A. Bailie, who had visited Gaseitsiwe, Setshele, and Kgama among other chiefs on a trip recruiting labor for the Kimberley diamond operations, had reported that the latter two were anxious to come under British protection. (Sillery 1952:55) To trace all the various conditions and events leading to the establishment of the Protectorate would entail a book in itself, and, in fact, this task has been admirably achieved by Sillery. (1952) In seeking "whether there is not some central cause from which have flowed the events which have been related" (1952:102), he sees first the pronounced acculturative influences of the missions which brought the Tswana into the British orbit and secondly tension between the Boer and Briton in southern Africa.

If there had been no Britons the Tswana would simply have been absorbed into the Transvaal and would today enjoy no independent status. If on the other hand there had been no Boers, Bechuanaland would, without a struggle, have become an ordinary British dependency, possibly a poor appendage to Rhodes' great dominions to the north. What gave it its peculiar importance—one can say in those days its only importance—was that it was not only a road to the north, but a road for which there were rival contenders. When the chiefs asked for a Protectorate they used the word in its literal sense: they meant protection against filibusters. In 1884–5, the political aims of the British Government to curb Boer expansion, Mackenzie's campaign for morality and humanity, Rhodes' vision of an empire in the north, all coincided, and the Protectorate came into being. (1952:103)

To this should be added the growing British fear of increasing German penetration in southern Africa.

When the decision finally came it came from Britain. Sir Charles Warren, the man who was to negotiate with the chiefs, had hardly arrived in Mafeking when he received the following telegram:

German Empire has been informed by Her Majesty's Ambassador at Berlin that Bechuanaland and Kalahari, as limited by first section of Order-in-Council of 27th January, are under British protection. As soon as practicable Warren should communicate with Sechele and Khame, and take care that no filibustering expedition takes possession of country, more especially Shoshong. (Sillery 1952:55) [11]

The Kwena chief, Setshele, had some doubts about the need or benefits of a protectorate but came around in the end.[12] Warren elaborated his proposals to the Ngwato, and Kgama accepted with the proviso that his laws against liquor should be enforced and that Ngwato lands were not for sale. He objected to the statement of boundaries in terms of degrees of longitude and latitude and instead offered his whole country, which, he maintained, extended to the Chobe and Zambezi Rivers in the north and to the Tati area and beyond in the east, reserving only 20,000 square miles around Shoshong for himself and his tribe.

Conditions in the nineteenth century—the constant wars and invasions, the rapidly recurring fissions and new amalgamations—were generally too unstable to permit either discernment or delineation of anything like state organization before the coming of the Protectorate. That state organization was at least partially underway seems indicated by the described absorption of conquered and refugee groups into the ward organization of the Ngwato and the beginnings of class stratification. Whether the Ngwato (or other Tswana) would have been able to maintain dominance over these groups, and hence maintain the order of stratification [13] without the intervention and support of some more powerful organization from outside, must remain problematical. Sillery has described the nineteenth-century situation in terms that are somewhat ethnocentric: "Before the coming of the Europeans it must be admitted that the story of the Tswana is one of migrations and wars apparently governed by no guiding principle other than fear of powerful enemies, want, family quarrels, or the caprice of petty chieftains." (1952: 102–3) Still, this summation is not altogether wide of the mark; and it would certainly argue against the likelihood that, in the absence of external intervention, the Ngwato would have indigenously developed a state.

Against this historical background it is now possible to confront in a more concrete manner both the question of Ngwato population density and the degree to which at any time the Ngwato may or may not have had a state. I shall address these problems in that order.

It is clear that the 2.5 average-density figure used in *African Political Systems* is derived from the 1936 population figures and the reserve boundaries imposed by the British administration. "The tribe occupies a reserve of 39,000 square miles in extent, much less than the territory it claimed when the Protectorate was established in 1885. Its population, returned in 1936 as 101,481, is by no means homogeneous." (Schapera 1940:57) It should first be noted that the reserve boundaries are quite arbitrary straight lines drawn on the map. Secondly, they mask important nucleations and concentrations of population within the reserves. For Bechuanaland in general (and including the Tswana) the population, both the African majority and 3,000 Europeans, live in the eastern sector near the railroad that traverses some 394 miles of Bechuanaland on its way from South Africa to Southern Rhodesia. Then, within this general concentration along the railroad, there was further concentration into large settlements. Practically all the Ngwato proper are concentrated in the capital, Serowe (population 25,000 c. 1940), along with some few *bafaladi* (foreigners). Most of the *bafaladi* are scattered through the rest of the reserve in some 170 villages ranging in size from settlements of under 100 to large centers such as Shoshong, Mnadinare, Bobonong, and Tonota, with populations in excess of 2,000.[14]

The comment by Schapera that the present reserve boundaries are considerably less territory than that traditionally claimed might lead the reader to suppose that Ngwato population was spread out over an even wider area in the pre-protectorate days and that the resulting population density was even less than 2.5. Actually the opposite is indicated by an analysis of the data.

The actual basis of the traditional territorial claims has been ably discussed by Sillery:

The tribes' title over huge tracts which they offered to the British Government was, to say the least of it, tenuous. Very little of this area was, or had ever been, in effective occupation. At the most they might be described as 'spheres of influence' visited by traders and hunting parties, and inhabited, if inhabited at all (e.g. in the neighborhood of the Botletle River) by refugees and other foreigners who for one reason or another gave allegiance to the ruling tribe in its distant capital. (1952:56)

In other words, claims to territory were not based upon occupation at one single time horizon but upon the totality of successive moves and occupations over time. The dynamics of this process can be greatly clarified by the application of Stenning's distinctions—transhumance, migratory drift, and migration.[15] It has already been noted that the Tswana, unlike other Southern Bantu, lived in large concentrated settlements and "durable, commodious houses," that is, in settlements that are intended to be relatively permanent. Transhumance, for the Tswana, involves the seasonal moves from the town to the arable, cultivated fields on the one hand and to cattle posts located in grazing areas on the other. Migratory drift is the gradual change of transhumance patterns over time:

since, at any rate with present agricultural and pastoral methods, the land and grazing round the towns are bound soon to become worked out, he must move his farm and his herds, and hence was devised the system of lands and cattle posts, appendages to the town, but at great distances from it. A man living at Serowe may have his farm twenty or thirty miles from the town, and his cattle post, as it is called, a hundred miles or more in the other direction. (Sillery 1952:200)

Beginning with both farm lands and cattle posts relatively close to the town at the time a settlement was first founded, the general trend of migratory drift would seem to be one of constantly extending transhumance trajectories. Hypothetically there are abstract limits to this process where the extension of migratory drift itself engenders migration, or a sudden and dramatic movement of the entire pattern. In the Tswana case this would involve a new settlement, with posts and fields relatively close by, and the reinitiation of a similar cycle. This last was not a feature of the Fulani process reported by Stenning. There migration was primarily due either to such ecological catastrophes as cattle epidemics or, even more frequently, to political and ideological conflicts with their neighbors. Among the Tswana, at least in the period studied, it would seem that migration most frequently occurred because of internal (largely succession) disputes and attack from predatory, militaristic chiefdoms. Depletion of water sources at the town center was an ecological factor sometimes causing migration. It has been obvious from the historical record that has been here examined that migration was a frequent occurrence in Tswana history. "But with the abolition of tribal war, better methods of finding and conserving water, and more settled political conditions, such mass movements have become rare (the last was when Kgama took the Ngwato from Palapye to Serowe in 1902) and are unlikely to be frequent in the future." (Sillery 1952:199)

The main Ngwato settlement had been constantly at Serowe for a period of 33 years up to the beginnings of Schapera's field investigations in 1935. When it is considered that in the pre-protectorate period the settlement shifted quite frequently,[16] the implications of the previous analysis should be clear. These implications are that it is highly probable that, under aboriginal conditions, Tswana fields and cattle posts were usually grouped much closer to their settlements than is the case today. Of course special conditions of defensive needs taken together with water requirements may have at times imposed conditions where cattle posts at least were far removed from settlements. But I believe it can be reasonably argued that the general tendency would be to begin by utilizing the areas closest to hand first, gradually moving out as these areas became exhausted. In this pattern a point would eventually be reached where a move of the entire settlement was dictated purely by the distance that had developed between field and town. The historical indications are that, for the nineteenth century at least, succession disputes and resulting fissioning or attack from other groups constantly triggered settlement moves long before these distance limits were reached. This conception is further reinforced by Schapera's observation that owing to increased use of ploughs (roughly one for every thirteen persons in 1936) and the importance of maize as a cash crop, especially among the Ngwato, "there has been a general increase in the average size of the fields." (1943:134)

Schapera has further noted that

The land cultivated by the Tswana is generally situated in the vicinity of the settlements where the people live. . . . Among the Tswana . . . the arable lands are located in special blocks or zones, often several square miles in extent, within which many different families have their fields side by side or very close together. These areas are reserved for cultivation, and people may not live permanently in them or establish cattleposts there. (1943:128) [17]

The preceding analysis would seem to be generally confirmed by the following quotation from Schapera:

The selection of arable land depends also upon its distance from home. This was an important factor in the past, when the people not only lacked wagons and other modern means of transport, but could not venture too far out for fear of enemies. It often happened, therefore, that a village would be moved when the land immediately around it became exhausted. Even now the inhabitants of the small villages found in the northern districts sometimes move away when their fields become unproductive. On the other hand, as we have seen, the bigger villages, and especially the towns, are tending to remain on fixed sites. Meanwhile, with the passage of time and the growth of the population, the arable land in the immediate vicinity has become taken up or exhausted. The people have consequently been forced to go farther out to cultivate, and the great majority *now have their fields too far away to be visited daily from their homes during the season.* (1943:131, my italics)

I have belabored this point because I feel it is necessary to have it firmly established before endeavoring to make projections back to the aboriginal situation from present-day population patterns. Beyond the estimates of total tribal and settlement population, there are no demographic figures available for the aboriginal period. These estimates provide a convincing indicator of population nucleation but not of average density. On the other hand, density figures arrived at by dividing estimates of total tribal population by either total area claimed or total area traversed in nineteenth-century wanderings would be largely meaningless. There is a way, however, through which a figure which is still crude and only approximate but probably closer to the mark than the others can be arrived at. Schapera, in his monograph on Tswana land tenure (1943:128), has given figures which illustrate the range of distances from settlements to fields for the following settlements: Molepolole (Kwena), Serowe (Ngwato), Mochudi (Kgatla), and Kanye (Kgwaketse). For Mochudi, these figures were supplemented by a map (1943: facing p. 128) of the cultivated and grazing areas so that greater precision could be obtained. For the others it would seem that, since fields do not extend out in a solid block to these limits on any side of the settlement, areas constructed using the average distances as radii would certainly not be less than the total of cultivated area. Using the map for Mochudi and these radii for the others, I calculated the following areas: Molepolole, 142 square miles; Serowe, 616 square miles; Mochudi, 150 square miles; and Kanye, 2,291 square miles. These areas yield densities of settlement population to cultivated land of 50, 40, 57, and 7 respectively. I then assumed, as an admittedly very rough estimate (although this is the approximate ratio indicated by the map for Mochudi), that grazing lands would be double those under cultivation. For the combined areas (three times the initial area) I then got the following densities: Molepolole, 33 per square mile; Serowe, 14 per square mile; Mochudi, 19 per square mile; and Kanye, 2 per square mile. The mean of these densities is 17 and, I believe, given the testimony that land use is more extensive in the present than it was in the past, I take this as indicating that the ratio of the populations of aboriginal Tswana large settlements

to lands in effective operation and constant use probably averaged in excess of 20 per square mile. These figures, of course,
are estimates pure and simple, but the alternative would seem
to be that aboriginal densities are simply unknowable.[18] I
apologize for the essential crudity of this figure, which is forced
upon me by the nature of the data, but I feel it is closer to the
mark than a figure of 2.5. It is reasonable to conclude, then,
that effective aboriginal Tswana densities were considerably
higher than the 2.5 figure, which is based upon arbitrary reserve
boundaries.

The final question that remains to be resolved is whether or
not or in what sense the aboriginal Tswana political organization (including, of course, that of the Ngwato) can be considered a state. Analysis here can be greatly assisted by a short
preliminary sketch of the indigenous political system based
upon Schapera. (1938)

The first point to consider is the office and powers of the chief
in traditional Tswana society. The office of chief was hereditary,
passing generally from father to son in order of the rank of the
wives who mothered the sons. Only members of the royal lineage could succeed to the office. The chief was not insulated from
the people by elaborate formal etiquette and taboo as was the
case in many developed African chiefdoms and states, but he
was treated with considerable outward respect. He had the right
to various forms of tribute, free labor for his fields and house
building, certain body servants and precedence in the choice of
land, building sites, and tribal ceremonies. He organized public
works and called out age-grade "regiments." He distributed
tribal land and regulated its use. He combined both administrative and judicial functions, and it was he who passed judgment
on the most serious cases.

This power was balanced by the power of several advisory
councils. The first of these was a small circle known as the
bagakolodi. Generally this was made up of the chief's own

senior relatives. It was rather informally constituted, and its membership was neither fixed nor limited. The chief was not bound to follow their advice, but he generally did not go against a majority.

The chief was further advised by a larger and more formal council of headmen which was summoned by him and dealt with such vital problems as making war, installation of chiefs, and projected legislation. "The chief will, in the course of debate, attempt to make them accept the opinion previously reached by him and his private advisors. But if the majority of the headmen are against it, he must abide by their verdict, unless he is looking for trouble." (Schapera 1938:78) Finally, there were several types of tribal assembly, with different names, convened for different purposes, up to and including the assembly of all the adult males of the tribe in the *kgotla*. Again, the chief was not bound to defer but usually did.

This type of organization would seem to fit the first set of criteria used by Fortes and Evans-Pritchard to distinguish states from nonstates. That is, the Tswana (including the Ngwato) had "centralized authority, administrative machinery, and judicial institutions." As to "cleavages of wealth, privilege and status," that is, social stratification, the situation is less clear. Early travelers such as Lichtenstein had only noted that the chief's houses were somewhat larger than those of the rest of the tribe. The chief had the right to certain tribute, labor for his fields and house building, and precedence in choice of land, but there is no firm evidence that the royal lineage as a group had such privileged access. In discussing rank and social classes Schapera reports the existence of three separate classes: "nobles" (*dikgosana*), who were agnatic descendants of any former local chief; "commoners" (*badintlha, batlhanka*), descendants of aliens incorporated long ago; and "immigrants" (*bafaladi, baagedi*), people of groups more recently admitted. (1953:36) The latter, he observed, are considered "on probation" but accepted as commoners if they remain. More importantly, he also declared that these class distinctions operated mainly in political life. I take this to mean that these distinctions were not important economically. In fact, with the exception of the restriction of the chiefship to members of the royal lineage, these distinctions do not seem to be crucial in the political life. Inner councils were composed of both "nobles" and "commoners" and all three "classes" participated in the general assembly, although the statements of immigrant spokesmen did not carry as much weight as the words of spokesmen from the other two groups. This does not constitute social stratification in the full sense of the term proposed by Fried as privileged versus impeded access to strategic resources.

There is one other class described by Schapera which might constitute at least incipient stratification. He refers to the members of this class as "serfs" (*malata*). They were mainly of Sarwa (Bushmen) and Kgalagadi (Tswana-Bushman mixture) stock.

These people, found in the country when it was occupied by the Tswana, were parcelled out in local groups among the chiefs and other leading tribesmen. They and their descendants were permanently attached to the families of their masters to whom they paid special tribute and whom they served in various menial capacities; such property as they acquired was at their master's disposal; if oppressed, as they often were, they had no access to tribal courts; and they lacked many other civic rights, including participation in the political assemblies. (1953:37)

At the present time, most the inequalities concerning these groups have been abolished and they are normally classed as commoners, but the Sarwa especially are still considered inferior by Tswana, and it is deemed degrading to intermarry with them. These groups present most of the aspects of submerged castes. A closer examination of their historical situation as described by Schapera alters the picture considerably.

These serfs apparently appear importantly in two different economic contexts—as herdsmen and as hunters. Wealthy Tswana or men of standing had hereditary servants who were Kgalagadi or Sarwa who looked after their cattle posts. In return the latter could use the milk of the cattle and, after the introduction of the plough, use oxen as draft animals. They were sometimes given heifers whose offspring then belonged to them. "Most people, however, rely upon their sons or other young relatives to look after the posts." (Schapera 1943:220) Here there is incipient stratification but apparently not of widespread economic significance.

The situation of the hunters was quite different. Over territorial districts there were placed either "royal" or "servant" overseers. Any Kgalagadi or Sarwa within the districts were the "serfs" of the overseer who was entitled to "appropriate whatever property they acquired." (Schapera 1943:260) This applied especially to such hunting spoils as ivory, ostrich feathers, and skins—all of which were important export items in European trade. "Royal" overseers appropriated these spoils themselves, whereas "servant" overseers returned them to the chief and were given a reward for their trouble. Overseers supplied the hunters with guns, dogs, and ammunition and visited them periodically to collect the ivory, ostrich feathers, or skins, leaving them the meat. It is instructive to note that as soon as the wagon roads were constructed the Sarwa and Kgalagadi began holding back these spoils and engaged in a "contraband" trade with the Europeans. The Tswana masters attempted to respond with severity by killing disobedient "vassals." This approach failed and was quickly abandoned. Schapera quotes an interesting comment from the pen of the missionary J. Mackenzie in 1871:

they found that severity did not answer their purpose, and so the masters now are in point of fact competitors with the European hunters and traders for the purchase of ivory and feathers from their own vassals. Of course they do not acknowledge that they occupy such a position, but the 'presents' which they now give their vassals are every year more handsome, and the whole transaction assumes more the appearance of barter than the levying of tribute. (Schapera 1943:261)

The relationship described here bears striking structural resemblance to the symbiosis between Bantu villagers and Congo pygmies as analyzed by Turnbull (1961). Here again the relationship was perceived by the villagers (and by anthropologists like Schebesta who took the village as their starting point) as domination and control by hereditary Bantu masters of the pygmies. To the pygmies this was a relationship to be utilized or ruptured to their advantage. Neither the Bantu-pygmy nor the Tswana-bushman cases are very convincing examples of class stratification. For the aboriginal Tswana, then, social stratification was rather minimal and limited to those proportionately few cases of clientship involving cattle herding. Tendencies toward further stratification were enhanced under the conditions prevailing in the nineteenth century, when many groups of diverse origin were incorporated into the Tswana ward organization as *bafaladi*.

The degree of social stratification among the Tswana takes on considerable significance when one considers the theoretical analysis of the evolution of the state offered by Fried (1960). It is Fried's contention that the state emerges under conditions of developing social stratification, and concerning the emergent state he has observed:

The first and most important task of an emergent state is to maintain general order both within and without. But evolving states generally lack the technical capacity to keep control of an entire range of social institutions; indeed, even the most tightly organized modern states cannot do so. That being the case, the emergent state in particular must maintain order by defending the keystone of that order—the order of stratification. (Fried 1964:188)

The maintenance of these two orders are what Fried terms the primary functions of the state. Their implementation by the emergent state in turn gives rise to several characteristic secondary functions, each associated with one or more particular institutions. In Fried's view these functions of the state never appear as a unified response to basic socio-cultural needs except in stratified societies that are on the threshold of becoming states. Furthermore, he feels that the coexistence of a majority of them can be taken as a valid indicator of the presence of state organization. This being the case, a full discussion of these functions should be helpful in classifying the Ngwato political system, and in fact the Tswana systems in general. As presented by Fried, the secondary functions of the state are:

(1) Population control (the fixing of boundaries and categories of membership, census).
(2) The disposal of trouble cases (the standardization of rules, procedure and officers for both civil and criminal cases tending towards codification).
(3) The defense and maintenance of sovereignty (this involves military and police power and forces and eminent domain).
(4) Fiscal support (taxation and/or conscription).

It seems clear that (1) was at least minimally present in the ward organization; on the other hand, this situation was strongly counteracted by the constant secession and fissioning from the political unit which was a pronounced feature of Tswana political organization. This fissioning was maintained at a constantly high rate throughout the nineteenth century. The process had begun at least as early as the beginning of the century, judging by the testimonies of both Lichtenstein and Barrow.

It seems that (2) was present in a fairly regularized hierarchy with the Chief at its apex. These were customary procedures rather than actual law codes.

Also present was (3), insofar as the Chief had the authority to call out the age regiments for military duty. This authority, again, was rather severely curtailed by the ability of dissident factions up to one-half of the tribe to move out and establish a completely autonomous and sometimes hostile politico-military unit. Eminent domain was present insofar as the Chief had the power to allocate agricultural and grazing lands and also building sites.

Under (4), conscription was represented in the power of the Chief to call out age regiments for work on his fields, building his house, or for public works. The first two were privileges specifically vested in the office of Chief.[19] These may also be considered taxation (taxation of labor services rather than product). The Chief was also entitled to one tusk of every elephant killed, ostrich feathers, and skins of all lions and leopards. Beyond this there was no taxation, so that in general it must be said that taxation was rather rudimentary in its development. It is important to point out again that both the power to collect tax and the amount to be collected was hemmed in and restricted by the capacity of large segments to withdraw from the political community and establish their own unit.

In fact this fissioning of the support structure, which was such a characteristic feature of Tswana political organization as far back as traditional history and the accounts of early visitors permit us to trace, sets rather important limits to the implementation of any of the primary or secondary functions of the state listed by Fried. Indeed Easton has devoted five pages of an overview article on Political Anthropology to a discussion of the rate of segmentation of the support structure as a crucial variable in the analysis and comparison of political systems. (1959:229–35) In the same article Easton criticized the dichotomous A and B typology of *African Political Systems* and suggested that instead political systems be ranged on a continuum in terms of the degree of differentiation and specialization of political statuses and roles. The advantage of the role differentiation is, according to Easton, that we can expect to find variations of other important political characteristics associated with each cluster point on the role-differentiation continuum. For example, we can hypothesize that significant increases in role differentiation will be accompanied by significant differences (1) in the criteria of recruitment, (2) in claims to the legitimate use of force as a sanction, (3) in continuity of political processes, and (4) in rate of segmentation of the support structure —to mention only a few variables. (1959:243–44)

It is Easton's contention that polities that rank low in political differentiation will also be those where:

(1) Recruitment to socio-political roles is largely ascribed.
(2) The claim to the use of legitimate force in sanctioning decisions will be only minimal.
(3) High-level decisions will tend to be episodic and made only when disputes involving the whole society require resolution.
(4) Segmentation of the support structure will tend to be high.

Specialized political statuses among the Ngwato and other Tswana was limited to the offices of Chief and headman, which are both ascribed by primogeniture in the agnatic line (first son of great wife) .

As to both (2) and (3), the Tswana would seem to rank higher on Easton's continuum than such genuinely acephalous groups as the Nuer or transitional systems such as the Logoli (Chapter VII) , but demonstrably lower than either the Zulu or the Bemba. Data concerning support-structure fissioning are not sufficient for the Logoli to allow comparison, but the Tswana would certainly rank above Nuer and below Bemba, though rather close to Zulu.

In terms of both the criteria used by Fried and by Easton, then, I should be inclined to argue that the Ngwato (and the same would hold for the Tswana in general) should be removed from the state column. On the other hand, they were certainly not an acephalous society. The chiefship among the Tswana was rather highly developed while the "royal" lineage which monopolized this office held a position in Tswana society not often encountered except in well-developed chiefdoms or emergent states. The members of this lineage held decidedly higher rank, its members had the influential voice in the councils, and also they headed up the various men's and women's age regiments. The managerial role of the Chief in the allocation of agricultural and grazing lands as well as in the coordination of production itself and the grouping of agricultural lands in ward blocks is not generally characteristic of African tribal economies. Also, the concentration of the population into large settlements structured into wards with a definite hierarchy up through ward headmen to the chief is more characteristic of state societies than it is of tribal organization. Indeed, one is reminded here (in a way that suggests intriguing evolutionary parallels) of such organizational forms as the Aztec *calpulli* or the wards of Peruvian Chanchan. Current historical research, using techniques and information from the fields of comparative ethnology, linguistics, archaeology, and the study of oral traditions, is already adding new dimensions to and perhaps new insights into Tswana origins and organization. This inquiry concerns the Empire of Mutapa (or Monomotapa) associated with the celebrated stone architectural remains at Great Zimbabwe. Abraham, who is currently engaged in ethnohistorical research into the subject, attributes the initial impetus to the Karanga or Shona ethnic group.

The bulk of the indigenous population of Southern Rhodesia belongs to the Karanga or Shona ethnic group; the Ndebele, nineteenth-century arrivals, although nominally of Nguni stock, are very largely assimilated Karanga; the Tonga, the Tavara, Helengwe, *Suto-Tswana*, etc., although ethnically distinct *seem always to have been under Karanga dominance from early times.* (Abraham 1964:105, my italics)

According to Abraham, who bases his assessment on oral tradition, archival material, and archaeological findings, the nuclear Karanga migrated from the vicinity of Lake Tanganyika into the region south of the Zambezi, arriving about A.D. 1325. (1964:106) The Karanga at this time were a relatively evolved patrilineal society familiar with hoe-agriculture and cattle herding, metal-work and masonry, and possessing feudal-like political institutions. The Karanga leader adopted the title of "NeMbire" which was passed on to his descendants and he was assisted by a certain Mutota Churuchamutapa, his son-in-law. The country south of that occupied by the NeMbire was occupied by Muslims and further to the south near the Limpopo was a group of people known to the proto-Karanga as "Varozvi" and regarded by the former as in no way related to them. There were also roaming Bushmen bands in the region. It is the Varozvi (or Rozvi) that are of importance here, for Abraham has noted:

The early Rozvi were possibly the bearers of Summers' Iron Age B I Culture, and Schofield has indicated typological analogues between the ceramics of this culture and that of early Suto-Tswana. Furthermore, the Rozvi dialects, as known to us at a much later stage, admittedly, are heavily impregnated by Tswana lexical and phonological characteristics, and it is therefore possible that the early Rozvi were a Tswana-related group. (1964:107)

Abraham continues:

The Mbire or people of NeMbire appear to have progressively assumed control of the centre and south of the country in the hundred years following their arrival, and NeMbire II despatched Mutota to install Chikura, son of the latter's daughter Senwa, as chief of the Rozvi but subject to the overriding authority of the Mbire. By the end of the fourteenth century a comparatively refined material culture, styled by Summers "Iron Age B II" was under way at the Dzimbahwe or sacro-political headquarters of the Rozvi *Mambo* or king—a culture whose main features were superior stone-masonry, elegant ceramics, the extensive use of gold, tin, copper, and bronze, and imported Oriental porcelain and glassware. (1964:107–8)

This research, if further substantiated, opens up intriguing hypotheses concerning the Tswana, hypotheses which, from the purely theoretical point of view, are rather attractive, to the present writer at least. In this context the puzzling aspects of Tswana organization are explained by conceptualizing the Tswana groups as having been formerly part of a developed stratified society. Tswana fissioning then began with the breakup of the Mutapa Empire. As subsections of Mutapa hived off, the Tswana would display the centralized leadership of the local units but not the social stratification of the whole society. It can be inferred, then, that the presumably pre-existing concentrated settlement patterns were reinforced by requirements of defense and water in the new environment while the breakdown of the original system of stratification and control led to increased fissioning of the support structure. Then, under the conditions of the nineteenth century, tendencies toward new social stratification became operative, but their full realization was truncated by the coming of British rule. Full evidence for the support of such a hypothesis is, of course, still unavailable, but the possibility of obtaining such seems to indicate that an attempt at a full and definitive classification of the Tswana political system is at present premature and likely to be abortive. The matter, then, for the time being at least, should be left open.

This leaves three alternatives. The first is the one mentioned above, which (although as yet backed by decidedly insufficient evidence) is frankly the one most attractive to me. Beyond this, it would seem that it can reasonably be argued that the Tswana polities were not states but should be ranged on a continuum of political development definitely beyond the acephalous societies. If this view be accepted, the rather large concentrations of population in single settlements would appear to be somewhat anomalous. Here it could be argued that the tendencies toward state development were inhibited by the chaos created by external intrusions during the nineteenth century and that the final crystallization of these tendencies was obscured by the imposition of colonial rule.

On the other hand, it could be argued that the Tswana (including the Ngwato), despite the rather low incidence of social stratification, should in terms of centralized chiefship, ward organization, and other factors be classified as states. In this case the very large indigenous settlements (themselves an important form of population density) should be borne in mind as well as the indications that *average* density for area actually occupied and utilized was probably much higher under aboriginal circumstances—certainly higher than 20 per square mile.

Most importantly, it should be noted that not one of these three alternatives contradicts the notion that state formation and population density are positively related.

THE THIRD of the low-density states presented by Fortes and Evans-Pritchard is the Bemba. The immediate puzzle confronting us, in terms of this group, is that of a political system of apparent complexity in association with a population density as low as 3.75 per square mile and a pattern of dispersed settlements which shifted every five years. The Bemba have seemed paradoxical in a number of ways to many anthropologists. Richards has expressed similar puzzlement, although in terms that seem the quietest of understatements, when she observes that the complexity of the political organization makes "an interesting contrast to the simplicity of the people's economic system." (1961b:25) We shall be concerned here with exploring the paradoxical population density–state formation relationship and shall find in our analysis that light is shed as well on other interesting problems about the Bemba. It will be seen that the paradox of the Bemba [1] is essentially an illusion created by the collapsing of history into an "ethnographic present." The Bemba state rose and flourished on the basis of a localized monopoly of the trade in slaves and ivory. With the coming of the British in the 1890s not only was this monopoly ended but the trade itself was eliminated and, with it, the effective functioning of the state. What have persisted are the traditions and complex ritual of a prior, and happier, day and a hollow shell of the state structure buttressed by British indirect rule. At the same time the Bemba economy has fallen back on an almost complete reliance on shifting cultivation supplemented by copper belt wages. The demographic correlates of the rise and fall of the Bemba "empire" largely confirm rather than deny the proposition that population density is related in a positive manner to state formation. In delineating this process, let us begin, as did Richards, with the economy and polity of the Bemba as it existed in the 1930s.

Richards' field studies among the Bemba were carried out between May, 1930 and July, 1931, January, 1933 and July, 1934, and a final return trip in the summer of 1957. Her accounts (1940b, 1959, 1961b) are all based primarily upon the first two tours, although the second edition of her *Land, Labour and Diet in Northern Rhodesia* (1961b) contains in its foreword some additions and emendations as a result of the 1957 trip. Primarily, then, the early 1930s form the ethnographic present for the Bemba as they confronted Richards in the field.

Bemba occupy an area on the northeastern plateau of Northern Rhodesia * between latitudes 9°–12°S. and longitudes 29°–32°E., an area which includes virtually the whole of Kasama administrative district and much of Mpika, Chinsali, Luwingu, and Mporokoso as well. There is a single rainy season in which the rainfall is described as more than adequate, but the soils of the area are generally poor, of a thin sandy character, and are covered by deciduous woodland, primarily of the type *Brachystegia-Isoberlinia*. The Bemba are primarily agriculturalists, practising a particular form of shifting cultivation called the *citemene* system after the native term for "cut garden." This involves pollarding the trees and piling the cut branches in small circular patches which are then fired to form an ash bed in which the seeds are sown. (Whitely 1951:1, 9–10) In general, the loppings from 6 to 10 acres of trees are piled on about one acre of land. Finger millet seed is broadcast over the burnt area and covered with the burnt surface soil. No further cultivation of the millet crop is required.

* As of October 24, 1964, the Republic of Zambia.

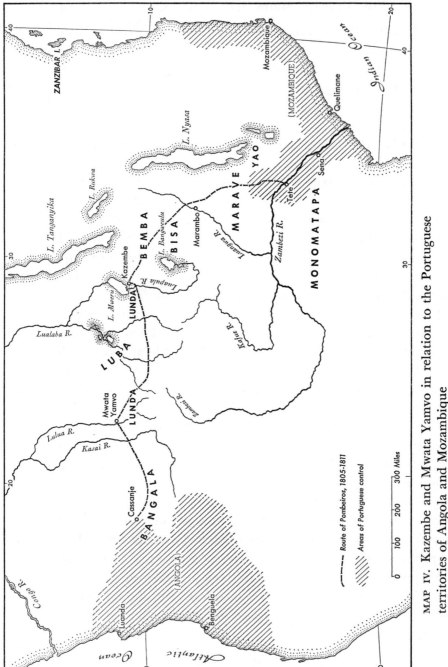

MAP IV. Kazembe and Mwata Yamvo in relation to the Portuguese
territories of Angola and Mozambique

From Ian Cunnison, "Kazembe and the Portuguese, 1798–1832," *Journal of
African History* **2**: 61–76, 1961

The method, though wasteful of otherwise useless woodland, is extremely reliable and the average yield of grain from wretchedly poor soils (about 1,400 lb. per acre) compares favorably with average maize yields on European farms on much better soils in Central and Southern Africa. . . . The great disadvantages of the system are that concentrations of population are impracticable and the rapid deterioration which occurs if the population-land balance is upset. As the trees take about 20 years to recover from lopping if not fire protected, from 120 to 200 acres of woodland are required to provide for an annual acre of finger millet, in perpetuity. (Allan 1949:86)

In addition to finger millet (*Eleusine coracana*), which is the main staple, Bemba also grow Kaffir corn, bulrush millet, Kaffir beans, Livingstone potatoes, pumpkins, edible gourds, cucumbers, melons, maize, cassava, sweet potatoes, and ground nuts.[2] This diet is supplemented by hunting, fishing, and the gathering of wild foods. Only a few goats or sheep are kept, and occasionally cattle are kept in the urban areas. The Bemba display ingenuity in the alternation of crops and the use of the more fertile soil of abandoned village sites. In general, their agriculture is regarded as less complex than that of a number of neighboring tribes. Furthermore, the material equipment of the Bemba is described as being of the simplest. This type of adaptation to environment forces the movement of the typical village to a spot a few miles away on the average of every four to five years. (Richards 1961b:18–21) There is neither appreciable cash cropping nor European settler farming in the area. It should be noted, however, that the opening up of the Northern Rhodesia copper belt placed considerable demands on native labor, so that by 1930 the percentage of men away at work at different portions of the year was from 40 to 60 per cent; and Richards, in fact, has termed the area a typical native labor reserve. (1961b:22–33)[3] These facts are neither surprising in themselves nor are they inconsistent with each other. Neither is a population density of 3.75 unexpectable under these circumstances. The puzzle lies rather in the correlation of these ecological, economic, and demographic factors taken as a whole and the political system described for the Bemba.

Richards' article in *African Political Systems* is still the classic account of Bemba political organization. This may be supplemented by other sources listed in my bibliography, particularly those by Richards, Brelsford (1944), and Sheane (1911). I shall content myself here with sketching merely the broad outlines, although at a later point I shall wish to scrutinize more closely some of the details.

The Bemba tribal territory is divided into approximately thirty-three semi-autonomous chiefdoms, all ruled by members of one clan, the *Bena nandu* or "Crocodile Clan." There were four major chiefdoms and twenty-nine minor ones dependent upon them. Of these, two, that of Mwamba and that of the Citimukulu, were far and away the largest and most pre-eminent; and at the time of the imposition of European rule the balance of power between the two was indeed very close. The Citimukulu, however, was the official paramount. His chiefdom lay at the center of the territory; and he held traditional pre-eminence by virtue of seniority, ritual relationship to the fertility of the land, and control of the sacred relics (*babenye*) by which he approached the ancestors of the tribe. More importantly, he controlled military and economic power rivalled only by that of the Mwamba. There were also specialist counsellor-priests called the *bakabilo* who controlled the rites of burial, succession, and installation as well as carrying out ritual for the tribe. (Richards 1960:180, 1961a:146) Hierarchical ranking was an important part of the system and was based upon closeness of kinship, real or fictitious, to the chief. Succession was in the matrilineal line within the *Bena nandu* passing to brothers and then sisters' sons. There were also special ranks for the "children of the chief" and the "grandchildren of the chief" who though not in the same clan, and hence not heirs, were nonetheless entitled to special privileges. "Royal women" also had a special position. Sisters of the chiefs were usually given villages to rule and there were two special offices, the *Candamukulu* and the *Mukukamfumu* to which the mothers of the paramount succeeded. The mother of the paramount was a highly honored person, took part in tribal councils, and had several villages of her own to rule.

In addition to the dogma of descent, the entire system was buttressed up by elaborate ritual and something akin to the ideology of "Divine Kingship." This proliferation of complex ritual and ideology should not be allowed to obscure the very marked decentralization of the entire system. "All chiefs and sub-chiefs had their own courts and collected their own tribute and approved the appointment of their own headmen." (Richards 1961a:146) [4] As one goes from what might be termed chiefdom to province, to district, to village there was a tendency for each smaller unit to mirror on a smaller scale the one above. In his own way the village headman attempted to emulate the court of the paramount. More important, each chief, including the paramount, directly ruled only his own district or *icalo*. It was from this unit alone and not from the chiefdom at large that tribute in labor and subsistence goods accrued. By the end of the nineteenth century the major chiefs had gained the power of appointing their own nominees to territorial sub-chiefships. These were not commoners but rather royal ineligibles—sons and, in one case, the daughter of a chief. These positions were replenished from the same source and so could not become local hereditary lines. This could be taken as indicating a tendency toward a tighter organization and a more developed chiefdom. Against this, however, was the tendency toward fission between the major segments ruled by the Mwamba and the Citimukulu respectively. At the time of the arrival of the first Europeans, the incumbent Mwamba had his own local *baka-*

bilo, was installing his own five or six subchiefs, and had his own important relics at his shrine. "He refused to succeed to the Citimukuluship because he said his own post was equal in authority." (Richards 1961a:146)

A glance back over the past few paragraphs will show that almost as soon as we began discussing the political system of the Bemba the temporal frame of reference shifted, perhaps imperceptibly at first, to the period of the nineteenth century and earlier. This is an important clue, not to be overlooked, and we are forced back on history in search of answers.[5]

This history, in turn, can only be analyzed meaningfully in terms of the development of trading networks in the region, a process in which the neighboring Lunda of the Luapula Valley played a crucial role. As there are also several important and recurring links of an economic, political, and traditional nature between the Bemba and the Lunda, it will be helpful to treat these two groups together. "The zero point of the Bemba is Lubaland in the Congo from which came their first chief, Citimuluba, his sister Bwalya Cabala, and the two subsequent chiefs, probably in the eighteenth century." (Richards 1960: 181) [6] The same zero point can be asserted for the Lunda. Their area at the time we first encounter them was between the upper Kwango and the Kasai and eastwards again to the Lualaba. Their traditions indicate neither large states nor powerful chiefs until the appearance among them, close to the end of the sixteenth century, of a small group of Luba ivory hunters. This led to the establishment of a chiefdom or state surrounded by satellite chiefdoms whose paramount rulers assumed the dynastic title of Mwata Yamvo. (Oliver 1962:128–29) Murdock cites a founding date of 1625 and attributes it to a Luba dynasty.[7] This Lunda complex expanded after 1675 until it was within 300 miles of the Atlantic coast. (Murdock 1959:286) From the very start the Mwata Yamvo's kingdom was in indirect trading contact with the Portuguese in Angola, receiving firearms, cloth, and other luxuries.

It is difficult in fact not to conclude that the whole state-building operation in this instance had an economic motive. The immediate perimeter of the Portuguese colony was dominated by the slave trade, and here warfare and destruction were the main result. Beyond this perimeter the main commodity of value for export was ivory, the hunting and handling of which, though highly lucrative, required large-scale organization of a political kind. . . . It looks very much as though it was in response to the economic stimulus provided by the Portuguese opening of the Atlantic coast that the process of state-formation in the vast area of Luba-Lunda domination was set in motion. (Oliver 1962:129)

The theme of guns and cloth for ivory (and later slaves) is a recurrent one through all the subsequent development we shall trace. There are other interesting parallels as well. The Mwata Yamvo appointed provincial governors and district chiefs who resided at his capital. They supplied troops and collected tribute of ivory, salt, slaves, and produce. The four highest formed a council called the Kannapumba which, together with the Lukokesha, or Queen Mother,[8] formed an electoral college to choose a successor. (Murdock 1959:286)

This may seem a long way from Northern Rhodesia, but the events are related and the general process all of a piece. If the Portuguese opening up of the Atlantic coast was a stimulus to Lunda development in the west, there are also good gounds for considering that the Portuguese presence at Sena and Tete on the Zambezi had a similar influence in the east. Toward the end of the seventeenth century and the beginnings of the eighteenth century there was a series of moves eastward by Lunda groups from Mwata Yamvo's capital into the region around Lakes Mweru and Bangweulu and the Luapula Valley. During the same period there was the movement into this general region of at least one Bemba group. By 1740 the Eastern Lunda were established on the Luapula under the first Kazembe. Tradition asserts that they came with guns, frightening the inhabitants into submission and incorporating followers on the way. Traditions also give as reasons for these incursions:

(1) To find more white men in the east.

(2) To gain control of the salt marshes of the Lualaba.

(3) To colonize a fine country to which they had heard a refugee had gone.

The first two of these are frankly economic and the third might also be so construed, depending, of course, on the definition of a "fine country." Lunda conquest was apparently not primarily a matter of either displacing or exterminating groups but was rather a process of entering into tributary and ritual relationships with lineage heads known as "Owners of the Land." District chiefs were appointed to rule and dwell side by side with these "Owners of the Land" in a manner strikingly similar to that employed by the Namoos among the Tallensi. (See Chapter VI) [9] The greatest expansion of this Eastern Lunda "Empire" was from approximately 1760 to 1860, when it stretched from the Lualaba in the west to the Chisinga country in the east and from Malungu territory in the north to that of the Bisa to the south. "Tribute is said to have come from centres throughout this whole district for some time." (Cunnison 1959:41) The Kazembes were in indirect contact with the Portuguese on the Zambezi through the Bisa, the major middleman tribe of the region, and through *pombeiros* or half-caste traders. Feelers were sent out and attempts were made to make this eastern trade with the Portuguese more direct. At the same time the Eastern Lunda remained in contact with and sent tribute to Mwata Yamvo. Thus there was, in effect, a transcontinental trade route operating indirectly through middlemen at each end. From Mwata Yamvo (c. 1798) Kazembe received goods from the west coast such as looking glasses, tea sets, plates, cups, beads, cowries, and woolen goods. In return he sent slaves to Mwata Yamvo which were destined for Angola and the Portuguese. By 1806

the kingdom of Kazembe was nearly at the height of its expansion, and he and the Mwata Yamvo together controlled a vast region of

Central Africa. The two centres were in constant communication. In 1806 the two Pombeiros followed a well-established trade route between them; and an individual of the Bisa tribe gave Lacerda good evidence that he was familiar with Angola. Thus there was transcontinental trade, and both potentates were in indirect contact with both sides. Also, both were trading on their respective sides through tribes which were in some measure under their control. The Bisa at this time were under Kazembe, though perhaps not very effectively, while the Bangala, Mwata Yamvo's middlemen, were a distant branch of the Western Lunda. (Cunnison 1961:65)

The Portuguese in the east were also desirous of entering more directly into this trade and three major expeditions were sent to the capital of Kazembe—that under Lacerda in 1798–1799, that of the Pombeiros in 1805–1811, and that of Monteiro and Gamitto in 1831–1832. The published accounts of these expeditions make possible the establishment of chronological bench marks and also give the first reports, though somewhat vague, as to the activities of the Bemba.

The precise relationship and the exact chronological synchronization of these developments with the earliest Bemba migrations into the region are still not clear and tend to be debated among the various specialists. Whitely gives the order of arrival as Bisa, Bemba, Lunda. (1951:8) Richards says:

The first [Bemba] arrivals apparently crossed the Lualaba River, which forms the western boundary of their present territory, about the middle of the eighteenth century, and travelled north and east until they established their first headquarters near Kasama, the present administrative centre of the Bemba country. (Richards 1940:85)

Coxhead (1914:3 fn 5) places the Bemba arrival some one to two generations before that of the Lunda in 1740, but Richards has noted: "The Bemba themselves are emphatic that they arrived with the Lunda and parted with them just south of Lake Mweru." (1961b:16) [10] It is quite possible, if not probably, that there were several separate and overlapping migrations of both groups, which then became telescoped and condensed in the traditions. It is noteworthy that, as the Lunda under Kazembe II moved east of the Luapula in the mid-eighteenth century, they "took care not to fight the Bemba whom they regarded as relatives of some sort." (Cunnison 1959:40) Yet by the end of the century Kazembe III had conquered and brought under tribute the Shila Nkuba, Nsenski, the fourth in a line of Shila Nkubas, traditionally established by Bemba offshoots. Traditions surrounding the original Nkuba indicate an early preoccupation on the part of the Bemba with ivory hunting and with ivory as a source of tribute.[11] It is also recorded that when the Bemba chief, the Mwamba, heard that his "mother's brother" (Kazembe III) was coming, he blocked the roads with human corpses and Kazembe respected the Bemba territory. (Cunnison 1959:154) These traditional accounts must all, of course, be treated with considerable circumspection, but their use in conjunction with the glimpses afforded by the early European accounts can help at least trace important broad outlines.

It is the diaries of the Lacerda expedition that permit establishment of 1740 as the probable date of Lunda arrival upon the Luapula. The same sources also make casual reference to the Bemba and their Citimukulu being in the north, but there is no indication of aggressive operations against the Bisa or other tribes as of 1798. On the contrary, the Bisa are described as being much larger than they were at the time of the British occupation and largely under the influence of the Lunda. The Arabs had not arrived and the Lunda were apparently carrying on a fair trade in ivory with the Yao and Anguru beyond Lake Nyasa and the Shire River. (Coxhead 1914:3) By 1810 Kazembe was at war with the Bisa, who were important middlemen trading with the Yao and with the Portuguese to the south. (Cunnison 1961:71) Then, in 1831, Gamitto's account described the Bisa as being fugitives in their own land from the invading Bemba, the Bemba having attacked some six years earlier. It seems a permissible inference that we have here at least a three-way struggle for control of the trade.[12]

Richards has expressed the opinion that the warlike bias of the Bemba did not develop until they began expanding against the Bisa and also the Lungu, Lala, and Cewa. (1940:86) If this be true, then Bemba militarism can be taken as a relatively recent phenomenon.[13] Richards is also quite clear as to the major further stimulus to this militaristic bias:

The Bemba are among those tribes which stood on a direct trade route of the Arabs, exchange of guns and cloth for ivory and slaves having apparently lasted from 1865 to 1893, such contact here, as among other Central African peoples, having led to the centralization of government and the increased power of the chief, who had the monopoly of ivory and hence of guns. (1959:165)

Actually the first real Arab contact may have come somewhat earlier. The year 1865 marks the first actual Arab invasion of the Lake Mweru region. There were individual Arab traders at Kazembe's capital from the 1840s on, and Gamitto reported two "Moors" as being there in 1831. Furthermore, as trade in slaves and ivory through middlemen tribes often preceded direct Arab contact, this trade and its control would seem a most important factor in the entire Bemba expansion. The type of contact to which Richards refers was not merely a matter of receiving a few guns from occasional traders. It would seem from the account of George Pirie that an entire party (or perhaps it was really two parties) of Arabs from Tanganyika entered the Bemba area armed with guns and one cannon. Kalongo, one of the leaders, established close ties with the reigning Citimukulu, while Kumba Kumba, the other leader, made similar arrangements with the Mwamba. Guns, gunpowder, shot, calico, and beads were traded for ivory and slaves. The Arabs successfully intrigued to reopen a dispute between the Bemba and the Ngoni, who had been, with difficulty, held to a stalemate some years earlier. In the attack upon the Ngoni the Arabs and their cannon interspersed themselves within the ranks of a combined Citimukulu-Mwamba force. The result was a major disaster for the Ngoni. Many slaves and cattle were captured, bringing into the hands of the Bemba chiefs the cannon, percussion caps, gunpowder, cannon balls, and—a substantial increase in prestige. "Kitimukulu's fame was now established, and he was greatly feared by the surrounding tribes, upon whom he continually made war, in order to establish his many sons in chieftainships, and to increase his number of slaves." (Pirie 1905:137–39)

This, then, was the period when the chiefs of the Crocodile Clan had extended their rule outward from the central Luwemba (Bemba) and Ituna provinces until their sway was acknowledged from Chosi River to Lake Bangweulu and their sphere of influence almost from Lake Nyasa to Lake Mweru; when the central provinces were fenced around by a ring of barrier outposts, stockaded villages astride the main trade routes and important ferries, where heavy tolls were exacted from all who wished to enter and trade in peace, and these in turn were flanked by minor stockaded villages along the frontiers; and when the Citimukulu ruled from a capital with both inner and outer stockade, divided into thirty-three quarters and surrounded by a dry moat.

The tribute was rigorously exacted from the border tribes; it is still the boast of the Awemba that they do not know how to hoe, that their only trade was war, and that the subject tribes supplied their various wants, the Wasenga bringing in tobacco, the Wabisa fish and salt, the Wiwa and the Winamwanga hoes, livestock, and grain. (Gouldsbury 1911:24) [14]

Also, "Elephant hunts, under the direction of the chief and with specialist elephant-hunters, formed one of the main sources of the wealth of chiefs." (Richards 1951:167) Iron was obtained mostly from the Lunda, although a few iron furnaces are still found in Bemba country. Important sources of salt were controlled, such as the major salt-grass area called Chibwa on the Luitikila River near Mpika.[15] Finally, Sir Harry Johnston, who in 1889 was the second British "pacifier" in the region (Lugard was the first), recorded a list of tribes possessing domestic cattle. He noted that "the Awemba on the Nyasa-Tanganyika plateau kept large herds." Richards, while de-emphasizing cattle as an important previous resource of the Bemba, nonetheless confirms the fundamental content of Johnston's report:

The Bemba are not a pastoral people. Not only is the country tsetse-ridden, but the people have no tradition or knowledge of handling cattle as have the contiguous tribes such as the Mambwe to the east. . . . Chiefs formerly possessed herds of cattle taken as the result of raids over the eastern border, but these perished in the Rinderpest at the end of the century. Sacrifices of cattle are made at the accession, and burial ceremonies of chiefs, but this rite may be of recent origin. (1951:166)

Speaking of the region's natives as a whole, but not necessarily including the Bemba, George Pirie reported: "it has been estimated that considerably over 1,000,000 head were in their possession before the rinderpest of 1894." (1905:132) [16] The data available for this period are, of course, insufficient to permit anything like a precise judgment as to the ratio of cattle to agricultural resources entering into Bemba subsistence or the ratio of resources obtained through raiding and tribute to resources indigenously produced. All of the indications are that both ratios were higher in the late nineteenth century than they have been at any time in the twentieth.

The coming of the British rapidly broke the very basis of Bemba power, both the power of the Bemba over other tribes and the power of Bemba chiefs over other Bemba. The British presence made itself felt in the form of first the African Lakes Corporation and secondly the British South Africa Company assisted by the British Central Africa Government. The British were able to exploit the divisions within the Bemba polity—

primarily the competition between the Mwamba on the one hand and the Citimukulu on the other—as had the Arabs before them. British fortunes were materially enhanced by the death, in 1895, of the incumbent Citimukulu. At this juncture, the Mwamba made overtures to the British, perhaps in an attempt to secure their aid in his bid for the top office. A company official who journeyed to the Mwamba's capital, however, found himself surrounded by Arab slavers and coast men, and the British request to build a station there was denied.[17] The Mwamba then sent an expedition which attacked the village at the royal burial grove at Mwalule and drove off the chief ritual priest [18] and all the villagers. British arms restored this village to its former inhabitants and held off a second attack by the Mwamba. Meanwhile Makumbu Chifwimbi, the actual next-in-succession, had appeared from hiding and with British assistance secured the office of Citimukulu. In 1897 a six-day battle was fought at the village of Chiwali, a Senga chief, on the border of the Mwamba-Bemba. This battle was between a force of Arabs and Mwamba-Bemba and the combined British-Senga forces. (Pirie 1905:140–47) The Mwamba-Bemba force was finally routed and Kapandansaru, the Arab chief, captured. The Mwamba-Bemba were driven in rout back across the Chambesi.

This little war had far-reaching results. External raids by the Awemba upon the surrounding tribes were checked, and the power of the Arab slavers was broken. . . . The Wemba kings, being now confined within their own boundaries, turned, as if in rage, upon their own people, and inflicted upon them atrocious mutilations and other horrors, which previously they had reserved for their enemies alone. Dissension naturally followed, but the most cruel punishments were meted out to the rebels, and many of the Awemba were sold into slavery by their own chiefs. (Gouldsbury 1911:42) [19]

The seriousness of this situation for the Bemba was drastically compounded in 1900 by smallpox, long endemic, which "during this year . . . became virtually epidemic." (Gouldsbury 1911:44) This was followed in the middle of the next decade by sleeping sickness.[20]

By 1900 the pacification was virtually completed and in that year an Order-in-Council placed northeastern Rhodesia under the control of the British South Africa Company.[21] The changes introduced meant the end of substantial power by the Bemba chiefs—all that remained was the form, buttressed up by a sort of indirect rule. The slave trade was abolished as was the killing of elephants unless caught in the act of actually ravaging gardens. These, of course, were the main economic props to the rule of the chiefs. Chiefs also lost the following rights: possession of slaves, possession of arms, right of mutilation, power to administer the poison ordeal, and the right to collect ivory tusks. (Richards 1940:114) The power to wage war on surrounding tribes and to exact tribute from them had already disappeared in the last decade of the nineteenth century. The people whose boast was that they did not "know how to hoe, that their only trade was war" were now forced back upon agriculture in an environment of low potential. Ordinances passed in 1929 tried consciously to build back some of the power and prestige of the chiefs. These were extended and further defined in 1936. Chiefs were:

given jurisdiction over definite territories and encouraged to issue orders on matters of hygiene, bush-burning, the movement of natives, the constitution of villages, etc. Native courts were also recognized and given jurisdiction over all cases except witchcraft, murder, issues involving Europeans, etc. (Richards 1940:117)

Chiefs were posted salaries which ranged from sixty pounds per annum for the Citimukulu to fifty pounds for the Mwamba and less in proportion for lesser chiefs. This was hardly wealth, nor in any real sense, compensation for what they had lost. In addition to loss of control of tribute, the ivory trade, and slavery, Bemba chiefs had found that their rights to *umulasa,* or tribute labor for the clearing of their fields and the building of their villages, had been undermined by the twin innovations of wage labor and labor migration. Given these changed conditions, it is not surprising that Richards entered a chiefdom where the *bakabilo* melted away from meetings because the chief could not find enough food to feed them, where princesses such as Canda we Eiya and Mulenga complained of difficulties getting their gardens made, and where the Mwamba could select a site for a new capital but would have to wait for a copper slump before he could obtain the labor to build it. As Richards says, "the art of chieftainship is difficult to practise even in the most advantageous conditions at the present time." (1961b:264)

It is clear then that the circumstances under which the Bemba system operated during the nineteenth century were quite different from what they are at the present. What we have are two quite distinct "social situations" which are not at all susceptible to analysis in a single synchronic context. The traditional political system still functions as an ideology and as such continues to help structure contemporary behavior. But it is just as clear that it does not function in the present in anything like the way it functioned in the past. Furthermore, the resource base was quite different in the past, with plunder from neighboring tribes and trade in slaves and ivory being supplanted by the present reliance on shifting cultivation and copper-belt wages. Consequently, it is inadmissible to use a present, or recent, population density to assess demographic relationships with the indigenous political system.[22] That is, of course, unless there is further evidence that this same population density was also generally true of the past situation.

There is reason, however, to question even the modern figure. The 3.75 figure used by Fortes and Evans-Pritchard is apparently taken from the following statement in Richards' article: "They (the Bemba) number today about 140,000, very sparsely scattered over the country at a density of an average 3.75 per square mile." (Richards 1940:85) It is necessary to emphasize that although this figure is for the modern period it is still very much in the way of an estimate and by no means a firm census figure. In fact, there seems to be considerable variability not only in the population numbers but also in the area to be used as a base. In one account Richards cites an estimate for 1934 by J. Moffat Thompson of 114,274 Bemba. *The Ethnographic Survey of Africa* mentions this figure also but tends to give greater credence to Richards' estimate of 140,000 (previously cited). In a recent paper Richards gave a figure of 150,000 as representing the Bemba population at the time of her visit in 1934. (1961a:136) It is probably impossible to measure precisely the "Bemba area" even under modern conditions. It is quite irregular and interpenetrates with the areas of other tribal groups. Further, there are pockets containing other tribes within the main Bemba area itself. *The Ethnographic Survey of Africa* estimates the area occupied by Bemba as 20,000 square miles. (Whitely 1951:1) Richards says:

The Citimukulu of to-day rule over their own territory only. It stretches from 29° west to 32.5° south, and covers the whole of the administrative district of Kasama and most of those of Mpika, Chinsali, and Luwingu, an area rather larger than that of Ireland. It includes much of the Bisa and Lungu territory occupied during the last century and now predominantly inhabited by them. (1961b:16) [23]

I have placed a grid over Richards' map of tribal areas (1961b), and the area there bounded as "Bemba" measures approximately 25,000 square miles. Using this as a reasonable base and the above three population estimates, we get the following results:

114,274	4.6 per square mile
140,000	5.6 per square mile
150,000	6.0 per square mile

All three of these estimates seem to contradict Richards' statement that "the density of the population never reaches a greater figure than 3.9 per square mile." (1961b:18) Actually, we are on rather safer grounds if we use the estimates per district contained on Map II in Pim. (1938) For the districts listed as "Bemba" by Richards we then get the following:

Kasama	6.67
Luwingu	7.86
Chinsali	3.46
Mpika	1.86

It is well also to include a cautionary note from Pim: "Even this, however, only tells part of the story, as even within districts there are great variations in density." (1938:7) [24]

If population data from the decade 1931 to 1940 leave something to be desired, the problems are only compounded when we try to assess the nineteenth-century situation, even at the moment of contact. For the most part we have only the somewhat casual observations of the early travellers, traders, explorers, and missionaries. These give us some idea as to the size of individual settlements, particularly capitals, but not even meaningful hints as to overall or average population density. About the only approach to a quantitative overview is afforded by the map of population density in Sir Harry Johnston's *British Central Africa*. (1897) This should be approached with some caution. In the first place, the map was not directly the result of Johnston's own survey. Rather, it was constructed by the Edinburgh Geographical Institute on the basis of data supplied by Johnston. The area covered was quite extensive and Johnston could not have had the same firsthand knowledge of his region as did C. W. Hobley, who personally mapped the much smaller area of North Kavirondo (see Chapter VII). In fact, the Bemba heartland was physically barred to the Europeans until the time that military conquest opened it up. Consequently, the data contained on Johnston's map is presented here as an impression only, and perhaps a clue, but in no sense a definitive survey.[25]

In the Bemba area Johnston indicates an area of about 9,500 square miles where the population density is 5 to 15 per square mile. There is then a center of population density with concentric zoning. This center is designated Marakutu and is in the area where one would expect that the Citimukulu's capital would be. It is not so designated on the map, and the name "Marakutu" is neither explained in the text nor in other early histories of the region. The outer zone around the center is approximately 314 square miles in area and is listed at a density of 15 to 50 per square mile. The inner ring contains a density listed in excess of 50 per square mile, covering an area of 20 square miles. Another reason for suspecting the accuracy of the map is that the capital of the Mwamba (called "Moamba") is also listed but no greater population density is indicated than that of the wider 9,500 square mile zone. The region of the Kazembe's capital in the Lunda region along the Luapula shows the same marked concentric zoning to an even greater degree. There is a rather wide and scattered zone of 5 to 15 per square mile density, an area of 1,256 square miles with an average density of 15 to 50 per square mile, and 157 square miles around the capital itself listed as in excess of 50 per square mile.

Another important component of the demographic pattern, and one which Fortes and Evans-Pritchard made an issue of theoretical discussion, is the question of the relative impermanence of villages.

It might be supposed that the dense permanent settlements of the Tallensi would necessarily lead to the development of a centralized government, whereas the wide dispersion of shifting villages among the Bemba would be incompatible with centralized rule. The reverse is actually the case. (Fortes 1940:8)

It is best to postpone final judgment in the matter until we have had an opportunity to analyze the Tallensi social and political system. It is nonetheless quite appropriate here to determine the exact empirical referent of "the wide dispersion of shifting villages among the Bemba."

In the first place, a careful distinction must be drawn between an ordinary agricultural village and a chief's village, or capital.

the Bemba live in small communities, the average village consisting of 30 to 50 huts, while that of the present Citimukulu numbers 150, and in the old days chiefs' villages reached higher figures still. (Richards 1961b:18)

A chief's village (umusumba) is very much larger than that of a commoner. Inhabitants of the capital are composed of relatives of the chief, his followers, and also a number of families which moved there originally to win royal favour and have become accustomed to court life. Since a chief's reputation depends largely on the size of his capital, and his councillors, courtiers, and administrative officers were drawn largely from his villagers, the umusumba is an important unit in the political machine. The late Nkula's village had about 400 huts when I visited it in 1931, that of the Citimukulu 150 in 1938. The capitals of pre-European days were evidently very much larger. These communities were divided into sections (ifitente, sing. icitente) and though nowadays there are nine ifitente at the paramount's village, there were formerly thirty to forty, according to native accounts. (Richards 1940b:91)

As to the smaller, basic agricultural villages:

The people are shifting cultivators, that is to say, they clear a fresh strip of the bush each year to make their gardens; and when the forest land round their village has all been used (four or five years) they move to a fresh site a few miles away, build themselves new huts and start cultivating again. (Richards 1961b:19)

This statement can be strictly verified only for modern conditions and, again, an examination of historical circumstances brings with it important qualifications:

Here as in other parts of Africa the establishment of European rule and the prevention of war has led to a far greater dispersion of the people than was possible in the old days when they tended to group themselves under the protection of their chiefs in large stockaded villages. At the present day the Bemba villages divide and subdivide as often as possible within the limits of the Government minimum of ten adult males.[26] (Richards 1961b:18 fn. 1)

Judging by the accounts of Livingstone (Waller 1875) for the year 1867 and Giraud (1890) for the period 1883–1885, the palisaded and moated village was the norm for the entire area from Lake Nyasa through to the Lunda settlements on the Luapula, although some few exceptions were noted. Livingstone reported that in 1867 the Citimukulu's capital had a triple stockade and that the inner palisade was "defended also by a deep broad ditch and hedge of a solanaceous thorny shrub. It is about two hundred yards broad and five hundred long." (Waller 1875:154) Giraud's account of the capital at the time of his visit seems to indicate that the outer palisade had been dispensed with. He estimated the area of the capital at a square kilometer containing some four or five hundred huts and granaries. There were three bomas in the northeastern sector of the capital complete with warehouses for slaves and ivory. One of these belonged to a coast trader and the other two to "princes of the blood." In addition there was the moated and palisaded central boma of the Citimukulu, in itself "un véritable village" and about 500 meters in diameter, and which in case of attack could serve as a refuge for the entire population. It was here that Giraud was entertained while the Citimukulu played for him on the accordian. (1890:254 ff.)

It is interesting to note that even in Livingstone's time (1867) communications with the coast (Bagamayo) were such that Livingstone could confidently mail out his dispatches to England and order supplies including coffee, sugar, candles, French-preserved meats, Port wine, and tinned cheese to be delivered to him at Ujiji. (Waller 1875:156) This was hardly an urban center in the same sense as Hausa, Nupe, or Yoruba cities of the same period, yet on the other hand it is a far cry from the small impermanent village of the shifting cultivator. The engravings in Giraud's account indicate very large, tall storehouses, and an extremely dense and compact settlement pattern, one hut practically touching the next. Livingstone, on the other hand, in 1867 tersely noted: "huts not planted very closely." (Waller 1875:154) Livingstone also encountered temporary villages built closer to cultivated fields and observed that sometimes the cultivated patches were enclosed with very high hedges. All of these features, of course, are to be expected under the conditions of warfare and slave-raiding then prevailing. It is true that, traditionally, capitals must be moved on the death of one chief and the accession of a new one, but even this concept is hedged with important qualifications. Writing in the modern period on the subject of Bemba chieftainship, Brelsford has devoted an entire section to the subject of "Permanent Village Sites." In it he observes: "We usually consider the shifting of villages a constant feature of Bemba life, but there are many chiefs and headmen who are definitely restricted in their power of movement." (1944:20)

Sites that were more or less permanent included fishing villages on the Chambesi, which moved about in a very limited area; the villages of headmen along the funeral route of chiefs; and the village of Chipashya, a ritual intermediary between the paramount and the other chiefs, and whose village must always be within a mile or two of the paramount's capital.

As to the chiefs, "Chitimukulu and Nkula are definitely restricted to almost adjoining sites when they wish to rebuild." (Brelsford 1944:21) The Mwamba, the Nkolemfumu, and all other chiefs except the Shimwalule may move about as they please.[27] Chief Makasa only moves in an area surrounding the confluence of the Mifunsu and Mombo streams, but this is because the remainder of his district has only seasonal water. Finally we come to the opposite extreme from shifting settlement in the village of Chief Shimwalule, the priest of the royal burial grove. "New houses must be built exactly on the foundations of the old ones so that the village, right on the edge of the burial grove cannot move." (Brelsford 1944:21)

To this it must be added that in the old days, according to Gouldsbury and Sheane (1911), there were fortified stations and villages stockaded across trade routes and at ferry stations and posts for the collection of tribute in the lands of subjugated tribes. These, of course, remained stationary or were moved according to the changing fortunes of trade and warfare, and not as a result of the exigencies of shifting cultivation.

Fortes and Evans-Pritchard, in addressing themselves to this question of shifting villages versus dense permanent settlements, seem to be first setting up and then knocking down a theory of political evolution or development. This is not made entirely explicit, but they seem to be suggesting that one might expect that centralized rule or the state should inevitably develop *sui generis* out of a dense, permanent, and stable settlement pattern. They then proceed to demolish this notion on the basis of their interpretation of the empirical evidence. Since I do not subscribe to this theory I see no point in trying to defend it.[28] It should be pointed out that the argument misses the mark with both the Bemba and the Tallensi, for with each the chieftainship came in from the outside. That is, it did not spring up *sui generis in situ,* as it were. We shall deal in detail with the Tallensi later, but all available data point to the fact that developed chieftainship entered northeastern Rhodesia with the Lunda migration, and that Lunda chiefs imposed their rule in a rather loose tributary network over the region, a network whose primary emphasis was the control of trade. The Bemba, in a way still not exactly determined, seem to have been a part of this general movement into the region with traditions of relationship to the Lunda and of a common Luba origin. Thus we have the splitting off of groups from regions of more advanced political development and the spread of this political organization into areas previously occupied by small clan and lineage groups—that is, by acephalous societies.

The very nature of this type of process has a bearing upon the question of density. Coxhead has noted that Bemba traditions insist that the area was uninhabited when the Bemba entered, although there are traces of a pre-Bemba, Bushmanoid occupation. (1914:3) Coxhead, himself, assumes that the area was practically uninhabited. Furthermore, we do not know the extent of Bemba political organization at the time of their arrival. The Lacerda expedition diaries would indicate that by 1798 there was among the Bemba a chief entitled the Citimukulu. We know nothing of his actual powers nor of the existence of a hierarchy of lesser chiefs, officers, and councilors. In short, we know that the Bemba had a titled chief; we do not know that at this time they had a state. Even if we assume that the Bemba hived off from the Luba already possessed of rather developed, political institutions, the problems of pioneering in a new and sparsely populated region would tend to inhibit the rate of state formation at least for a period. On the other hand, if it be assumed that state-like institutions were just emerging in 1798, then we have a rather shallow time depth for the process of state formation in the area and a shorter time for the effects of state formation to be felt upon population. Coxhead has indicated a belief that the Bemba migrations were triggered by population pressure in their original homeland, but this view is largely speculative. (1914:4) We should want to distinguish those cases where the processes leading to state formation and higher density were operating together within a single region from those involving migrations into new and largely unsettled areas. This becomes a most important consideration when we come to compare the densities of the Bemba to those of the Logoli, where the latter were just beginning to show evidences of development in the direction of state-like institutions but had been for some time existing on the borders of an expanding node of population density and state formation.

Finally, if we assume that the Bemba state did not really begin developing until the period of Arab contact and influence, then the time span is really very short. I would certainly argue that the question of time span is an important one in assessing the relationship of population density to state formation and that, other things being equal, the state of longest relatively continuous duration will display the greater densities.

In any event, when a full diachronic perspective is taken, the Bemba case is no longer a paradox, and furthermore it strikingly confirms rather than denies a positive correlation between population density and state formation. Johnston's density estimates must be viewed with some caution, but they may as well be on the low side as the high. When taken together with all indications of depopulation at the end of the nineteenth century (loss of cattle, epidemic, war, and civil war), they would certainly seem not too high. Furthermore, even if we do not have positive proof of higher average density we do have proof of greater nucleation and permanence of settlements.

We have better information for the neighboring and putatively related Lunda in the Luapula Valley. Cunnison, who has studied these people in historical depth as well as through recent field studies, has given a picture of more or less continuous population growth in the region after the establishment of the Lunda state. "Immigrants who arrived after the establishment of this Lunda state were attracted generally for peaceful ends. They came for what the Luapula Valley and the power of Kazembe could offer them." (1959:42) Gann has also noted of the Kazembe-Arab relationship:

In turn Kazembe received powder and guns from them and thus found his position further strengthened. Kazembe was well placed for raiding. He commanded the resources of the Luapula Valley, rich in fish and cassava, and so he was able to maintain a large population concentrated in a small area. Sharpe for instance thought that his stockade contained as many as twenty thousand people. (1954:35)

All indications are that Bemba development mirrored this process, although on a smaller scale. Particularly, it must be noted that the internal subsistence base within Bemba society was much less productive and reliance upon the products of others correspondingly higher than was the case for the Lunda —hence the ideology of the spear versus the hoe.

Much remains to be learned of Bemba history but the broad outlines seem clear. The Bemba came from outside into what was at least a sparsely populated area. The greatest part of the development of the Bemba state (and perhaps its entire development) took place under the conditions of the trade in slaves, ivory, guns, cloth, and other products. During this period population in the area grew and hence the average density went up. With the coming of the British both the trade in slaves and the hunting of elephants was brought to an end. The basis of the Bemba state was destroyed although a hollow shell remained, weakly buttressed by Indirect Rule. The Bemba, once predatory and militaristic, although traders as well, were forced back upon shifting cultivation in an agriculturally unproductive area and upon Copper Belt labor migration for support. The processes which brought about the destruction of the state—war and civil war—brought depopulation in their wake, a depopulation that was intensified by epidemics—both of men and cattle. This same period that has seen the decline of the Bemba state has also witnessed a decline in population density.[29] Such a historical sequence hardly lends support to the position advanced by *African Political Systems*.

CHAPTER VI. The Classical Segmentary Societies I:

The Nuer and the Tallensi

THE BALANCE of the cases adduced by Fortes and Evans-Pritchard—the Nuer, Tallensi, and Logoli—are all familiar names to students of ethnographic literature. This is because they are almost invariably cited as prototypes of a certain category—the acephalous, segmentary society. This prominence, in turn, can be attributed largely to their selection for pioneer studies of social structure by British social anthropologists. They have thus become trail markers for those researchers who followed. Middleton and Tait (1958), for example, use the Nuer and Tallensi as reference points for further subdivisions within the class; while Eisenstadt (1959:206) frankly lumps all three together as "Classical" Segmentary Tribes. Though differing to which among the three are most typically or "classically" segmentary (Eisenstadt 1959:206; Middleton 1958:12–13), they are all agreed as to the validity of the acephalous and segmentary label. It is the alleged segmentary nature of these societies which, when taken together with the fact that Fortes and Evans-Pritchard adduce for them densities which are uniformly higher than those of their "state" societies, or societies with centralized institutions, makes these three important cases in the density–state formation controversy. As we have seen, the "state" societies presented in argument by the editors of *African Political Systems* were supposed to lie in the 2.5 to 3.5 per square mile density range, while the Nuer is said to have 7, Tallensi 171, and Logoli 391 per square mile. I shall analyze the latter three in this order.

The Nuer case is not really problematical in terms of our argument, and the reason that the Nuer appear problematical is an illusion created by the very low densities adduced for the three states. It has been seen that 20 is a more realistic figure for the Zulu than is 3.5. The 2.5 for the Ngwato masks present-day concentration along the railroad and aboriginal concentration in large settlements, as well as possible densities as high as 20 for land then currently occupied and under use. It is true that 1931 Bemba densities were very close to and slightly under the Nuer figure of 7, but evidence indicates a rather marked decline since the period of effective functioning of the Bemba state. Johnston's map (1897) was seen to contain a range of 5 to 15 per square mile for the sizeable area of 9,500 square miles and a range of 15 to 50 per square mile in an inner area which was over 314 square miles in extent. Thus viewed, the Nuer are not really high but low in density, and that is just what Evans-Pritchard said they were:

The total Nuer population is *round about* 300,000. I do not know the total square mileage of the country, but to the east of the Nile, where there are, on a rough estimate, some 180,000 Nuer, *they are said* to occupy 26,000 square miles, with a *low density* of about seven to the square mile. The density is probably no higher to the west of the Nile. Nowhere is there a high degree of local concentration. (Evans-Pritchard 1940b:276–77, my italics)

In another source Evans-Pritchard gives a range of 4 to 10 per square mile for the Nuer, with an average of 5, and this is clearly below all figures of the other three groups heretofore mentioned, except for the Reserve boundary average of 2.5 for Ngwato. It would be quibbling, however, given the general imprecision of the figures, to insist on one or the other average for the Nuer.[1]

The real problem, then, is not so much with the "low-density states" but with the "high-density" acephalous societies, of which there are two: the Tallensi of northern Ghana and the

Logoli of Nyanza province, Kenya.[2] Each of these poses rather serious problems in classification, so I will devote a chapter to each—the remainder of this chapter to the Tallensi and the chapter following to the Logoli.

THE TALLENSI

The Tallensi data present a problem of more serious proportions. The figures given in *African Political Systems* (p. 239) are for the administrative district of Zuarungu, of which Taleland comprises less than half. The density of this district (171 per square mile) is higher than that of Kano Province (138) and considerably higher than that of the following districts or provinces: Zaria (56), Sokoto (45), Kumasi (54.5), Buganda (50.7), and Bunyoro (24.2). The basis in every case is that of colonial censuses for 1931. (Kuczynski 1948, I: 420, 599; II:252).[3] Thus Tallensi densities rate high in comparison with similar and contemporary figures from the areas of such state systems as Hausa-Fulani (Kano, Sokoto, Zaria), Ashanti (Kumasi), Buganda, and Bunyoro. Even the more modest estimate of 100 per square mile that Fortes uses for Taleland proper (1945:4) is well within the range of major state systems that I have examined. Nor can this density be dismissed as a purely post-European contact phenomenon. Both Fortes and Cardinall (1925:1-2) cite evidence which would give respectable antiquity to the permanent and relatively dense occupation of the area.

Cardinall does note conditions in the decade 1921–1931 which would have served to swell this density. This was the considerable population movement southward out of the French Sudan. Although Kumasi was the reputed lodestone, the Northern Territories were also considerably affected. In discussing the "Settlement of strangers. . . . not only in the pleasant easy land of the south but in the hard and difficult areas of the north," Cardinall states:

The increase is particularly noticeable along the northern frontier. In 1921 the Northern Mamprusi District comprised the present districts of Navrongo, Zuarungu and Kusasi. In that year the population was returned at 257,949 and a decade later at 365,465, an increase of 41 per cent in an area which is almost overcrowded. An overflow took place into South Mamprusi where the increase appears as 112 per cent. (1931:152)

Unfortunately the redistricting mentioned in the quotation makes it impossible to adjust accurately the density figures. Part of the difference may be attributable to increased efficiency of the census itself. Even assuming that the full 41 per cent was uniformly felt (and of course there is no justification for such an assumption) we are left with a density of 122 per square mile for Zuarungu and 72 for Taleland proper. Both are sufficiently high to merit further consideration.

The segmentary and purely acephalous nature of Tallensi society would at first blush seem equally closed to question. The classification as mentioned previously is deeply rooted in the literature in a respectable lineage that extends from Fortes himself through Middleton and Tait (1958) to Eisenstadt (1959). Closer examination of some further statements by these same writers can, however, give rise to some healthy misgivings. For instance, within two pages of attesting the acephalous nature of the Tallensi, Middleton and Tait remark:

Chiefships of a very modified sort in West Africa are often part of a European administration (Kissi, Basare) or other alien administration in a heterogeneous society (Dagomba among Konkomba or Mamprusi among Tallensi, societies of Group II). But these 'chiefs' had little indigenous authority. (1958:17)

A year later, without further clarifying the issue, Eisenstadt noted: "The mutual specialization and interdependence of corporate lineages and clans is manifest among the Tallensi in the two types of *chiefdoms,* the na'am and the ritual tendaam (Custodian of the Earth)." (1959:206, my italics) The final and perhaps prophetic irony comes with opening the covers of

Fortes' own original study of Tallensi (1945). The frontispiece of the volume is a portrait of Na Naam Biong, Chief of Tongo, shown in full ceremonial robes and wearing the traditional red fez, symbol of office. We seem confronted, then, with what might be entitled the "paradox of the chief in an acephalous society." Fortunately Skinner, from the vantage point of his Mossi studies, has been able to view this problem in fresh perspective and has pointed the way to a definitive resolution of this problem. After surveying data both from Fortes' own accounts and from that of his predecessor Rattray, all pointing to a Mamprusi origin of the Namoo clans (holders of all local chiefships, including Tongo), Skinner concludes:

These data certainly suggest that prior to the arrival of the British, the Mamprusi were either incorporating Tale country into their kingdom or losing their hold on the Tallensi. Fortes' insistence on the acephalous nature of Tallensi society stems from his failure to consider that these people had been defeated and dispersed by the British after the turn of the century and had probably lost a great deal of their organization. The society he describes can be compared to a modern community arbitrarily divorced from its nation state. (1964:7)

This would indicate that, far from being in the midst of a classical segmentary society, we are actually in the presence of significant indigenous state formation. The matter is certainly worthy of closer scrutiny. Following Skinner's lead we shall delve deeper into Fortes' own material, as well as that of his predecessors Rattray, Cardinall, and Binger, in an attempt to delineate concretely the actual indigenous status of the Chief in this society. This task can adequately be undertaken, however, only within the context of the region, its history, and wider relationships in the superorganic environment.

The country of the Tallensi, called "Taleland" by Fortes, occupies less than half the administrative district of Zuarungu in the Northern Territories of the former Gold Coast—modern Ghana. It is in the Sudanese zone of savannah or orchard bush.

Zuarungu is on the Trans-Volta plateau, whose undulating monotony is broken by a scattering of bouldery hills 100 to 500 feet in altitude. Just 4 miles north of the river are the most conspicuous of these hills—the Tong Hills, which are more or less the heart of Taleland. This is the area of the oldest and densest settlements, an area which spreads out like a fan to the west, north, and east. The total population of Taleland, according to the 1931 census, was about 35,000, and Fortes has estimated the total area to be about 300 square miles. So neither in area nor in total numbers are the Tallensi as important a people as their position in anthropological literature might indicate. The average density for this region is, as Fortes has observed, 100 per square mile. (Fortes 1945:4) Fortes, however, notes that nearly a third of this population is concentrated within a radius of 2 or 3 miles of the Tong Hills—or within the small area of 28 square miles. As these are frankly rough estimates, nothing more than an apparent precision is lost by rounding to 30 square miles, and we get an effective density for this small area of 400 per square mile. By the same token, the average density for the remaining 270 square miles is dropped to 80 per square mile. Tongo, the administrative capital and one of the densest settlements in the country, lies about one mile to the north of the hills.

The sacred dancing ground at Tongo today [4] marks the homestead of the original Tendaan. A mere stone's throw away, marking the site of another ancestral homestead, is the grave of Mosuor, founder of Tongo. Tradition has it that Mosuor fled Mampurugu [5] after losing a fight for the succession to the office of Naab, or paramount chief of the Mamprusi state. His approach toward Tongo was observed by the Tendaan, who fled to the hills. Here the myth diverges slightly, Namoos claiming that Mosuor's red fez and gown of cloth were the source of terror, while elders of the Gbizug clan (in which this particular Tendaanship is vested) claim, perhaps with greater realism, that it was rather the horses and guns which accompanied Mosuor. At any rate, Mosuor waited by the water hole until the Tendaan reappeared and there seized him. The Tendaan instructed Mosuor in the taboos of the land and the two slashed wrists and drank each other's blood, pledging themselves and their descendants to perpetual peace.

Upon Mosuor's death his eldest son, Nangkamung, wished to succeed immediately, but a younger son insisted that the death must first be ceremonially reported to the Mampurugna'ab, the "Fountainhead of their chiefship" (na'am). Upon the failure of the eldest to comply, the younger went in secret and was invested with the chiefship by the paramount of Mamprusi in return for a payment of 100 cattle. What is of even greater importance is that, upon his return to Tongo, the eldest son removed to Yamalaug, leaving the younger as Chief of Tongo. Another of the brothers settled at Sie (beside Yamalaug) and a third at Biuk, thus establishing four patrilineal subclans in all. Further colonies have continually hived off from these nuclei, the myths in each case recording ritual arrangements with the local tendaans. (Fortes 1945:22,40) Taken collectively these myths both mark the genesis and serve as charter for what Fortes deigned to call the "major cleavage" in Tale society.

The point of primary importance is that a major cleavage runs through the whole of Tale society. On the one side stand communities or part of communities the members of which are generally agreed to be descendants of immigrant Mamprusi. These are the Namoos. On the other side stand similar groups who claim to be and are accepted as the descendants of the aboriginal inhabitants of the country and earlier immigrants whom they absorbed. (1945:27)

These, of course, are the Talis [6] clans. Fortes also records that these two groups are distinguished not only by myths of origin but also by differences of totemic and quasi-totemic usages and beliefs, and politico-ritual privileges and duties connected with the ancestor cult and the Earth Cult. (1949:2) The most important point to note as pertains to the "politico-ritual" sphere is the almost exclusive monopoly of the secular chiefship by the Namoos. (Fortes 1940:255; Manoukian 1952:46) In short, we have here strong symptoms of two subcultures and definite political and social stratification which are only blurred by Fortes when he subsumes them under his principles of "segmentary differentiation" and "dynamic coherence." (1949:2) Fortes goes on to note that these two groups never combine for mutual defense but such warfare as exists is usually between them. "One might even describe them as a kind of civil war, since they sprang from the cleavages inherent in the social structure, particularly the cleavage between Namoos and non-Namoos." (Fortes 1945:242) His explanation of this state of affairs is that this type of war keeps the cleavages alive, preserves the unity of corporate groups, and is at bottom a tension-resolving mechanism. And, his own assertion of cultural and economic homogeneity notwithstanding, Fortes has himself reported considerable economic differentiation, such as between chiefs and headmen on the one hand and ordinary Tale on the other.[7]

That all of this is not purely a local phenomenon is also clear from Fortes' account:

It is widely known among the Tallensi that groups of people claiming to be of Mampuru origin are found scattered throughout the Northern Territories and the adjacent parts of the French Haute Volta. *Though they have no political or social ties with them,* Tale Namoos assert that they are of the same stock . . . as the Mossi in French territory, the Dagomba in British territory, and the various clans claiming Mampuru origin among the Gaurisi, the Namnam, the Kusaasi, the Bulisi, and other neighboring groups. (1945:66, my italics)

At this juncture Fortes has missed the wider regional interconnections just as surely as in the foregoing he missed the true significance of the internal differentiation. The italicized statement that they "have no political ties" is simply not correct.

Had he said "no *direct* political ties," one could not quarrel
with the *factual* correctness of the statement, though one would
be forced to point out that it tended to blur rather than clarify
the political reality. Since Tongo is a political subdivision
under Mamprusi, the chain of command and hence direct
political ties do not go to commensurate subunits in Dagomba
or in Mossi but *up* the hierarchy to Mampurugu. Political ties
between the largest divisions of the "Tri-Dominion" (Mossi-
Mamprusi-Dagomba) were maintained at the top level. On this
point Cardinall is quite clear. He quotes from the *Journal of a
Residence in Ashantee* of Dupuis, who was British Consul at
Kumasi in 1821 when Dagomba had been brought under the
dominion of the Ashanti. The *Journal* notes that the Dagomba
capital of Yendi and other large towns were under an annual
tribute of 500 slaves, 200 cows, and 400 sheep and cloths, and
that the smaller towns were taxed in proportion. Cardinall then
continues:

The Grunshi, Busani, Konkomba, Tchokossi, and other independent tribes were raided regularly to procure the necessary number
of slaves, and when hard put to it the Na of Dagomba asked his
relatives of Mossi and Mamprussi to help him in his payment. Be it
noted that these three kingdoms seem never to have forgotten their
family ties, and to this day observe the relationship by an interchange of messengers on all occasions of great national importance.
(1925:9)

The more local direct ties are also clear. Fortes himself notes
that the crucial act of conferring the chiefship on Tongo and
other Tale chiefships belongs to a single elector, a subchief of
Mamprusi.[8] Competition was between lineage segments to
raise the necessary purchase price of the na'am, and Fortes also
reports that the "cost" varied from 8 cattle up to 70 cattle as
well as many cowries, depending on the importance of the
chiefship involved. In addition many gifts had to be given to
the elector's (the Kuna'aba) elders to obtain their good offices.
(1940:257) Manoukian has noted that after investiture the new

chief returns by a special road which is supposed to be the one taken by the original invaders from Mamprusi and that he must be welcomed into the community by the Tendaans, who present him to their Earth Shrines for blessing. (1952:49) Years before one of Rattray's informants among the Tallensi had told him of a Sumri who did not become a *Na* (chief) because he never went back to Mampurugu to be invested. Instead he became only *golog'dana* or "owner of the drums." Rattray permitted the informant to finish his account and then carefully rechecked.

> I asked this informant if a man could not become a Chief in a new country independently of Mampurugu. He replied he could not do so unless 'he went to Mampurugru (near the present town of Nalerugu, the former capital of the Mampruse State) whence spread all the black race.' (Rattray 1932,II:341)

Chiefs in Taleland called the Kuna'aba *ba* (father) indicating loyalty and ceremonial deference. They protected his clansmen when traveling in their territory and he reciprocated; neither made war on the other's community. Yet, while reporting these facts, Fortes goes on to note that the Kuna'aba has "no economic, juridical, administrative, or military rights sanctioned by the native political system over any Tale chief," and that his only real modern power is the sanction of force represented by the British administration. (1940:257) Here Skinner's comment that probably a good deal of the indigenous organization had already been lost (previously quoted, p. 119) is an important consideration. That the power in the old days resided at the top is clear in Rattray's account when he reports that about the time of the fourth succession after Mosuor the Mampurugna'ab placed one of his sons as chief of Kurugu and placed Tongo under Kurugu. (1932:340) For a time after this Tongo chiefs were invested from Kurugu. Rattray's own summary of the Tale political system is both succinct and forthright:

The history of the ruling class of almost every Talense town follows these lines. This upper class were scions of the Kings of Mampruse, from which place, according to themselves, the black race, i.e. the upper classes of Moshi, Dagomba, and Mampruse—and, just possibly, Ashanti—sprang. (1932, II:344)

Ironically enough, that what is involved here is a wider regional economic and political network can be seen in the very demographic pattern itself and has been noted in these terms by the geographers, thus giving a measure of independent confirmation to our argument. Harrison Church (1961:365) in discussing the high density of Zuarungu terms it an extension into Ghana of similar areas in the Upper Volta. Glenn Trewartha, while observing that the population concentration in the northern Gold Coast (Ghana) is "something of an unsolved problem," goes on to point out:

It appears to be part of an interrupted east-west Sudanese belt of denser settlement which reaches from French Guinea in the west to Lake Chad in French Equatorial Africa. . . . The densest settlement area in the extreme northeast is the southern part of a more extensive and very ancient area of population concentration in the upper Volta region, chiefly in the French Sudan. (1957:57)

A glance at Fortes' map of the distribution of Mole-Dagbane-speaking peoples is also very instructive. (1945:5) The shaded area, which plots the distribution, spreads like a giant squash from Salaga in the south to above Ouahiguya, covering Dagomba, Mamprusi, and Mossi. The major roadway from Kumasi through Salaga to Ouagadougou runs like a backbone along its western edge and corresponds closely to the former major caravan route from Salaga on to Ouagadougou and thence to Timbuktu. Tongo is located slightly to the east but within easy striking distance of a major juncture in this artery, where a western leg branches off toward Bawku, itself an important trading town on the former French frontier. (Boateng 1960:195–96) It was along this trade route [9] that Krause trekked in the summer and fall of 1885, traveling with a caravan from Salaga in the south to some 400 miles northwest of Ouagadougou (Skinner 1962:245); and Binger, traveling in the other direction, passed through a few years later. Evidence from current historical research is mounting that these routes and such nodal centers as staging areas, termini, crucial junctures, major markets, and major way stations played a crucial role in state formation in the region.

Rattray was the first to point out that the political systems of this region were the results not of migrations of entire peoples, but of small armed bands of mounted soldiers of fortune, perhaps refugees from Sudanic states, who settled down among the indigenous peoples establishing chiefships. (1932, I:xii-xv) Fage, accepting this in principle, has made the further and fruitful observation that the process of state formation tended to flow along the caravan routes as they were extended southward toward the forest and the coast, and that the invaders were those who had lost out in trade or succession at home. (1959:27) Most recently Wilks (1962:340) has made the suggestion that these invaders or strangers were warrior bands hired to guard the caravans. Further, it is clear from Cardinall's account that the chiefships were not always imposed from the outside. After noting that the chiefs of the most outlying districts were often those exiled from the centers, Cardinall continues:

In the country which these exiled Chiefs dared not venture there were no Chiefs. But heads of families had heard of the proximity of the Mamprussi *nenamse* (pl. of naba), and for various reasons, such as protection, ambition, pride, etc., went to pay their respects, presenting cows or other gifts. (1925:20)

They were given medicine, usually earth from the *naba's* compound which conferred power over the recipient and at the same time delegated power from the donor. This is of theoretical interest in terms of parallels among the East African Alur and elsewhere. These various processes are none of them mutually exclusive and probably all were operative in varying degrees, depending on the situation. What is important to note is that, whether trade followed the flag or the flag followed trade, the correlation between the two is marked.

This caravan route has another important aspect. Both Fortes' account and that of Manoukian would make the powers and privileges of Namoo chiefs appear rather minimal. Outside their own lineage their powers were limited to arbitration with the consent of both parties, with no means of enforcing decisions or legislative powers. Special privileged access was limited to the produce of all locust-bean trees, vagrant humans, and animals found dead in the bush. Nothing is said of their relation to trade or markets. It is clear that something is missing here because Rattray's account of the Mampruse Constitution includes an account of considerable tax and tribute funnelling in to the Mampurugnaba from divisional and lesser chiefs, including a proportion of the ferry tolls collected, war spoils, captives, and others. (1932, II 559–60) We have here a double anomaly—lineage segments competing by means of considerable gifts and rewards to obtain positions which are not particularly rewarding, and a tributary network that has an end but no seeming beginning.

Skinner has pointed out that among the Mossi no caravans were allowed to pass which did not pay taxes and that those who were derelict in this were attacked by the *nakomce,* mounted nobles acting for the district chiefs. "Wise caravan leaders not only paid their taxes but established close relationships with the chiefs in order to receive adequate protection from some nobles who illegally attacked and looted the caravans." (1962:246) Add to this the ferry tolls, market tolls and fees, and payments for special titles that these subchiefs could confer, and we have several lucrative sources of income that would largely have dried up after the British pacification.[10]

Furthermore, in an ironic reversal of fortunes, certain ten-daans, in particular the Golibdaana, in the post-pacification period were beginning to outstrip Namoos in material wealth through their control of a lucrative oracle in the Tong Hills at the time Fortes was there. (1945:253–58) This cult drew adherents, and hence wealth, from as far away as Accra. Tale society was apparently anything but self-contained; anything but stable.

Cardinall recounts that the caravans came from the north and dealt in slaves in the markets of Salaga and Kintampo to the south, returning with quantities of kola nuts. These were not small groups but major expeditions protected by as many as three hundred armed men. That both caravans and markets were raided from the Tong Hills is also clear from his account. One story recounts how the people from the Hills crossed the river near Dua (10 to 15 miles away) from the Tong Hills base, ambushing a caravan and capturing many donkeys. This would presumably include what the donkeys were carrying, though it is not so explicitly stated. In addition, the main Tallensi market at Bari was "raided many times" from the Tong Hills. (Cardinall 1925:97–98) Binger's account of his trip through this region contains an interesting drawing of a "Construction Sacrée" of the Gurunsi.[11] (1892, II:39) This shows an extremely concentrated compound, apparently fortified, atop a heap of immense boulders. Down a long ladder (which could apparently be retracted in defense) streams a line of warriors brandishing spears and heading in the direction of a caravan which is proceeding on its way through the tall grass beneath the boulders. The same Sumri, who did not return to be invested and hence became only "owner of the drums" is described in the same account as being a son of the Mampurugna'ab who failed in a succession dispute and was driven out and eventually settled down atop the Tong Hills (see p. 124). We may well have here a parallel to those nobles described by Skinner as

illegally raiding caravans. Unfortunately the historical accounts
are not yet sufficiently detailed to tell us if indeed this was the
case. Perhaps we have parallels to the nakomce, acting on behalf
of the chiefs, or perhaps the "real Talis" (non-Namoos) had the
practice of raiding from the hills, and the establishment of the
Chiefship in the region was part of an endeavor on the part of
the Mamprusi to contain and pacify them. Initially, at least, the
latter would seem likely, and it may well be with the breakdown of Mamprusi authority in the late nineteenth century
that the Talis returned to their old ways. In either case, this
would explain why Kologu (Kologo, perhaps the Kurugu of
Rattray, see p. 124) had a decided interest in, and did in fact
establish, authority and chiefship over the Tong Hills area.
(Cardinall 1925:19) In any event, there is ample evidence that
there were major sources of wealth, revenue, or just plain loot
above and beyond the local subsistence products of the land.

The "major cleavage" then extends far beyond Taleland,
indeed, throughout the entire Tri-Dominion, its distribution
being largely isomorphic with the wider demographic, linguistic, cultural, and political patterns, and the network of markets
all linked by the major trade and caravan routes. The myths,
whose historicity Fortes eschews (1945:27), are all of one piece
forming a single cycle which stands as a charter validating both
the political system—the relationship between Namoos and
tendaans—and the common origin of Mossi, Dagomba, and
Mamprusi.[12]

Nor was the social and political structure by any means either
stable or static. Cardinall interprets the precolonial period as
one of constant flux. (1925:11) This may express too great a
reverence for the Pax Britannica, but there is a certain truth in
it if it be taken to indicate shifting centers of power and
influence and the rise and decline of the power of the various
states relative to one another. If, on the other hand, it be taken
to mean that this period was one of pure chaos rather than de-

velopment, it is highly misleading except for the period of the late nineteenth century, when the British and French were moving in and the slave raiders of Samory and Babatu were ravaging the region. Though the full history of the development is yet to be told, the main outlines seem to be emerging. Fage (1959:28) cites the fifteenth century as the probable date of arrival of the founding ancestors of the Dagomba and Mamprusi. Binger estimated that the peak of Mamprusi power and geographical spread was during the seventeenth century, or two centuries before his visit to the region in 1887–1889. (1892 II:38–39) This estimate may be somewhat speculative, but Binger was clear in his belief that the situation he viewed in the late nineteenth century was one of diminished Mamprusi power. Shifts in trade route orientations undoubtedly affected the varying fortunes of the politics involved, as did shifts in military and political power bring shifts in the routes and direction of trade. When to this are added the ravages of the late nineteenth century, the effects of the British pacification, and the loss of considerable Mamprusi and Dagomba territories when the Germans annexed Togoland (Bourret 1952), the total picture is one of considerable socio-cultural change— change that was still underway when Fortes was in the region.

Undoubtedly, the exact nature, extent, and degree of power of the Mamprusi state at any given time will be debated and redebated at least until firmer historical evidence is obtained. What historical evidence there is must nonetheless be employed if the analysis is to be at all meaningful. We have seen that the application of a purely synchronic approach which eschews all history as "conjectural" has obscured rather than clarified the political reality. One may suspend judgment on some of the inferred historical details, but, as to the broad outlines, the evidence assessed here would seem to make abundantly clear that we are dealing neither with a stable situation nor with a homogeneous society. Rather, the picture is one of broad regional interrelations, considerable historical depth, and important developmental processes in the combined and interdependent fields of economic, social, and political organization.

Furthermore, it is clear that the local demographic picture as of 1931 had been considerably influenced by migration, and that the relatively permanent dense settlement pattern which existed previously was part of a wider pattern that was intimately tied in with the significant development of trade through the region and the concomitant formation of states. In fact, studies by Fage have indicated that the Mamprusi was apparently the parent state in the state-formation process that produced Mossi and Dagomba, and that the Mamprusi line is still recognized as senior by the others. The primary significance of this for us here is in connection with a further statement by Fage that the first state established lay to the north of modern Mamprusi, and could perhaps be regarded as the latter's ancestor, and that from this locus power was extended north to establish the Mossi states. If this be the case, the general Tallensi area could well have been the geographical hearth for the formation of all three states. In short, if evidence from this region is to be brought into the debate concerning population density and state formation, it can only reasonably be brought in under the column "state."

Actually, however, it is neither just nor reasonable to simply transfer the Tallensi density figure from the acephalous column to that of state. We are confronted here not with the average density of a state system but with that of one of its parts. To compare Tallensi densities with the averages of other societies, then, is in effect to compare a local nucleation in one with the overall average of the other. For this reason, the Tallensi figure should be excluded from further discussion.

The Logoli

THE LAST society in the density sample of *African Political Systems* is the Logoli of the North Kavirondo District, Nyanza Province, Kenya. The Logoli are only one of approximately twenty tribal groups which together constitute the some 300,-000 Bantu-speaking peoples of the District and are collectively known as either the "Bantu Kavirondo" or by the more modern designation Luhya. (Mair 1962:53) It is the Logoli alone and not the entire Luhya whose density is cited by Fortes and Evans-Pritchard. This case at the same time represents the smallest area of any in the sample—52 square miles—and the highest density—391 per square mile. (Wagner 1940:191) Both this area and the density, however, are in need of further clarification before proceeding with the argument.

For unstated reasons Wagner has cited the population density of South Maragoli [1] alone. North Maragoli, also occupied by Logoli, had in 1937 a population of 25,451 in an area of 43 square miles, yielding a density of 591.88. If one is to refer to the density of the Logoli, it would seem more realistic to use the average for the total 95 square miles of both locations, which is 482 per square mile. This would indeed be the case were it not for one further complication. Apparently the boundaries on which the official 1932 population estimates (used by Wagner) were based were not accurate. Writing in 1947, Norman Humphrey, the Senior Agricultural Officer of the Kenya Colony, noted that a field crew check with a new and more accurate map had indicated a serious underestimation of the size of Bunyore

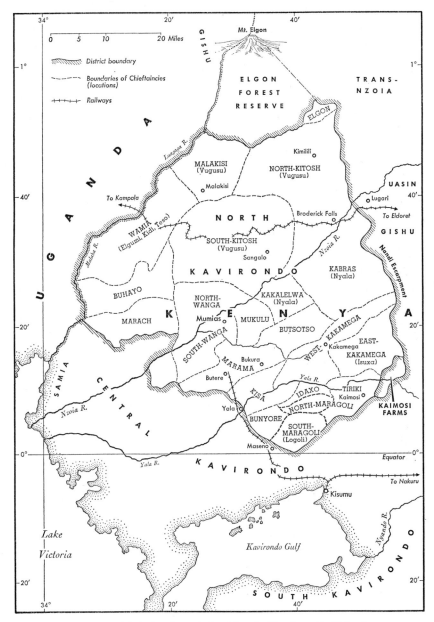

MAP V. The Chieftaincies of the North Kavirondo District
From Gunter Wagner, *The Bantu of North Kavirondo*, Vol. I, Oxford University Press, 1949

(or Bunyole), which adjoins Maragoli and which was noted for its population density of over 1,000 per square mile.[2] Humphrey concluded that the Maragoli-Bunyore boundary was still not accurately known, and that only by combining Bunyore and Maragoli and extracting the average of the two could anything like an accurate estimate be given. I shall follow the same procedure here, but with the 1932 population figures used by Wagner. The total population of 76,506 in a total area of 122 square miles gives an average population density of 627 per square mile. The ensuing discussion will show that the problem is historical and regional and by no means limited to the Logoli of the ethnographic present. Consequently, this combination simplifies rather than complicates the problem.[3]

It would seem, then, that a genuinely high density, one higher than reported for any state system except Ruanda, was obtained in these three locations in 1932. This poses a problem only in relation to the alleged acephalous nature of the societies involved, and it is to this side of the question we must next address ourselves.

There is no question but that the acephalous and segmentary character of North Kavirondo society is well-established in traditional anthropological literature. Radcliffe-Brown explicitly recognized the problems involved in delineating Kavirondo political organization in the Preface to *African Political Systems.* (1940:xiii) His attempt there to attribute law and organized legitimate authority to what Wagner had described as a lynch group has become one of the classic cases in political anthropology.[4] Eisenstadt (1959:206) has listed the Bantu Kavirondo among his Classical Segmentary Tribes, and there is nothing in the more recent discussion by Mair (1962:53–57, 66–68) which would contradict the applicability of this designation. It was Wagner, of course, who performed the field studies upon which all of these secondary interpretations were based. His conclusions are both clear and succinct: "There is no

political structure as distinct from the kinship and social structure; that is, there exists no system of institutions that serve
explicitly and exclusively the purpose of maintaining the tribal
unit as a whole." (1940:201) In an earlier source (1939:28)
Wagner had already pointed out that in his opinion there was
no tribal organization overruling the authority of the clans.

Norman Humphrey, the former Senior Agricultural Officer
of the Kenya Colony, casts some doubt upon these designations:

It would seem that he (Wagner) regarded them as chiefless societies,
his description being generally in accordance with conditions found
among the Kikuyu. On the other hand, all the evidence given to the
Land Tenure Committee was to the contrary and to-day a denial of
the alleged old chieftainships is likely to be met with an indignant
rejoinder. (Humphrey 1947:15)

This Report [5] was the result of a seventeen-day investigation by
a special committee. Testimony was taken in eight different
"locations" and evidence was sought from representative elders
of every tribe in North Kavirondo.[6] The Report notes that
keen interest was taken in the proceedings and that many hundreds gathered in each place to listen. (Kenya 1931:1) As it
presents a composite picture of the overall political organization
of the Bantu Kavirondo which is somewhat at odds with that
presented by Wagner, it is important to consider at least some
salient sections.

Land and the tribe are regarded as one and indissoluble.
Debatable questions having to do with the land or its people
were, by custom, "decided by the tribal elders sitting in con-
clave under the chosen chiefs," and a clan could become a separate entity only if it became completely and territorially severed
from its tribe. (Kenya 1931) The basic unit of land administration was the *lugongo,* or ridge, and this was under the patri-
archal rule of an elder called the *liguru,* usually the senior
member, by primogeniture, of the clan or subclan occupying
the particular ridge. No one could hold land apart from his

family except under the tribal authority represented by the
liguru or the elders. "Even a clan member could be evicted
from his land and driven out of the clan for misconduct, if the
chief and the elders so decided." (Kenya 1931:4) [7] Furthermore, each tribe is reported as having its chief, who was head of
all the clans. In most cases the office descended in the clan of the
eldest son of the common ancestor except in cases where unpop-
ularity or incompetence of a potential incumbent were important factors, or where factionalism had led to the splitting off
and departure of the senior line. Among the Wanga tribe,
which was most important in the area, the chief had a special
title, *Nabongo*. Other tribes also had specific names for the
office, but among the smaller and less important tribes, the chief
was simply known by a term which could be translated "senior
chief" and indicated his authority over clan heads. The tribal
chief was regarded as the final *omumali we kina,* or adjudicator,
and he decided disputes which were either referred up from the
clan heads or appealed by the disputants. Most importantly:

He could impose fines of stock or grain on those who had been
guilty of breach of the peace or other offences against tribal custom,
and such fines were his. The trophies of game killed or found in the
kitsimi land (bush or uncultivated land not within *lugongo* boundaries—RFS) and he took annual tribute from the clans. (Kenya
1931:5)

This picture is sharply at variance with that presented by
Wagner:

Political authority thus remained inarticulate. It was not linked up
with clearly defined rights and privileges, such as are usually associated with institutionalized chieftainship. The leading elders of a
clan or sub-clan were merely those persons whose opinion carried
most weight when public matters were discussed on the *oluhia* and
who were called to perform sacrifices. They had no rights that were
inherent in their office, such as to collect tribute, to enact laws, to
call up warriors for a raid, or to grant or refuse residence of
strangers on clan lands. There is no generally accepted term for a

clan or tribal head, but a leading elder is referred to by a variety of terms which can also be used with regard to any respected and honoured person. Finally, there was no formal appointment and installation of the head of a clan or sub-clan. (1940:235–36)

These conflicting results are, in part at least, due to differences in the type of investigation and area covered. The Land Tenure Committee endeavored to draw a composite picture for all North Kavirondo. Their report, therefore, suffers from the inevitable deficiencies of any composite—similarities are stressed at the expense of differences, and it is virtually impossible to say conclusively just what statuses, institutions, or offices were claimed for a given specific tribal group such as the Logoli, Nyole, or Wanga. Had they supplemented their conclusions with even an appendix which gave some indication of tribal variation in specific and significant offices or institutions, their work would have been much more valuable to anthropologists; and it would be easier to assess the exact degree of difference between the two accounts. Its virtue is, of course, its generality, broadness of tribal coverage, and, purported at least, typicality for the region. Wagner's account, despite its title,[8] is strictly and avowedly limited to only *two* tribal groups. He says:

In none of the approximately twenty tribal groups which make up the 300,000 Bantu Kavirondo has political integration reached a very high degree, but it differs sufficiently in the various tribes to make generalizations from conditions in one area impossible. The following analysis, therefore, claims to apply to the two sub-tribes only of which a detailed study has been made, viz. the Logoli in the south and the Vugusu in the north. (Wagner 1940:198)

What has been said here concerning detailed study holds in a general way for Wagner's full monograph (1949, 1956) although in the larger work the Logoli and Vugusu material is supplemented by data from most of the other tribes of the region—material which was either gathered on shorter personal trips or gleaned from the studies of earlier investigators, official accounts, and others. Nonetheless, the work and the resulting generalizations are heavily concentrated around the Logoli and Vugusu material. This is not a criticism, nor does it diminish the value of the work. It would obviously have been difficult, if not impossible, to carry out a truly detailed study in more than two different groups in the time he had at his disposal.[9] Nor should one quarrel with his selection of these two. The choice had several advantages in the way of control and comparison including the geographical spread between north and south, as well as marked differences in population density, degree of reliance upon cattle, and settlement pattern.[10]

From the standpoint of the study of political organization, however, the results of this selection are somewhat different, for the very choice of north and south groups involved the omission of the center, which was inhabited by a very important group—the Wanga.[11] All of the sources are agreed that, here among the Wanga, political development was the highest in all Kavirondo, and all are agreed as to the marked centralization of political authority. Wagner himself, who admittedly did not engage in fieldwork among the Wanga,[12] states cautiously that the clan of the Wanga chiefs "already in pre-European days commanded an authority extending—at least at times—beyond the tribal limits." (1949:14) Wagner's self-imposed limitation as to the coverage of his statements on political organization must, particularly in the light of more recent overviews and classifications, be both underscored and remembered.

Admittedly it is a difficult task to assess precisely and classify Wanga political organization. There is no fully systematic and comprehensive account on the order of Richards' study of the Bemba, for example. The greatest detail concerning political institutions is to be found in an article in the *Journal of the Royal Anthropological Institute* (43, 1913) by K. R. Dundas, a British administrator. This is unfortunately sketchy, at least by modern standards. It may be supplemented from the writings of the missionary N. Stam (1920, 1929), who gives a parallel account of the traditional history and some information on "Divine Kingship." His accounts are, quite naturally, concentrated on beliefs and customs associated with the supernatural. In addition, several facts of considerable significance can be gleaned and pieced together from the accounts of the earliest travelers and administrators in the region: Thomson (1885), Hobley (1898, 1929), and Jackson (1930).

Evaluations in this matter have ranged somewhat widely. Some writers have tended to see the Wanga chiefdom as largely created by the schemes of the late chief Mumia in conjunction with the imposition of British rule. This view has overlooked its earlier history. Dundas tends to the other extreme, indicating his belief that it was well on the way to becoming another Buganda. Perhaps the most measured view is also the most recent. D. A. Low, who wrote the section "The Northern Interior, 1840–1884" in Volume I of the *History of East Africa* (Oliver 1963), calls the Wanga polity a "substantial little chiefdom," and notes that the authority of the Wanga Nabongo, or paramount chief, bore many similarities to that of the rulers of the neighboring Busoga states. (1963:310) I shall not add my own assessment at this point, but first give a short sketch of the major historical developments and the main outlines of political institutions, so that the reader may have sufficient ground for judgment of his own.

The peak of Wanga political development apparently came toward the middle of the nineteenth century under Nabongo [13] Shiundu.[14] At this time the Wanga dominion extended from Samia in the west to Kakamega in the east, and from Bukusu in the north to a southern boundary along the Yala River. (Low 1963:310) The Yala in turn marks the northern limits of Bunyole and Maragoli. Stam attributes this ascendancy of the Wanga to the arrival of Swahili traders from the coast who brought guns and allied themselves with the Wanga against their enemies.[15] It is to be noted that the major Wanga centers, Mumias (formerly Shiundus) and Sakwas,[16] were located at a crucial ford and crossing of the Nzoia River, the major river of North Kavirondo. This afforded a strategic position for the collection of tolls as well as a convenient resting stop and supply depot for caravans. Some tendencies toward fission had also manifested themselves, and in Shiundu's reign, his brother, Sakwa, established his own center with some autonomy a few miles away. The exact role of the Swahili traders in this event is not made clear but, by the death of Shiundu, Sakwa had emerged as pre-eminent among the Wanga. This prompted Mumia, the son of Shiundu, to extend his use of Masai warriors, strengthen his ties with the Swahili, and then send out feelers to the Europeans when they penetrated the region. This dual division within the Wanga polity persisted to a degree down to the coming of British rule. There does not seem to have been any great antagonism between the two centers, however; and they were used alternately by caravans without any apparent friction, judging by the accounts of Thomson, Hobley, and Jackson.

By the time of Sakwa's death, Mumia was again ascendant and was able to secure the succession (at Sakwas) for his favorite, Tomia. (Dundas 1913:24) Because of his dominant position and close ties, the British made Mumia Paramount Chief over all North Kavirondo in 1894 (Wagner 1949:14) and placed his brothers over Samia, North Kitosh, Marama, and Wahola. (Stam 1929:147) [17] This, of course, gave official British sanction to Mumia and the ruling Wahkitsetse Clan and served to consolidate their position as well as the general dominance of the Wanga in the region. Furthermore, a major expedition which included a company of Sudanese, a levy of one thousand armed Baganda under Chief Kakunguru, a column of Mumia's spearmen, and a volunteer detachment of two hundred local Uasin-gishu Masai had succeeded, with considerable difficulty, in destroying the military power of the Kitosh (Vugusu) tribes directly to the north, undercutting the rammed mud walls of their fortress villages with combined Hotchkiss and machine-gun fire from British-manned guns.[18] This ended the threat from the last significant Wanga enemy in the region. (Hobley 1929:81–87)

British support and the network of Sudanese garrisons they established in the region were not the exclusive, nor even primary, sources of Mumia's strength at this time, however. For, during the regional Sudanese mutiny of 1897 when the Mumias station was manned only by a half company of Sudanese and fifty armed Swahili and Nyamwezi porters in the employ of the local Smith-Mackenzie transport agent, Mumia was able to summon quickly one thousand of his own warriors and hold the Sudanese to a standoff. The officially sanctioned and dominant position of the Wanga chiefs remained right down to the thirties; but in addition to their official support, they apparently wielded considerable sub rosa power and influence as well. Suddenly in 1928 the *Native Affairs Department Annual Report* noted the following: "Politically the year has been one of comparative peace, except in North Kavirondo, which has been disturbed by a persistent agitation against the vague but powerful overlordship of the Wanga family." (NADAR 1928) By 1929 this had become known as the Anti-Wanga movement. Apparently the movement was initiated by acculturated Luhya occupying subordinate posts in the government offices in Nairobi and elsewhere, and, at first, directed against Mulama, chief of the Marama location and brother to the aging Mumia.

One by one in the years immediately ensuing, the other brothers of Mumia originally placed by the British in charge of various locations [19] were made the targets of propaganda attack and litigation. In December of 1928 a head-on clash was fought between members of the various factions on a football field in Butere; in 1932 the retirement of Murunga was demanded, there was trouble on the Wanga-Buhayo boundary, and the Wanga-South Kitosh border was reported ablaze as the result of attempts by Murunga to set up a coffee plantation there. In Waholo (Buholo) Were was astutely playing off Bantu against Luo and encouraging the illegal immigration of Nilotic Ja-Luo to enhance his faction. But by 1934 the Native Affairs Department could report the Wanga as largely "home in Wanga" with Mulama deposed and Murunga retired from Kitosh to be chief of South Wanga, although agitation still continued for the latter's full removal. (NADAR 1928–1934) These events are noteworthy not only in sketching the persistence of Wanga-Wahkitsetse power until its final demise, but in highlighting the degree to which the whole topic of "chiefs and chieftainship" was a politically "loaded" issue at the time. Depending upon one's faction and situation, there were both cogent reasons for claiming and for denying the traditional right of chiefs. It was in this environment of conflict and contention that Wagner had to carry out his field work.[20]

It seems that the mid-nineteenth century and pre-European florescence of the Wanga was due largely to its strategic position astride the long-distance caravan route from the coast.[21] Sir Harry Johnston records that one of the first caravans to come across Nandi and Masai country from Mombasa halted in Kavirondo "waiting for permission to enter Uganda." (1902, I:218) The permission was refused on grounds that the Kabaka, Suna, was dead and his successor, Mutesa, not yet duly installed. This is informative as indicating a chain of political communications, at least between Buganda and Kavirondo via Busoga. Maps in Wakefield (1870) and New (1873) indicate trade routes from the coast through Kavirondo to Buganda and mark off by name such Wanga "capitals" and supply centers as Shiundus (later Mumias) and Sakwas. All the early Europeans —Thomson, Hobley, Jackson, Lugard, the trader Stokes, and the German Dr. Peters—used these as headquarters and supply stations and comment upon the abundance and cheapness of supplies.[22]

While the full flowering of the Wanga polity can be attributed to the catalytic influence of trade from the coast, it is not at all clear to what extent a chiefdom may have developed here prior to this contact. The environmental diversification within a relatively small region,[23] the close proximity of different ethnic groups with different ecological adaptations and economic specializations, as well as the nearness of the Busoga states and Buganda would make this latter eventuality at least likely. There is, unfortunately, no solid information one way or the other. The genealogy of Wanga Nabongos includes some six names between Shiundu and Wanga, the tribal ancestor, but there is no proof of the actual power or status of these, and the traditional history is largely an account of wars and conflicts and miraculous exploits by the ancestral Nabongos.

There was, at the time of contact, a regional trade network which was to a considerable degree independent of the long-distance carrying trade, and some elements may either have been entirely indigenous or stimulated from the interior rather than the coast. Hobley (1898) said that the major occupations of the region were cultivating, cattle-rearing, and trading. He cited the accumulation of cattle, sheep, and goats as the goal of trading but did not indicate just who the traders were. Goats, sheep, or hoes were traded at Mumias for brass wire, which was exchanged in Busoga for more goats and sheep. These in turn were taken to Samia, the main ironworking center, and converted by trade back into hoes. The result, according to Hobley, was a doubling of the initial outlay. The Wa-Milambo who inhabited large islands in Lake Victoria (near Ugowe Bay) were engaged in the specialized production and trading of salt. Packaged in banana leaf, this salt was traded up and down the entire eastern shore of the lake and exchanged at one to two strings of beads per packet. The ivory trade was the monopoly of Mumia and a few others as it required a large reserve of cattle. (Hobley 1898:365–70) Tribes of Kakamega and Kabras held trade relations with the Nandi through their women (Hobley 1929:88), and in Logoli-land indigenous and precontact markets were the meeting and trading places of Logoli, Isuxa, Nandi, Nyole, Luo, and Idaxo. (Wagner 1956:162)

The political developments which took place within the historical and economic background we have described for the Wanga were, indeed, a far cry from those Wagner has described for the Logoli and the Vugusu. The main outlines, at least, have been recorded by Dundas (1913:19–75), and his is by far the most complete account available. It was his contention that the Wanga were ruled by a royal dynasty. (1913:20) Although there is no systematic discussion of social organization, it is clear that clans were externally ranked and (at least in the case of the dominant, or "royal" clan) internally ranked as well. These, of course, are features of the "conical clan" first discussed by Kirchhoff (1955) and elaborated by Fried (1957) and associated with Chiefdoms and emergent states.

The ruling clan was the Wakhitsetse, and its members, especially the heads of the component lineages, enjoyed many privileges denied to the common people. According to Dundas, these privileges diminish as one moves out from the dynastic line and cease in the case of the younger members of the more distant branches.

There was a special rank, the Itawkho, to which all the sons of the Nabongo were elevated upon the accession of his successor. The Wakhalivu Clan (which see below) apparently had some veto power in this elevation. Commoners could only address Itawkho by a special term of deference and never by name. Finally, Itawkho were distinguished by their privilege of wearing copper bracelets, the symbol of royal rank.

With some exceptions there was no clearcut difference between the privileges of the Nabongo and other Itawkho; and, again, with some exceptions, district chiefs enjoyed, in their own districts, privileges and prerogatives mirroring those of Nabongo. All chiefs were entitled to one tusk of every elephant killed or found dead. All lion and leopard skins were claimed by the chiefs, who rewarded the hunters with a small present and some beer.[24] Only the Nabongo, however, could wear a leopard-skin cloak or sleep on a lion skin. No one was permitted to sit on a stool in his presence, and his sons were not permitted to sit on stools at all until after his death.

In addition to the Wakhitsetse, three other clans had special status and performed specialized roles in the political systems: the Wakhalivu, the Washikava, and the Wachero. Of these, the Wakhalivu were the most important. Their elders formed the Nabongo's official council and he was, ideally, expected to be governed by their advice. They had a say in the elevation of Itawkho, and, as keepers of the secret of the reigning Nabongo's choice could, in practice, have an influence on the succession.[25] Wakhalivu young men also performed important functions. They were the Nabongo's official police and messengers, collecting fines, executing punishments, and making arrests. In return for these services they received special fees or a share of the fines (in kind) assessed.

The Washikava, on the other hand, seem to have been a more subordinate group in an emerging social stratification. It was their task to build the Nabongo's village, make roads, and the like. Dundas reports that in Shiundu's time they were worked very hard and treated with severity.[26]

The Wachero were the royal undertakers. They guarded the ill or dying Nabongo, permitting none except Wakhalivu elders to enter. Wachero also had the task of strangling the Nabongo when he was demonstrably near death.

The burial of the Nabongo was markedly different from that of commoners. The Wachero stripped the body of all adornment and handed the copper bracelets into the safekeeping of the Wakhalivu. The corpse was then wrapped in the hide of a newly slaughtered bull and lowered, in a sitting position, into a hole in the center of the hut. A tube for sucking beer was placed in his mouth and an inverted pot was placed over his head, which was left protruding from the ground. Then, after the head had decayed, the pot was tamped down over it and all was covered with earth. A year later, when his successor had been able to amass resources for a major food distribution and feast, the bones were removed by the Wachero and washed and anointed with butter. The new Nabongo led the procession to Matungu, the ancestral burying ground, where the grave was simply marked with a few stones. There was apparently opportunity for interregnum clashes, even at this late date, for the successor, according to Dundas, was heavily guarded to protect him against rivals. (1913:29) The new Nabongo visits the site periodically thereafter for the purpose of making sacrifices to Wanga and other royal ancestors who lie interred there.

Upon return to the capital the Nabongo made presents of bullocks to all the various clans, and it is significant that at this ceremony the leaders of all the clans acknowledged the new Nabongo as their chief. (Humphrey 1947:16) The Nabongo did not attend the ensuing feast, but he and all his brothers went into seclusion for four days while the historic sacred spears and royal ancestral stones were displayed outside. Finally, on the night of the fourth day, a circumcised member of Wakhalivu placed the copper bracelets and leopard-skin cloak upon the incumbent, and other bracelets were bestowed upon his brothers in order of seniority, elevating them to Itawkho rank.

The Nabongo's mother was also regarded as being a most important person and possessed great influence in both domestic and tribal affairs.

She exacted large contributions in money and in kind from the king and the Itawkho; and is, in consequence, reported to be enormously rich. Should these contributions not be forthcoming, she threatens to make use of the power vested in her by virtue of her custody of the sacred spears; a threat that rarely fails to have the desired effect. (Dundas 1913:30)

Dundas has also provided a short account of Wanga laws and penalties (1913:49–55), including the observation that all major cases were handled by the Nabongo alone. Some of the penalties listed, such as a month's imprisonment in the stocks or hard labor in the Nabongo's plantations, would seem to be likely post-European innovations.

In cases of feud the chief dispatched an armed force which surrounded the village involved, and a penalty of two cows and two bulls was imposed. After the case was heard, a further fine of fifteen head of cattle was imposed, of which five went to the chief's headmen and the balance to the injured party. The list of offenses and penalties covers a wide range from murder to theft, but a number of specific items show strong traces of European influence. In short, we have here a state, though on a small scale and newly emergent.

Close examination of Wagner's material reveals that within the Logoli, too, there were strong tendencies in the same direction in both the realms of political organization and economics. In fact Wagner himself includes an important qualifier to his general view that there was no authority above the clan, a qualifier which was not stated with sufficient emphasis, apparently, to have continued into the subsequent literature.

As regards submission to political leadership, the largest groups, both among the Logoli and the Vugusu, are the exogamous, patrilineal clans *or clan groupings, consisting of one larger and several smaller clans,* but not the whole tribal society. (Wagner 1940:200, my italics)

Wagner amplifies this situation in his monograph. After listing the thirty-two Logoli clans, he says:

By far the largest and most important of these clans are the Mavi (14) and the Yonga (31). With these two clans rested essentially the leadership in warfare; they controlled the most extensive tracts of land and to each of them was affiliated a number of smaller clans which submitted to their leadership both in times of peace and war (see below p. 388). The Mavi and the clans politically attached to them inhabit the northern part of the chieftaincy, and the Yonga, together with the allied clans, the southern part. Of the two clans, the Mavi again surpass the Yonga both numerically and as regards the influence wielded by them. In their clan, for instance, was vested the hereditary office of the tribal priest who performed the semi-annual *ovwali*-sacrifice addressed to the Supreme Being and to the clan and tribal ancestors (cf. below, p. 290 sq.). The Mavi clan also supplied the majority of the leaders (cf. vol.ii) whose authority was recognized by other clans of the tribal community, as well as the present tribal chief nominated by the British Government. (1949:58).

Opposed to the tendency of clan fission and segmentation is the process whereby small clans, unable to maintain their own independence effectively, become *avavute* with larger clans. This is, the two clans engage in ritual friendship, perform certain rites together, refrain from intermarriage, and engage in mutual defense and support in warfare. The initiative is said to have come from the smaller clans which needed the protection of the larger. (1949:71,388) In the socio-political realm, then, the process of chiefdom-building would seem to have been at least partially underway.[27] These processes were not limited to the Logoli. The Loxova and Mbo clans were the largest among the thirty-four clans of the Tiriki and from their ranks the most influential clan heads were chosen. Among the Marama, clans who later joined the tribe and who could not trace descent from the common tribal ancestor were called *emikuru,* or veranda-poles, because they support the big clan the way veranda-poles support a roof. (1949:62–64) There were also strong economic tendencies at work toward the development of chiefdoms. The pre-European Logoli markets, where members of not only different tribes but different linguistic groups as well came together for trade, have been described in a text collected by

Wagner (see page 144 above). These imply a higher political authority, although this is not described. Wagner does mention, though, that disputes were arbitrated in the market and the produce of the unruly seized by force. Market dues in kind were charged and collected, but members of the Dindi clan, whose members had organized and controlled the market, were not charged. The ultimate distribution of these dues is not given.[28]

It would seem then that the acephalous label cannot be applied to the Logoli without some important qualifications. As to its (largely post-Wagner) application to the Bantu Kavirondo as a whole, such a classification only does violence to the facts and seriously vitiates any serious comparative work that is at all developmentally oriented. A reclassification, however, is essentially beyond the scope of this work. In terms of density, it is the Wanga who are most important at the time of contact, so let us return to a consideration of the demographic pattern as it was then.

In October 1898 the *Geographical Journal* carried an article by C. W. Hobley, who in 1896 had made a compass survey and map of both North and Central Kavirondo, traveling throughout the area in the course of the survey. The article, which gives a short geographical and ethnographic summary, is most valuable to us for what it says about population:

It is difficult to form an accurate idea of the population of the country under control, but it is roughly estimated that the population does not much exceed 200,000. The most thickly populated tract is a line roughly following the Nzoia river, a strip about ten miles wide, running parallel with the left bank of that river. (1898:362) [29]

In short, at the turn of the century the high density was not in the Nyole-Logoli pocket at all but exactly where the political development was—the Wanga State.

This density was also commented upon by Joseph Thomson, who in 1883 was the first European in the region. Although his impressions were based on a familiarity with the area considerably less than Hobley's, some of his remarks concerning his trip from Kabras down the Nzoia valley to "the chief town of Upper Kavirondo," Kwa Sundu,[30] are quite illuminating:

What most impressed me was the surprising number of villages, and the generally contented and well-to-do air of the inhabitants. (1885:481)

Almost every foot of ground was under cultivation.

We passed along a perfect lane of people, all carrying baskets of food which they were dying to dispose of for beads. There were honey, milk, eggs, fowls, beans, &c., &c. (482)

Food at Kwa-Sundu was surprisingly cheap and apparently inexhaustible. Four men's food in flour was got for one string of beads, eight men's food of sweet potatoes for the same, a sheep for fifteen strings, and a goat for twenty strings. Such were some of the prices which ruled. Fish also from the Nzoia was added to our fare, so that we were in a veritable land of Goshen. (487)

And further on down the Nzoia toward the lake:

The extraordinary density of the population was to us a matter of great wonder. (491)

Lord Lugard (Perham 1959, I:386–88) and Sir Frederick Jackson (1930) also commented on the density of the Nzoia River–Wanga area, but only Hobley unequivocally pointed to it as *the* major concentration of population in the area.

The shift in the density node, from the center of the district (Nzoia River–Wanga) to the southwestern corner of the Native Reserves (Bunyole-Maragoli locations), was the result of a process which took place after the British State had imposed its rule over the entire area and as a result of a postcontact process involving acute acculturative pressures upon the Bantu Kavirondo. The important factors in this process include: full pacification of the area and the establishment of the Pax Britannica; the establishment of Native Reserves with fixed boundaries and definite locations for specific tribal units; the stimulation of temporary migration outside the reserves for wage labor on

European estates, the railroad, or for work in various government services; marked development of cash-cropping for export; the introduction of European techniques and implements in agriculture; and the introduction of medical facilities, dispensaries, veterinary stations, and others. Finally, in 1931, the problem was dramatically compounded by the discovery of gold in the vicinity of Kakamega, the consequent influx of Europeans and South Africans, and the hiring of even greater numbers of African assistants. As many (but usually not all) of these factors have been operative in producing other cases of seeming abnormal densities, it seems useful to give a brief historical sketch of the process here. Such a sketch should serve two further important functions. On the one hand, it completes the "explanation" of the high density in the Nyole-Logoli locations; and, on the other, it serves to delineate the complexities underlying the density figures in the postcontact period. This should serve as a cautionary note to those who would readily adduce higher density figures from individual cases in this period and then attribute them to indigeneous and acephalous societies.

We have seen how, in an area of relatively high agricultural potential, the development of the Wanga chiefdom was greatly stimulated by its strategic position on the east-west trade route to Buganda. With the establishment of political authority and coordination in that region, the preconditions were met for successful and relatively peaceful trade and the stimulation of even higher production in agriculture. When the Europeans appeared along the same trade routes, trade and friendly political ties were established with them by the Wanga rulers. Between 1890 and 1895 a British administration was established in North Kavirondo, the first European officials were stationed at Mumias, and the District became part of the Eastern Province of Uganda. Wanga arms participated in the military actions against Kitosh in 1895, and by 1900 the process of pacification in the entire area was largely over. In 1896 the Slater Road, which was constructed for oxcarts, reached Mumias from the East. This, of course, served to further enhance the position of Mumias as a major nerve center.

However, in 1901 the Uganda Railway finally reached Kisumu, at the head of the Kavirondo Gulf, some forty miles to the south of Mumias. This achievement at one stroke rendered obsolete the old caravan routes, the Slater Road, and the strategic economic position of Mumias. Politically, Mumias remained as the headquarters of the District administration while Kisumu (Port Florence) became a major railhead and port of transshipment for goods bound for Uganda. (Wagner 1949:32) Until 1928, when a direct line was completed across northern North Kavirondo to Uganda (Hill 1949:473), the major route for Uganda-bound freight and passengers was by rail from Mombasa to Kisumu and then by steamer across the Lake. Then, in 1902, Kavirondo was severed from Uganda and placed under the Kenya Colony and Protectorate. This was also to have profound consequences, for with this administrative change was to come the system of Native Reserves and later the influx into the region of populations displaced by exclusive white settlement in Trans-Nzoia, Western Nakuru, and along the Uasin Gishu Plateau. (Fitzgerald 1942:248). While Mumias remained as the administrative headquarters for North Kavirondo, Kisumu became headquarters of the entire Nyanza province and of Central Kavirondo and Kisumu-Londiani as well. (Wagner 1949:7) [31]

All of this meant rather rapid and drastic acculturation for North Kavirondo. As early as 1902 Sir Harry Johnston could note the draining of the marshes and the sprouting of piers, wharves, hotels, and residences in corrugated iron at Port Florence and lament that his chapter on the eastern province would before long "only possess the value of describing an aspect which in many details has ceased forever to exist." (1902:40) By the 1920s a perceptive visitor to the region would note the gangs of Kavirondo at the Kisumu station on their way to work all over the Colony—work on the railway, on the farms, the new harbor, or the public roads.

Shouting, jostling, laughing, provided with dried fish, lumps of meat for the journey, they crowd into the long native carriages and are firmly locked in. More than half the police are Kavirondo, and a large percentage of the King's African Rifles, so that the continual stream of outgoing and returning labourers and the work of the innumerable missions in their country, they are more touched by Western influence than any other tribe. (Buxton 1927:127)

Wagner, too, on his way to carry out his field work would comment on the "great changes" since the days of Joseph Thomson, as leaving behind the sprawling township of Kisumu and the bright green of the Indian sugar plantation, he cautiously maneuvered his car through the hundreds of Africans, mostly women and children on the road, carrying either their maize, sorghum, bananas, or vegetables to the Kisumu market or the large boxes or suitcases their husbands would carry with them to the European Highlands or the coast. The trip beyond through Maragoli to Kakamega, that bit of the Rand in East Africa, would carry him past the neat goalposts of the football fields, traditional native huts, village schools, the crossroads dukas of the Indian traders and the occasional square, red brick home, topped either with thatch or corrugated iron, that was the home of an African teacher, trader, or chief. (1949:8–9)

In the decade 1921 to 1930 a government hospital had commenced operation at Kakamega, an agricultural extension service had been inaugurated, and a veterinary station set up; ten native dispensaries had been opened in the District, a regular ambulance service was in operation, and the "North Kavirondo Taxpayers' Welfare Association" had been founded under the lead of the Church Missionary Society. (Wagner 1949:34)

Undoubtedly many of these events had the general effect of

increasing population density, but it would seem that most crucial influences on the demographic pattern were the development of maize as a commercial and export crop and the growing practice of labor migration. Given the somewhat arbitrary limits of the Reserves, Bunyole and the two Maragoli Districts form a wedge in the southwestern corner of the District closest to Kisumu, which was a major market and the communication funnel through which both goods and labor had to move. As such, Kisumu served as a magnet, inducing a more southwesterly concentration of population, while the boundaries of the Reserve served as a dam tending to bottle this concentration within Bunyole and Maragoli. Emphasis on this process should not be permitted to obscure the role of vital ecological factors as well. Both Bunyole and Maragoli were favored with an optimal combination of soil fertility and rainfall pattern which permitted high productivity and two crops per year. (Humphrey 1947:33; Wagner 1949:15) [32] The government records show that as early as 1905 the natives of the southern part of the District were selling their produce at Kisumu. (Wagner 1949:33) The official history of the Kenya and Uganda Railway records that until 1908 no *export* traffic was derived from Kavirondo and that all traffic loaded at Kisumu came from Uganda or German East Africa. By 1913, however, Kavirondo had become the railroad's best customer and was producing more than 28,000 tons of freight. "This remarkable advance had given rise to proposals for the building of a branch line from Kisumu to Mumia's, and the preliminary survey had been made." Work on the direct line to Uganda, however, led to the decision to abandon this scheme at this time. (Hill 1949:334, 337) The idea was advanced again from time to time, and finally a Kisumu-Yala branch 32½ miles long was completed in 1930. (Hill 1949:478) *The Report of the Agricultural Commission* of October 1929 noted: "There is a large export of maize from the Central and North Kavirondo District; indeed the Yala

Branch of the Railway is being built to serve this important and purely native producing area." (Kenya 1930:36) Despite the pressures of the depression, which forced curtailment of several other extensions of the railway, the Yala Branch was extended on to Butere "nearby the old caravan post of Mumias." (Hill 1949:481)

As to labor migration, Wagner reports that by the end of 1937 a total of 31,078 Bantu Kavirondo were employed by Europeans, including those working in the gold fields. This, he estimated, corresponded to 9 per cent of the total population or to 44 per cent of the male population between 15 and 40 years of age. (1949:38) He carried out a detailed inquiry into the occupational activities of 360 married men registered in the taxation lists of one headman in the location of the Yonga clan of South Maragoli. The results showed that 147 of them were either permanently or temporarily employed away from home. In Nairobi, 250 miles away, there were 96; in farming areas 100–150 miles away he counted 21; and in the mines or in other European employment in the reserve, 30. (1939:34) In the gold fields, which in 1932 extended over 420 square miles, in 1935 there were 4,515 Bantu Kavirondo out of a total of 6,814 native miners. The number of Europeans amounted to about 300. (1949:38)

I have gone to some length to sketch the effects of the colonical period upon the population-distribution pattern and density of North and Central Kavirondo not only because this is important in understanding the Logoli densities, but also because similar inflations of density have occurred where the colonial state has been imposed upon previously nonstate societies, and Native Reserves, large-scale land alienations, cash-cropping, and so forth introduced. I would maintain, in this as in similar cases, that the different time horizons—precolonial and time of ethnographic field work (which was inevitably in the colonial period) —be kept carefully separate and not merged or collapsed into a single "ethnographic present." This is merely minimal. Ideally we should want a full diachronic sequence.

Let us then review the demographic evidence for these two time horizons. Hobley, in 1898, gave a population estimate that indicated an average density circa 70 per square mile for North and Central Kavirondo. What is more important, he stated unambiguously that the most thickly populated tract was along the Nzoia river, which was the center of the Wanga state. (Hobley 1898:362) He also mentioned in another source that the population of the Logoli (called by him Awa-Lakoli or Maragoli) was "large." (1902) If the average for the area is in the vicinity of 70 per square mile, the average for the ten-mile-wide strip along the Nzoia River could well exceed 100 or even 150. In light of Hobley's statements we should assume that the Logoli densities at that time were high but not nearly as high as those of the Wanga. This is, of course, as we would have predicted. Nonetheless, the Logoli case does pose certain problems for our position. If Wanga densities can be considered to have been in the range of 100 to 150 per square mile, then certainly Logoli densities could have been as high as 70 per square mile. This admittedly is guesswork, but certainly they could not have approached too closely to those of the Wanga without Hobley's having noted *two* tracts of population concentration. Certainly it is stretching reason by all bounds to suggest that a man who surveyed and mapped the region would have entirely missed an area of higher population density than the one he reported. This, of course, places the 391 figure used by Fortes and Evans-Pritchard into proper perspective. In 1898 the population density of the Logoli was anything but 391, and anyone who has entertained the notion that Logoli population densities (or any other African population densities) have been in a condition of stable equilibrium over the past half-century or so is belied by the facts.

If even this seem too conjectural, the opinions of the Africans themselves as well as those of the ethnographer may be consulted:

There is a consensus of African opinion that the southern locations of the District (Maragoli, Kisa, Bunyore, Tiriki) are far more densely populated today than they used to be. . . . As far as the available data indicate, the annual increase in population averages somewhere between 0.7° and 1.2% for the whole District. It probably lies well above the average in the comparatively healthy, prosperous, economically progressive and largely Christianized southern locations. Moreover, in addition to the natural increase in population, the very fertile soil of the southern part of the District attracted an influx both of clans from neighbouring tribes and of individuals. It seems, therefore, quite probable that the population of Maragoli has doubled during the last fifty years. (Wagner 1956:92)

Still, a density of perhaps 70 per square mile is high compared to the densities we have adduced for the precolonial era among the Zulu, Ngwato, and Bemba. But the far higher densities of the Fort Jameson Ngoni must be borne in mind, as well as the still unresolved historical problems concerning the Ngwato. More importantly, it must be emphasized that we are dealing here with a localized nucleation of population—95 square miles is not a very large area. In this sense, it should be remembered that Johnson's density map of the Bemba gave an area of 314 square miles between 15 and 50 per square mile. Within this area there could well have been peaks of 70 or over. Nonetheless, the full implications of this case must be faced, and those are that definite density thresholds for state formation cannot be elicited at least under conditions of what Fried (1960:713) has rather aptly termed the "murky mirror" of secondary state formation.[33] On the other hand, the murky mirror can be cleared to an extent if we realize that a distinction should be drawn between those cases which arise or exist on the borders of existing and often expanding states and those which do not. Most of Kavirondo was linked by ties of trade to Busoga, which in turn was linked to Buganda. It is entirely conceivable and perhaps expectable that, under the influence, though not actually formal control, of neighboring states, nonstate societies can maintain rather high densities without the full emergence of the state.

Secondly, it must be re-emphasized that the Logoli, as reported by Wagner, displayed definite tendencies toward state development both in the ascendancy of certain clans to positions of dominance and the concomitant hierarchical ranking of clans and in the development of markets under attested political control. Given the contiguity of the Logoli to the Wanga and the subsequent blurring of aboriginal political conditions by the political controversies and intrigues against the Wanga which marked the 1930s, it would be tempting to hypothesize that, at the turn of the century, the Logoli were actually under the Wanga state. Actually, there is no tangible evidence that I have seen to support this contention. It is true that Wanga traditions indicate Maragoli connections (Stam, 1920; Dundas, 1913) but this, in the absence of other evidence, is rather tenuous ground on which to stand. Of course, this may have been the case. We simply do not really know. Nonetheless, I wish to make it absolutely clear that I do not hypothesize any such situation on the basis of available evidence. In sum, I feel that the Logoli case enforces certain modifications and refinements of my initial position (that is, one must be prepared to accept high-density nonstates along the borders of state systems or as neutral zones between states). I do not feel that this case (or others like it) can be taken as negating the thesis of a general relationship between population density and state formation.

Ironically, although the Logoli would seem to present the most cogent single case so far against my contentions, and in favor of the propositions advanced by the editors of *African Political Systems,* it is one of the most important cases in strengthening the approach developed here. It indicates rather strikingly how densities can be inflated by postcontact changes. Seventy per square mile (and I have deliberately used a high figure) and 391 per square mile are rather different quantities. As such this case provides a rather convenient transition to our next chapter, which contains a survey of the present population pattern and an analysis of what meaningful extrapolations can be drawn from it. As we shall see, *most* of the exceptions to my hypothesis are, like the Logoli: (1) small in area; (2) situated along the borders of indigenous states, and/or subject to pronounced colonial pressures, including reserves, labor migration, cash-cropping, alienation of lands for European settlement, and more.[34] Let us turn, then, to a consideration of a broader overview of the relation between population density and state formation in tropical Africa.

Population Pattern

DETAILED and intensive study of the cases presented by *African Political Systems* has now been completed. From a purely quantitative point of view the results can best be seen if arranged in two tables, the first representing estimates of the average population density at the time of contact and the second giving the figures for the decade of the 1930s, the period during which these societies were studied by the anthropologists contributing articles to *African Political Systems*. (Tables I and II) [1] These results do not at all confirm the position taken by Fortes and Evans-Pritchard; instead, they give general, though not perfect, confirmation to the hypothesis that population density and state formation are positively related. The Logoli stand out in a rather anomalous position on both tables, but modifications of my hypothesis have already been introduced to account for its 1898 density, and the 1932 density has been interpreted as a product of the colonial situation.

In Chapter II it was observed that the sample in *African Political Systems* lacked representivity because, on the one

TABLE I

Range of Average Densities for Sample
in *African Political Systems* at Time
of Contact

Nuer	under 7	Bemba	15–50
Ngwato	15–20	Logoli	50–70
Zulu	20		

TABLE II

Range of Average Densities for Sample
in *African Political Systems* at Time
of Ethnographic Study (1931)

Ngwato	2.5	Zulu	30 (approx.)
Bemba	6	Logoli	500
Nuer	5–10		

hand, food-gathering bands were excluded from consideration, and, on the other, no cases were drawn from the major indigenous state systems. A clearer demographic picture is gained if data is added from the Bushmen and BaMbuti Pygmies at one extreme and data from Hausa-Fulani and Ruanda-Urundi, major states from the Western Sudan and the Lacustrine Region respectively, at the other extreme. As the population estimates for the Bushmen and BaMbuti pertain to the decade of the 1950s, it is advisable to carry out the comparison with all of the other cases with data from the same decade. The results are given in Table III in order of ascending density. Bunyore-Maragoli (Logoli here combined with Nyole out of necessity because of undetermined boundaries) is the only markedly anomalous case; but it must be remembered what is being compared. The combined areas of Bunyore and Maragoli total only 122 square miles. This is against over 20,000 square miles for Ruanda-Urundi. It is instructive to note that "since half the large population of Ruanda-Urundi occupies only one-quarter of its territory, it is evident that there is an unusual concentration of people within a restricted area—more specifically the high plateaus of the central portion of the mandate." (Trewartha 1954b:169) This means, in fact, an effective density of 400 per square mile over an area of 5,000 square miles.

Gourou states the densities of 294 per sq. km. (761 per sq. mi.) prevail over 1.2 per cent of the country's area and that in some localities densities exceed 400 per sq. km. (1,036 per sq. mi.) . Such a concentration of rural population is nowhere approached in Europe or North America; it is equalled only within a few small regions of Africa and elsewhere in the world probably only in Monsoon Asia and the Caribbean region. (Trewartha 1954b:175)

Thus, in Ruanda-Urundi, over an area of 251 square miles, there was in 1951 a population density of 761 per square mile. This effect (from 187 to 400 to 761 per square mile depending on the area used) is what I call the "areal-relative" aspect of density and is a most important consideration when comparing the average densities of two widely disparate areas. Viewed in this perspective, the Logoli case appears considerably less anomalous.

TABLE III

Range of Average Densities of Sample
from *African Political Systems,* with the
Addition of Some Food-Gathering Bands
and Major Indigenous States, for the
Decade of the 1950s

Bushmen	0.25	Schapera 1956:35
BaMbuti Pygmies	0.66	Turnbull, personal communication
Western Tswana	2.50 (avg.)	Schapera 1956:35
Nuer	7–10	My estimate projected from Evans-Pritchard 1940
Bemba	7.50	Central African Statistical Office—187,000 Bemba, 25,000 square miles—1952:7
Zulu	46.00	Schapera 1956:35
Hausa-Fulani	100.00 (approx.)	Prothero 1956:171
Ruanda-Urundi	187.00	Trewartha and Zelinsky 1954b:176
Bunyore-Maragoli	766.00	Humphrey 1947:2

Table III, then, gives even more marked confirmation to the hypothesis that high density is correlated with state organization. Of course, such a selection is not fully representative of all Africa. Nonetheless, the table covers a much wider spectrum of types than that embraced by the discussion in *African Political Systems*. As far as it goes, it indicates a marked positive relationship between state and population density.[2]

A small sample intensively analyzed still remains a small sample. Although I believe it has been sufficiently demonstrated that the six examples from *African Political Systems* do not show what they purport to show, I feel it is still important to confront the problem in a more comprehensive manner. The balance of this chapter, then, will be given over to that effort, which will take the form of an assessment of the overall distributional pattern of population in most of sub-Saharan Africa and its implications for the population density-state formation relationship.

It will be recalled that Fortes and Evans-Pritchard concluded their remarks on demography with a reference to "evidence from other African societies." (Fortes 1940:8) This statement carries with it the implication that there is further and considerable support for their position to be found in a wider survey.[3] These implications invite further inquiry.

This involves certain problems in method. I have already indicated my belief that contemporary demographic data can only be used with great caution in making inferences concerning the precolonial period. On the other hand, estimates by early travelers, explorers, missionaries, and others are neither sufficiently plentiful nor accurate to be used in a broad comparative study. Finally, it should be obvious that an intensive, case-by-case analysis such as has occupied the preceding five chapters is out of the question for the hundreds of societies of precolonial Africa. There is, I believe, a reasonable alternative.

Particularly within the last decade, population geographers

have been mapping Africa's contemporary population distribution and analyzing the main patterns as well as the factors considered crucial in their formation. A dot map representing the
population pattern for all tropical Africa has been constructed
by Trewartha and Zelinsky. (1954a) In addition, there have been
specific maps and studies of more localized regions and single
countries.[4] Making due allowance for areas where colonization
and its concomitants have strongly influenced the pattern, and
making further allowance for such factors as pronounced slave
raiding, epidemics, tsetse fly zones, and more, these sources
provide a generally accurate picture of the aboriginal population patterns at the time of colonial take-over. (Kimble 1960,
I:104; Trewartha 1954b:187–92) It has already been observed
(Chapter VII) that in small localized regions such as Kavirondo, postcolonial changes including among others cash-cropping, labor migration, and the imposition of tribal reserves can
drastically alter the population pattern. It seems doubtful, however, that less than a century of colonial rule could have had the
same marked effect upon the population pattern of the entire
African continent. This means that the broad pattern is
more closely representative of the aboriginal and precolonial
pattern than are the more detailed patterns of small local regions.

It should, of course, be emphasized that given the general
imprecision of African demographic statistics, it is only permissible here to talk about the relative density of one area to another. Neither anthropological analysis nor demographic
studies in Africa have reached a general level of precision where
it is possible to specify meaningfully absolute densities. In fact,
in the African instance, Trewartha and Zelinsky are quick to
point out that the basic population statistics upon which any
such map must be constructed are still so inaccurate that the
map can make no claim to represent absolute densities.

Where population data are available for tropical Africa (Appendix II), they are universally characterized by meagreness of detail and relative unreliability, as compared to the census material published by the more advanced nations of Europe and America. . . . The result is that there is a large probable margin of error in all African population counts—generally, it appears from the available evidence, on the side of underenumeration. The size of this error is such that it masks any discontinuities that might be introduced into Figures 1a, 1b [the density maps] by the use of material that varies in publication date by as much as a decade from country to country. The most that can be hoped from these statistics is that the degree of error does not vary too greatly regionally and their synthesis in Figures 1a, 1b affords a moderately good picture of relative distribution, if not of absolute number. (1954a:137)

I believe that these maps and studies can be used as a field for the testing of hypotheses on the correlation between state and population density in a manner that is both economical and reasonably definitive. This will mean, of course, a slight reduction in area from sub-Saharan Africa to tropical Africa as defined by Trewartha and Zelinsky.

This will exclude the area of South Africa, but exclusion is both advisable and reasonable—advisable, because more than any other region of Africa this region has been transformed by the rise of a European-dominated, modern industrial state, and reasonable because we have already dealt with the aboriginal situation there in some detail. Also:

Tropical Africa . . . excludes the dry tropics—the regions to the north of the 17° N parallel, the Somaliland colonies, South-West Africa, and Bechuanaland—because of the thinness and nomadic behaviour of their population and also because of the inadequacy of their statistics. The reason for the omission of Ethiopia and the Anglo-Egyptian Sudan is almost total absence of population data for these countries. (Trewartha 1954a:136) [5]

What I propose to do here is to follow Trewartha and Zelinsky's (1954a) analysis of the demographic pattern supplemented by material from Church (1961), Gourou (1961), and others and to ascertain to what degree there is conformity to a correlation between high-density zones and state formation. I shall start with the broadest outlines of the pattern as delineated by Trewartha and Zelinsky and then refine the analysis by assessing relationships within these bands.

As far as possible I shall endeavor to use census materials for the decade 1951–1960, with a preference toward the earlier years of that decade, as these years more than others provided the important basis for the Trewartha and Zelinsky survey. I am interested in distributional patterns sufficiently broad as to reflect the aboriginal population pattern yet recent enough to be based upon census figures rather than what were often merely the guesses of early explorers or missionaries. Trewartha and Zelinsky's general survey of 1954 would seem still the most serviceable survey for this purpose to date. Where census and other demographic materials outside this decade show relevance, I shall not hesitate to use them.

Trewartha and Zelinsky begin by observing that:

. . . tropical Africa can readily be divided into three major population regions: 1) a relatively dense West Africa-Sudan area (average population density about 11 persons per km.²) which includes the western portion of the French Cameroons, the northern section of French Equatorial Africa and all the lands westward therefrom; 2) a sparsely populated Central African area (average density 3.4 persons per km.²) embracing the remainder of the French Cameroons and French Equatorial Africa, the Belgian Congo excepting its northeastern parts, and the whole of Spanish Guinea, Angola, and the Rhodesias; and 3) an East African area (average density of 10.3 per km.²) characterized by a complex alternation of high and low densities in which are included Kenya, Tanganyika, Uganda, Ruanda-Urundi (along with the bordering section of the Belgian Congo), Nyasaland, Zanzibar, Mozambique, and Madagascar. (1954a:142)

These broad regions are, of course, too gross for our purposes, but may be further reduced to subregions which are eminently serviceable at least for first-stage analysis. I shall analyze these main regions then in this order:

I. West African-Sudan Region.
II. East African Region.
III. Central African Region.

The West African-Sudan Region is further divided by Trewartha and Zelinsky into three zones of higher density and one of lower density generally as follows.[6]

A. Guinea Coastal Zone—southern Ghana to western Cameroons and 100 to 200 kilometers deep. Highest density.
B. Sudan Belt—interrupted high density—from southwestern Mali across Upper Volta, northern Ivory Coast, Northern Nigeria and northern Cameroons to extend in an attenuated fashion into Chad.
C. Atlantic Coastal Belt—high density. Senegal to Sierra Leone.
D. Middle Belt—stretches from west to east between A and B and is marked by generally low density and nodes of higher than average density both attributed in large part to slave raids by states both north and south.

The Guinea Coastal Zone contains one of the densest concentrations of rural population in all tropical Africa. This is the Ibo area of southeastern Nigeria. As of 1952 average densities were 269 per square mile with densities of 500 per square mile covering 10 per cent of the region and some portions displaying densities up to 1,700 per square mile. (Hance 1964:174) It is the general consensus among anthropologists who have worked in the region and among typologists who have classified indigenous political systems that the Ibo were stateless or acephalous prior to the coming of the British. This means that this case constitutes a major exception to my hypothesis on the relationship between density and state formation. Here high densities extend over large areas and they cannot be explained as having arisen subsequent to colonization.

As of the sixteenth century the Ibo area was bordered on both the west and the north by state systems—Benin to the west and Igala and Jukun to the north. At this time Benin was expansive, reaching its peak in the seventeenth century. (Fage 1962:92) Benin apparently had an important influence at least upon certain sections within the Ibo region. (Dike 1959:21–23) Benin type kingships developed and persisted through the nineteenth century at Aboh on the west bank of the Niger and at Onitsha on the east bank, as well as among other northern Ibo. Thus far we have a situation analogous to certain East African cases to be discussed in this chapter where population densities developed along the frontiers of pre-existing states. However, from the seventeenth century on Benin was in decline; and a comparison of maps of state systems in Nigeria for the sixteenth and nineteenth centuries respectively in Hodgkin (1960 after p. 52) reveals marked shrinkage of both Benin and Jukun, with Tiv appearing on the latter map between Igala and Jukun. As will be seen, however, unlike the Logoli-Wanga case where the Logoli densities were high but lower than Wanga, all indications are that well in advance of the colonial period the densities in the Ibo region were higher than the densities of any of these states. Consequently, I feel that this case deserves detailed treatment, and shall devote the next chapter (Chapter IX) to its full consideration. For the rest of the Guinea Coast area the situation is quite clear.

Next in order of density is the Yoruba region of Western Nigeria, a region and people characterized by complex political organization and very large concentrated settlements. Ibadan has a population of over 600,000, and four other cities exceed 100,000 in population. (Hance 1964:174) This urbanism is of an indigenous nature and cannot be attributed to colonial rule. In 1851 Ibadan had 11 miles of walls which afforded protection to farmers who by day cultivated land as far as 6 miles away. Harrison Church has estimated that the population at this time

was in the vicinity of 60,000. (1961:463) For the present, the
areal-relative quality of density is again notable. According to
the 1952 census of the Western Region, Yoruba districts have
an average density of 160 per square mile. However, for Ibadan:
"Within the 8½ square miles inside the old walls, the population density is about 54,000 per square mile, averaging 24 per
house and up to 100 per compound." (Church 1961:464)

Moving westwards from Nigeria, density progressively dimin-
ishes, but we are still within a generally dense zone and also one
of significant state formation, particularly in the period of the
European commercial influence along the coast (slave, gold,
and palm-oil trades). West of Yoruba were the states of Porto
Novo, Cotonou, Whydah, Alladah, and Abomey, which were
finally organized under Fon hegemony as Dahomey.

In Ghana this region saw the early Akan forest state of
Akwamu (early seventeenth century) (Wilks 1961:31) and the
later Fanti states and Ashanti. Of course population densities on
the immediate coastal area were greatly influenced by European
contact and trade. It is instructive that local states did arise in
response to this trade and as part of the same general process
that saw population increase in the region. Contemporary
population density maps, such as that by Hilton contained in
Barbour (1961:96–97), still display the correlation between
population density and state. Aside from the direct coastal area,
other zones of density are found around Kumasi (Ashanti),
Tamale (Gonja), and in the northern region analyzed in terms
of the formation of the Tri-Dominion (Mamprusi, Dagomba,
Mossi) in Chapter VI. It is also instructive to note, with Harrison Church, that the highest rural density in Ghana is associated
with the Ashanti state of New Juaben. Density here is 671 per
square mile, and Church notes the areal-relative nature of
density, although cryptically—"Had the state been larger, the
density of population would have been far less." (1961:167) I
do not feel that this should be taken as an assertion that big

states are necessarily less dense, but rather that when one is dealing with truly small areas peak density and average density become one and the same. Nonetheless (as we have observed already for Ruanda and will shortly observe for Hausa Fulani and Yoruba), larger systems of perhaps lesser average density will display even higher peaks.

It is noteworthy that both the A and B belts have been associated with significant state formation. The Sudan Belt (B) is associated with a rather impressive inventory of states which have arisen and fallen in the area over a time span of a millenium and a half. These include ancient Ghana and Mali, Songhai, Mossi-Mamprusi-Dagomba, Hausa-Fulani, and Bornu-Kanem. There is a nodular quality to this pattern which gives the effect of a series of rather large islands of density rather than a continuous distribution. This is largely attributable to pronounced functional interrelation between trade-route junctures and state formation in this region; to the decline of states as trade-route orientations shifted; and, reciprocally, the shift of trade routes after the collapse of states, as in the case of the Moroccan conquest of Songhai.[7]

The areal-relative quality of density should be noted when making comparisons in this area as elsewhere.[8] As of 1952 the region of northern Nigeria associated with the Hausa-Fulani emirates had an average density generally in excess of 100 per square mile. Within this area Kano Division had an average density of 230 per square mile; and, within a radius of 20 miles (1,257 sq. miles) around Kano city, the average density was 360 and approached 1,000 in places. (Prothero 1956:171-73)

Exceptionally high densities are to be noted for the Kabrai Massif in extreme northeastern Togoland and adjacent Dahomey.

The average population, over more than 1,000 square miles and embracing between 200,000 and 235,000 people with a yearly increase of 5,000-6,000, is 180 per square mile. Yet the environment is so rugged that only one-third of the land is cultivable. Thus the effective average population density is about 500 per square mile, but reaches 1,500 per square mile in some mountainous cantons. (Church 1961:423)

Church attributes this to intensive cultivation and fertile soils. The Naoudemba, Lamba, and Kabrai (especially the latter) all build tiny terraces and manure and irrigate their crops. All these people are described by Murdock (1959:87) as being stateless. However, this region is in the general orbit of the state formation described in Chapter VI for northern Ghana and the Upper Volta. This may be a case either of another Tallensi situation or one of population density and terracing both developing in mountain refuge areas as a response to raiding by states. This in itself is a secondary effect of state formation. Conclusions concerning this case should await further studies of the history of the region.

Further west, generally high population densities in the Fouta Djallon massif of Guinea are associated with state organization since the Fulani conquest of 1750. (Murdock 1959:417)

Densities along the short Atlantic Coastal Belt are further associated with colonial influences and the establishment of ports, trading and administrative centers, and naval bases (Dakar and Freetown). Indigenous state formation was present among the Serer and Wolof of Senegal. Also, a recent article by D'Azevado (1962) has pinpointed precisely this Atlantic Coastal Region as one of significant increase in population density and concomitant state formation, particularly among the Temne in the precolonial period. Labouret (1941:43) has specifically noted the attractive force of Dakar as an international port and administrative center in inducing densities as high as 417 per square kilometre (1,080 per sq. mile) on Cap Vert.

Both the general low density and the higher than average nucleations around defensible refuge areas in the Middle Belt

(D) are explained as a response to slave raids from states both to the north and south. (Trewartha 1954a:153; Hance 1964:174)

We should not leave the West African area without consideration of the Tiv of Nigeria, who, because of the Bohannans' work there, have become an important case in the ethnographic literature. Tiv are described as acephalous and are included as an important case in the Middleton and Tait edited volume, *Tribes Without Rulers.* (Middleton 1958) Ethnographically the Tiv are described as subsistence farmers. "Soil and climate, however, permit the Tiv to participate both in the grain cultivation of the north and in the yam farming of the south. Tiv are subsistence farmers." (Bohannan 1958:34) The average population density is rather high for a segmentary and acephalous society, though by no means as impressively high as the Ibo and other groups we shall encounter. "The average for Tiv Division (64 per square mile) means little; there is a steady increase from the 25 or fewer per square mile north of the Benue to the 550 per square mile along part of the southern border." (Bohannan 1958:34) This picture seems rather problematical until we turn to the work of the geographers and demographers.

In discussing the Peasant Export-production Economy Buchanan and Pugh note:

Two main export regions may be distinguished: a northern zone, centering on Kano City and characterised by production of annual crops such as cotton and groundnuts and with an outlier *in the benniseed* and soya bean producing region *of Benue Province,* and a southern zone, extending across the high-forest region and characterised by the production of perennial tree crops, such as cocoa, palm produce and rubber. (Buchanan 1958:101, italics mine)

Further on, benniseed, or sesame seed, is described as a prime example of an "ethnically localised crop" or a crop whose cultivation is limited to one ethnic group and its cultivation listed as "virtually a monopoly of the Tiv people." (Buchanan 1958:

141) Export production is described as beginning when the imposition of taxation forced the Tiv farmer to find a cash crop. Output in the 1930s was relatively small (2,000 to 3,000 tons), but in 1937 it had exceeded 11,000 tons, while in 1955 as much as 19,000 tons to the total value of 883,000 pounds sterling were exported. The Tiv may be a subsistence farmer; he is also and perhaps primarily a peasant.

Furthermore, Bohannan tends to treat Tiv densities as a purely internal matter involving the expansion of the Tiv. The population geographers would tend to take a different view.

Areas of medium population density are found for the most part adjacent to the areas of higher density. Katagum Division (85 per square mile) of Bauchi Province and Potiskum Division (69 per square mile) of Bornu Province are the most easterly extensions of the population concentration of which Kano is the focus. Idoma (86 per square mile) and Tiv (73 per square mile) divisions of Benue Province and Igala Division (72 per square mile) of Kabba Province *are on the northern fringe of the provinces of the Eastern Region where the greatest population concentration and highest densities in Nigeria occur.* (Prothero 1956:172, my italics)

These are important points for anthropologists to ponder, for the rather idealized models presented by Bohannan have led prominent anthropologists to generalize important theoretical conceptions from the Tiv as if they represented a proto-typical case of purely subsistence-oriented, shifting cultivators.

When it is further noted that Bohannan explicitly documents the emergence of big men with certain definite political functions, the Tiv case becomes even less a riddle, and comparison is invited to the Ibo as analyzed in Chapter IX.

A man of prestige, on the other hand, is a man whose wealth generosity and astuteness give him a certain influence over people and formerly allowed the purchase of slaves and thus the formation of a 'gang' to furnish safe-conduct to those strangers who paid tribute and to rob those who did not. These men, then, had a certain measure of physical force (no longer available to them) at

their command. Unless they were also elders, however, they were
ultimately controllable by the powers of witchcraft and magic lying
within the hands of that gerontocracy. (1958:54)

For my part, I will follow the population geographers and
interpret the high density node in south Tiv and its effect upon
the overall Tiv average *not* as internal pressures of Tiv expan-
sionism but as the simple pressure upon the Tiv from the
considerably higher and larger density node in southeastern
Nigeria which is to be explained in the next chapter.

The West African-Sudan area, then, in its pattern of population would generally confirm expectations of a positive relation
between population density and state formation, with the major
exception, of course, of southeastern Nigeria. I do not pretend,
of course, to have "explained" the density pattern of West
Africa in all its nuances and shadings. There are, to be sure,
variations within this pattern which can be explained only
by ecological factors such as soil, climate, topography, and
others, as well as by factors both cultural and historical not
accounted for in such a broad and general survey as I am
engaged in here. I am necessarily working at a rather high level
of abstraction and generality, and what is being sought is either
general confirmation or general denial of the proposition that
high densities are associated with state formation. With the
exceptions noted, the West African-Sudan Region offers rather
striking confirmation.

An analysis of the East African Region also offers rather clear
support for my hypothesis. Here the region may be conveniently broken down into a coastal zone of interrupted high density representing the city states and coastal enclaves that grew
up in response to the Indian Ocean trade and an area of much
higher indigenous density in the Interlacustrine Region. Here
the association with state formation is most pronounced. The
inventory of states is rather impressive. Major state systems
include Buganda, Bunyoro, Ruanda-Urundi, and Ankole, while

lesser states include Haya, Zinza, Busoga, Alur, Toro, Wanga, and Sukuma. This list is by no means exhaustive. The population densities range from Ruanda-Urundi, which as we have noted has densities as high as any in the tropics, through Buganda with an average density of 116 per square mile (Apter 1961); Ankole, 90; Toro, 74; and Bunyoro, 33—these last three all as of 1959. (Taylor 1962:96, 42, 17) These are all former states. Of Bunyoro it is instructive to note that the rather low density can be attributed in large measure to the following:

The total area is 6,011 square miles, of which 4,847 square miles are land and swamps and 1,164 square miles open water. Much of Northern Bunyoro is occupied by a National Park and sleeping-sickness areas and there are some hundreds of square miles of forests and swamps. It has been estimated that about 2,350 square miles are actually available to African cultivation and grazing. Of this, only about a quarter is actually used. (Taylor 1962:17)

Large areas in the southern part of the territory occupied by the former Busoga states, once densely settled and cultivated, are now depopulated due to sleeping sickness. (Fallers 1960:20) South of Lake Victoria the area of the Sukuma chiefdoms had a density of 53 per square mile. (Cory 1953) As of 1957, the five Sukuma districts of Mwanza, Kwimba, Maswa, Shinyanga, and Geita yielded a combined average density of 62. (Porter 1966) To the north of Lake Albert the Alur were expanding what Southall has termed a "segmentary state" at the time of British penetration. Southall (1953:267) has estimated the average density of this area as 100 per square mile at the time of his field work.[9]

Within the stateless groups, densities of pastoralists are generally quite low. That of the Masai (Murdock card, 1958:1097) is 4.6 and Turkana (Gulliver 1953:53) 3.4. The Nandi, also primarily pastoral but with supplementary agriculture, have rather high densities, averaging 66 per square mile in 1938 (Kuczynski 1948,2:150). Huntingford (1953:3) cites considerable confusion in the various Nandi counts. It should be noted that the Nandi have been crowded by the coming of white settlement in Kenya and the loss of lands to the settlers. The average density of Nandi for 1962 as calculated from the figures in Porter (1966) has climbed to 170.

Several apparent exceptions to the propositions that high density and state formation are linked appear in this area among agriculturalists (and some mixed pastoralists) whose indigenous organization is described as acephalous and whose present densities are impressively high.

It is interesting to note that the combined density of North and South Maragoli, home of the Logoli which were analyzed in Chapter VII, was 1,440 in 1962 on the basis of the data in Porter (1966). Neighboring Central Nyanza (formerly Central Kavirondo), inhabited primarily by the Luo, had an average density of 406 in the same year ((Porter 1966).

The Chagga of Tanzania, formerly organized in small chiefdoms, now maintain high densities associated with agricultural cooperatives and the growing of coffee as a cash crop on the fertile slopes of Mt. Kilimanjaro. For example, the 1957 density of Moshi District, largely occupied by Chagga, is calculated to be 289 per square mile on the basis of figures in Porter (1966). In the extreme southwestern district of Uganda, bordered by Ruanda-Urundi on the south, the Congo to the west, Lake Edward on the north, and Ankole on the east, is the most densely populated area of Uganda, the Kigezi District. This is a compact hill, lake, and mountain region, most of it above 6,000 feet.

According to Purseglove, the total area is 2,040 square miles, of which 1,969 square miles is land and swamps and 71 square miles open water. . . . The northern part descends into extensive flats below 4,000 feet bordering on Lake Edward. A large section of this area is taken up by the Queen Elizabeth National Park and a forest, and is infested with tsetse fly. . . . Purseglove estimates an average density of population on cultivable land and pasture in the occupied parts of 356 per square mile, with as many as 720 people to the square mile in the densest area in 1945. (Taylor 1962:114)

It should be noted that this is a different type of density from simple arithmetic or average density. In 1959 the average density for the area, which extends 70 miles from north to south and 30 miles from east to west, was 260. (Taylor 1962:114) The Kiga people are classified as acephalous but it should be noted that they are in a rather small area and wedged in between two states—Ankole and Ruanda. The area has been swelled by immigration from Ruanda, and Purseglove estimates that the population increased by 75 percent between 1931 and 1948 alone. (1951a) There was also in this general area the kingdom of Mpororo, a buffer state between Ankole and Ruanda. Kiga boast that they were never subjugated, but there are reports that they were from time to time at least under relations of clientship to Hima in Ankole or Tutsi of Ruanda. (Richards 1960:280–81)

Another group along the borders of the state system are the Amba described by Winter. (1956, 1958) The area which is on the borders of Toro is very small, comprising only 164 square miles. Of this, about 80 square miles lie in the Bwamba forest, which is an eastward extension of the great Ituri forest. Only about 84 square miles are consequently available to the Amba. These are also a group classified as acephalous and included in *Tribes Without Rulers*. (Middleton 1958) However,

There was always a certain amount of contact between the people of Bwamba and the people living to the east, beyond the mountains. The Nyoro and the Toro, in their turn, claimed sovereignty over the Bwamba but in actual fact the exercise of this sovereignty seems to have consisted of little more than occasional raids and irregular exactions of tribute. (Winter 1956:3)

Furthermore:

Towards the end of the last century there seems to have been an attempt to unify Bwamba by the introduction of a new political philosophy. Whether this new movement sprang completely from the ambitions of a few individuals, whether it was a response to an insight into the internal limitations of the traditional system, or whether it was due to the realization of the weakness of Amba in the face of raids from organized kingdoms to the east, is not known. What happened is that one of the lineages in Bwamba began to claim that it was a branch of the Babito, the royal clan of Bunyoro and Toro and that one of its members was entitled to be recognized as king of Bwamba. (Winter 1958:157–58)

The viability of this movement never met the test. Soon after its inception Bwamba was forcibly incorporated into the Kingdom of Toro and Toro into the Uganda Protectorate. Today the Amba are peasant cultivators with coffee and cotton as cash crops, and the opening up of the road from Fort Portal has facilitated the export of these commodities but has brought with it considerable immigration from Toro. (Winter 1956:4)

Cases such as these last two cannot be taken as serious exceptions. They are along the frontiers or in the buffer zones of indigenous state systems, and even the fragmentary history offered by the ethnographers indicates direct influence from the states themselves upon these societies. Furthermore, their population has expanded during the colonial period under conditions of cash-cropping and immigration from outside. Finally, it should be noted that we have here very small areas. When these are compared to the larger areas of, say, Ruanda-Urundi, we are in effect comparing a node to an overall average; and nodes within the state systems vastly exceed densities such as that of Amba though not so much that of the Kigezi, which is demographically part of the Ruanda density pile anyway. Then too, small areas tend to inflate the effects of equal immigration.[10]

No survey of East African population patterns would be complete without including the very high densities characteristic of the Kikuyu, and to a lesser extent the Kamba, Reserves of Kenya. Both areas were reported as densely populated by early travelers along the caravan routes from the coast to Buganda.

Low has pointed out (1963) that in both cases there was evidence of the emergence of "big men" and the beginnings of more elaborate political organization arising during the period from 1870 on, when the caravans began in significant number to use the northern route which traversed this territory. These developments were truncated by the coming of colonial rule. Today the very high densities in these regions are the artificial creations of the colonial policy of zoning large areas of the choicest lands for white settlers. Fitzgerald has cited an aggregate of 12,000 square miles (1942:256) appropriated for white settlement only. A decade later this appropriation totalled 16,700 square miles. Added to this, of course, are most of the elements we noted for Kavirondo—cash-cropping, labor migration, and others. This is such an artificial situation that I feel it should not be used to test developmental generalizations about indigenous state formation.

The precolonial situation would seem to pose more serious problems, but we need to know more about the actual densities of that period (we have only rather impressionistic and qualitative statements) and also more about the degree to which indigenous political institutions were developing. Finally, density maps of the region reveal two bands of higher than average density, one stretching northwestward from Dar es Salaam and Bagamayo on the coast, through Sukumaland, to Haya on the southwestern corner of Lake Victoria. The other roughly parallels this first band but lies to the north. This latter band begins at Mombasa and stretches across Kamba and Kikuyu territory through Nairobi to Kisumu on the Kavirondo Gulf. Both of these bands generally follow the routes of the present railroad lines and the older caravan routes. The southern route, which was the older, was associated with several chiefdoms and small states. The northern route, which was only in general use from the mid-nineteenth century on, passed largely through the area of acephalous groups, although, as mentioned above, local "big men" were emerging among both Kikuyu and Kamba.

The coastal zone is a rather thin and interrupted one with nucleations around the old port-of-trade city states such as Malindi, Mombasa, Dar es Salaam, Kilwa, and Quelimane, and the European ports such as Moçambique. The coastal band is a reflection of the increase in density and concomitant city-state formation that came with the east coast and Indian Ocean trade, a trade that dates back at least two thousand years. (Oliver 1963)

Trewartha and Zelinsky's sparsely populated Central African zone (average density 3.4 per square kilometer or 8.7 per square mile) includes that part of former French Cameroons not included in the West African-Sudanese zone, all of the present Congo except its northeastern parts, former French Equatorial Africa, and the whole of Spanish Guinea, Angola, and the Rhodesias. (Trewartha 1954a:142) The northeastern region of the Congo is associated with the state-building activities of the Azande, although further inflated by immigration from the poorer districts of Equatoria Province in the Sudan. Kimble (1960:92) observes that the most thickly settled zone in Central Africa runs roughly from east to west between 4° S. and 8° S. from the Atlantic Coast as far east as the Kasai Province of the former Belgian Congo. Although, as will soon be seen, it is difficult to assess the degree to which these present patterns can be taken to be indicative of those of indigenous Africa, it is still interesting to note that this band roughly corresponds to the area of the former Kingdom of the Kongo to the west and the hearth of Luba-Lunda state formation towards the center.

Were it true that this Central African area was devoid of state formation, our task would be rather easy and this chapter nearly complete. This, however, was not so. Nevertheless, certain important points that were distinctive of this region should be noted.

(1) State formation in this area never had the high incidence it had in either the West African-Sudanese zone nor in the Lacustrine Region.

(2) As compared to the two before-mentioned zones, state formation in Central Africa had generally a relatively shallow time depth.

(3) Depopulation, particularly during the period of the slave trade but also in the early colonial period, had more drastic impact on this region than on either of the others.

I shall discuss these points in the above order.

For the Equatorial Bantu, who, as the name would indicate, are distributed along the equator, Murdock gives the following summation:

Only the Lengola, Mituku, Rega, Songola, Topoke, and northern Babwa recognize paramount chiefs over groups of settlements, and none has an elaborate political structure. The Equatorial Bantu observe no significant caste or class distinctions, except for slavery, and the Amba, Bira, Fang, Kumu, and Rega do not even keep slaves. (1959:282)

For the central Bantu, whose distribution is to the south of the Equatorial Bantu and includes the 4°S.–8°S. zone noted by Kimble and extends further to the south to around 10° in the west and 20° in the east, Murdock sees significant state formation whose incidence is equalled only by that of the Sudan-Sahara fringe.

Genuinely complex states occur with a frequency probably greater than anywhere else in Africa south of the Sahara-Sudan fringe. In addition to powerful tribal states among the Bemba, Chokwe, Kimbundu, Kuba, Luapula, Vili, Yaka and formerly also the Buye and Tumbuka, the province had two empires of even greater magnitude at the time of first European contact. (1959:297) [11]

The two "empires," which could be described with somewhat greater accuracy as rather loose federations, were the Lunda state of Mwata Yamvo and the Kongo Kingdom. Murdock's contention that the frequency of genuinely complex states in this region [12] is greater than in the West African forest zone or in the Interlacustrine area is debatable and ultimately hinges on more operational definitions of "genuinely complex." Specifically, it is to be doubted if any of the states listed could compare in either complexity or centralization to Buganda. Nor is the inventory as long as for either the West African zone or the Interlacustrine area.

As to time depth, Kongo compares favorably with the states of the forest zone of West Africa and perhaps to the Interlacustrine Region as well.

When the Portuguese discovered the estuary of the Congo in 1482, they found themselves in contact with one of the largest states in Africa south of the Sahara, and with one of the very few large states situated anywhere near the coastline. This was the kingdom of the *Bako*ngo, a Bantu people whose king, the *Mani*kongo, had his capital at *Mbanza*kongo, the modern San Salvador in northern Angola. (Oliver 1962:125)

Oliver, in another work, dates the foundation of Bito dynasties in Bunyoro and Buganda by immigrant Lwo (Luo, Lwoo) at the beginning of the sixteenth century or even earlier.[13]

The nucleus of the Kongo Kingdom, including the entire section directly ruled by the Manikongo through a hierarchy of appointed chiefs, is given by Oliver as the area to the south of the Congo estuary bounded by the Congo on the north, the Dande River on the south, the Kwango River to the east, and the Atlantic on the west. (Oliver 1962:125) This is an area of roughly 60,000 square miles by my own estimate. The population of this region was estimated by a seventeenth-century missionary at about 2½ million. (Oliver 1962:125) This estimate, if accurate, would give the area a population density of slightly over 40 per square mile, and this is after more than a century of the slave trade, which had brought chaos and depopulation to the Kongo Kingdom, as shall shortly be seen. Luba and Lunda development came later, in the region between the Kwango and the Upper Kasai out of reach of Portuguese depredations along the coast, but indirectly stimulated by the demand for ivory emanating from the Portuguese zone.

From the traditional history it seems that the Lunda had no large states or powerful chiefs until there appeared in their midst, ivory hunters who proceeded, by diplomacy and prestige as well as by force, to build up a 'Sudanic' state whose kings took the dynastic title of Mwata Yamvo. (Oliver 1962:129)

From this center soon radiated a mushroom growth of Luba-Lunda satellites until by the middle of the seventeenth century a loose federation covered a very large area of the present southern Congo as well as Northern Rhodesia and western Angola. The very rapidity of this spread would indicate that at this stage the process of state formation would have rather slight effects on the average density of the region. In fact, this type of state formation, spreading rapidly along transcontinental trade routes, would tend to leave its traces more in local nucleations such as that of the Luapula valley than it would in a markedly increased average density of the region. We have also dealt with the Eastern Lunda and the Bemba in some detail in Chapter V and consequently there is no need to trace it in depth here.

State formation in the Central African Region was, for the most part, so bound up with the slave trade that depopulation was as much a part of the process as population increase. More specifically, successful centers in the trade (such as Kazembe's on the Luapula) tended to build up localized nodes of density, while less favored areas—areas without states, guns, or exceptionally advanced military organization (such as the Ngoni) — were systematically raided and depopulated.

Duffy has given us an eloquent picture of the effects of this trade upon the Kongo Kingdom. Speaking of the 1520s, he says:

Twenty-five years of slaving, during most of which Afonso had innocently inflamed Portuguese desires by his lavish gifts of slaves to Manuel and his subsidy to the missionaries (the slaves being a form

of currency), had left their mark on the Congo. The traffic was causing revolts and fears of depopulation. (1961:17) It is impossible to
overestimate the importance of the trade in the Congo during the
first half of the sixteenth century. Everyone engaged in it: merchants, priests, ship's officers and men, the king's officials. . . . In
vain Afonso complained that the Portuguese who scattered through
his realm like locusts were depopulating his lands. . . . By 1600 the
Congo kingdom was a shambles; the trade through the mouth of the
river had probably averaged over five thousand slaves a year
throughout the century. The Congo trade went on for another two
hundred years; during much of the time the only European contact
with the interior was through the slave trader and his half-caste and
African agents. (1961:137-38)

Angola followed suit: "Angola remained the supply-base for the
Brazil slave trade, and during the seventeenth and eighteenth
centuries was converted into a howling wilderness." (Oliver
1962:128) On the eastern end of the Central Zone similar
effects can be attributed to the Arab slave trade:

The Arabs had remained near the coast for a thousand years until
1840. Within eighteen years their caravans, armed posts and agents
advanced as far as the upper Congo, halfway across Africa. The
Zenj traders carried Swahili into the interior, making it the lingua
franca of East and Central Africa, but they also generated an
unprecedented series of ferocious tribal wars. Settled agriculture
was disrupted. Bantu villages were enslaved or massacred, and the
population declined sharply. (Wiedner 1964:111)

Gann, who has given us an important study of the differential
response to the slave trade of such states as the Bemba, Lunda,
Ngoni, and Lozi, confirms the impression of large-scale depopulation of areas in East and Central Africa as a result of the trade.

A few areas in Central Africa managed to remain free from the
scourge of the traffic in human beings. The great majority, however,
did not. . . . Everywhere there was the same story of burnt villages, of slaughter and the devastation of crops. The loss of life
caused by these raids must have been enormous, though it is of
course impossible to give any exact figures. Burton, a British
explorer, estimated that in order to capture fifty-five women, the

merchandise of one of the caravans he observed, at least ten villages had been destroyed, each having a population of between one and two hundred souls. . . . The trade must have constituted a severe drain on the manpower resources of Central Africa. (Gann 1954:39–40)

For the Congo, Trewartha and Zelinsky have noted that estimates of the population on the eve of European occupation range from those based on flimsy data to fantastic guesses. (1954b:165) Here, the first years of European rule seem to have brought even further depopulation:

The first years of European rule—the Congo Free State period of 1885–1908—constituted a period of reckless and dangerous exploitation of both natural and human resources which quite likely resulted in an absolute decline of population. Even today it is possible to detect the unhappy character of that era in the demographic characteristics of the older elements of the Congo population. (1954b:165–66)

Nonetheless, Kimble feels that:

Although the European occupation has brought many important changes of detail, many of the lineaments of this rather arbitrary pattern appear not to have radically altered. So far as the Belgian Congo is concerned, it can be shown that the areas of currently high and low population density are inherited from the pre-European era and that recent changes have, for the most part, merely accentuated the differences. (1960,I:104) [14]

Kimble cites the recent flow of migrants from Angola eastwards into the upper Zambezi valley and the sizeable increase in the rural population of Katanga Province, both of which areas were once emptied by Arab slave raiders, as testifying to the importance of cultural-historical factors rather than physical ones in explaining the population distribution.

Although it is possible to agree with Kimble and Trewartha and Zelinsky that the basic distribution of population within the Congo area reflects in accentuated form the broad outlines of the period preceding European penetration, it is known that the slave trade had been having its effects for several centuries, and these effects are more difficult to judge. To the extent that reasonable inferences can be drawn, and taking into consideration both the relatively shallow time depth of the Luba-Lunda-Bemba states as well as the attested depopulation of the Kongo Kingdom, we would thus seem to get general confirmation of our hypothesis that higher density is associated with state formation.[15] In short, both the northeastern corner of the region (Azande) and the southern (4°S. to 8°S.) band of higher than average density were the general areas of state formation for the region.

It remains to note that a survey of rural African densities in Central Africa by R. J. Shaul, contained in Barbour (1961), comments that: "The areas of densest African population in Northern Rhodesia are the Luapula valley and parts of Fort Jameson, Petauke, Mongu and Kalobo districts." (Barbour 1961:44–45) The Luapula valley is familiar to us as the headquarters of Kazembe (Lunda), Fort Jameson is the area of the Ngoni, Petauke is along the Moçambique border, across which there has been considerable migration, and Mongu and Kalobo districts are in the heartland of the Barotse Kingdom.

The high densities in the Shire Highlands south of Lake Nyasa are attributed by Trewartha and Zelinsky to the influence of European settlers.[16] The African rural population of Southern Rhodesia is concentrated largely in an arc that reaches from a point south of Bulawayo (the former Matabele capital) eastward through Shabani and Fort Victoria to Umtali and Salisbury (the modern capital). (Prescott 1962:562) Southern Rhodesia is not a reasonable test case because of the pattern of enforced territorial segregation under white rule there and the appropriation of the majority of agrarian land by Europeans.[17]

Obviously, a single chapter survey such as this cannot claim to be exhaustive and undoubtedly there are single case exceptions we have missed. It is also true that this survey has demonstrated some exceptions to my hypothesis. In some cases these exceptions are covered by the modification to the hypothesis concerning higher than average densities along the borders of indigenous states. For others, postcolonial change seems the rather obvious answer. For still others, a ready explanation is not immediately at hand and would require analysis in depth of the type undertaken for the cases of *African Political Systems.* Such a task is beyond the limitations of this paper. I shall, however, in the next chapter offer an explanation for one of these exceptional cases (the Ibo of Southeastern Nigeria) which can stand as a model for the type of analysis and explanation which might be offered for the others as well. For the rest, let it be noted that our general survey has nonetheless demonstrated a decided general positive relationship between state formation and population density.[18]

CHAPTER IX. High Density and State Formation
in Southeastern Nigeria: The Ibo Problem

IN THE last chapter we traced the broad outlines of tropical Africa's population pattern, demonstrating that where reasonable inferences could be drawn from the present pattern concerning the situation in precolonial times there was a significant general relationship between areas of high density and the formation of indigenous states. Exceptions were found to consist for the most part of small (in area) but rather high-density nodes, often distributed along the boundaries of developing indigenous states, and having much, if not all, of their present high density attributable to postcolonial changes. One very important high-density area was noted which did not conform to this pattern, the Ibo region in southeastern Nigeria, a region both large in area and among the highest in tropical Africa in density. Furthermore, it is an area to which the labels "segmentary," "acephalous," or "stateless" are usually applied, both by ethnologists who have worked in the area and by those engaged in the comparison and classification of indigenous political systems. As such, then, it constitutes an important problem in any attempt to establish that in Africa high density and the formation of states were generally associated. For this reason, I feel it is proper to devote an entire chapter to its analysis.[1]

In general my procedure will be first to discuss the density pattern itself as well as its relative antiquity and then, after establishing that the population must be considered to have been significantly dense rather early in the precolonial period, to go on to the really crucial problem—the alleged absence of state

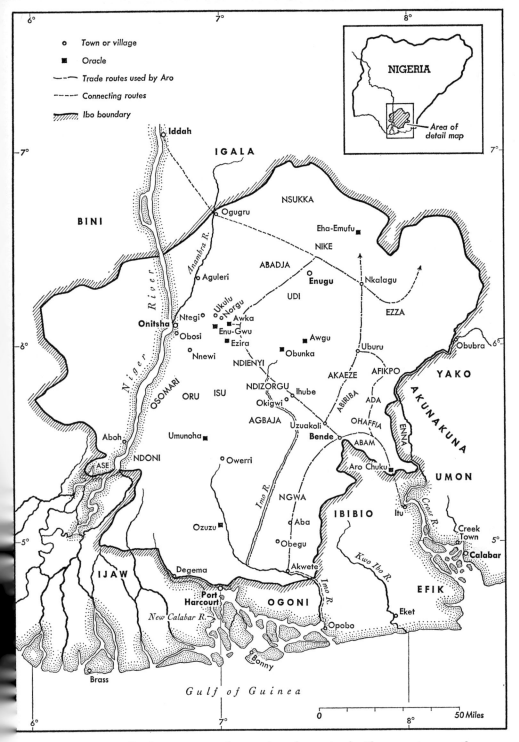

MAP VI. Settlements, oracles, and trade routes in Ibo country, southern Nigeria

From Simon Ottenberg, "Ibo Oracles and Intergroup Relations," *Southwestern Journal of Anthropology* 14: 295–317, 1958

formation. I believe that it can be shown, if one considers fully what is known of historical development in the region, that what must be regarded as a certain type of state did arise in the region and that, by concentrating on certain crucial political functions (relegating all others to local rule), it was able to weld the entire inland region into a single, functioning trade network. This may be regarded at least as "partial state forma-tion." Analysis here will concentrate on the major oracle, slave trading, and mercenary organization of the Aro Chuku. Finally, it will be shown that the major shift from the slave trade to the trade in palm oil which was characteristic of the last half of the nineteenth century tended to weaken seriously though by no means destroy the Aro control of the region. At the same time, strong tendencies toward the formation of larger units mani-fested themselves in the struggle of the Delta Trading States for control of the hinterland oil markets and oil-producing regions. By this time, however, the British state was becoming more and more a major partner to this struggle and intervened consis-tently to fragment and amputate the establishment of hege-mony by individual Delta States. The outcome of the entire process was the emergence of a single state supreme over the region, but that state was British. An attempt will also be made to show the reciprocal relationship between the development of trade and the development of denser populations, the trade stimulating densities higher than would have been feasible had subregions within the area been economically isolated and self-sufficient. On the other hand, the trade tended to stimulate some aspects of state formation (the control of markets, trade-routes, and warfare) but to inhibit others. With this general schema in mind, I shall turn now to a more detailed considera-tion of the region's density.

There can be little question that the Ibo region in south-eastern Nigeria constitutes one of the greatest nodes of rural population density in all of sub-Saharan Africa. It may indeed be the major node. Writing just over a decade ago, Trewartha and Zelinsky cited the uplands of Ruanda-Urundi as containing the densest populations in all Tropical Africa. (1954a:143) Recent evaluations of the 1953 census of southeastern Nigeria would indicate that this region is at least the front-rank contender for this distinction. Ruanda-Urundi, with a combined area of nearly 21,000 square miles, was cited by Kimble as having an average density of 220 per square mile in 1958. (1960,I:89) Trewartha and Zelinsky cited an average density for Ruanda-Urundi of 191.1 per square mile and noted that some tracts exceeded "300 or 400 persons per km.[2]" This is equivalent to 777 per square mile and 1,036 per square mile respectively.

It is instructive to compare the density pattern of southeastern Nigeria to these figures: "According to the 1952 census the region had an average density of 269 per square mile, but 10 percent of the region had over 500 per square mile and parts had as high as 1,700 per square mile." (Hance 1964:174) For the southeastern Nigerian Region as a whole the 1953 census gives a total of 7,971,000 in an area of 46,065 square miles. This yields a density of 173 per square mile, which for an area this size is a significantly high density. If the three typically Ibo provinces of Ogoja, Onitsha, and Owerri are taken by themselves, one gets a population of 4,929,000 in an area of 16,231 square miles, which yields a density of 303.7 per square mile. These gross averages only tell part of the truth, however. Thus J. H. Jennings has noted:

The larger population revealed at the Census increases interest in certain areas of dense population extending in a broad north-west-south-east band across the region from Onitsha to Calabar. Within this band is Orlu Division registering at this Census a density of 873 persons per square mile; on population maps based on divisional boundaries this area stands out as the most congested. This new map, however, suggests that the area to the south-east has even greater densities, in the northern part of Owerri Divisions and the southern part of Okigwi Division. An area of 1500 square miles de-limited arbitrarily in the five divisions of Owerri, Okigwi, Orlu, Onitsha, and Awka, not including the town of Onitsha, contains 1,500,000 people, giving an overall rural density of 1000 people per square mile. This density is approached farther to the south-east in small areas around Ikot Ekpene and Uyo, between Aba and Calabar, and again in an area around Nsukka in the far north. (Jennings 1957:416–17)

Prothero, too, has observed that:

The highest densities (over 600 per square mile) are found in divisions which lie for the most part between the valleys of the Cross and Imo Rivers and between the Imo River and the River Niger. They form two concentrations; in the Aba-Ikot Ekpene-Uyo Divi-sions of Calabar Province and in the Orlu-Okigwi Divisions of Owerri Province. They are the highest average densities found in Nigeria and for that matter in West Africa, and are indeed among the highest for the whole continent. (1955:166–7)

If the development of these densities could be attributed to the colonial period and the imposition of British rule, they would not pose a theoretical problem in terms of their relation-ship to state formation any more than do the high densities in the north coastal Java plain which Gourou (1961:110) has traced to the influence of Dutch control of that region. A simi-lar explanation can hardly be brought forward for southeastern Nigeria, however. Although we have nothing in the way of re-liable quantitative estimates for the precolonial period,[2] the very nature of the density and the large area involved bespeak a rather respectable antiquity. Furthermore, authorities on the Ibo seem agreed that Ibo population was quite dense in advance of British penetration of the interior.

Ottenberg expresses the view that densities between 400 and 1,000 per square mile developed in Ibo country prior to any "major influence emanating from direct contact with European culture." (1961:219) Jones, moreover, attests to the antiquity of both the density of population and a complex network of trade routes and markets.

Field studies in the Eastern region have shown that the region possesses a highly developed system of distributive trade. This system is not recent in origin but appears to have been developed over centuries of slow and unimpeded growth. The overall pattern was the import of salt, protein, and of bulk foodstuffs by the over-populated areas of the hinterland, in particular the Ibo hinterland, which paid for this by the export of their labour, skilled and un-skilled. The skilled labour was in the form of craftsmen and artisans, for example 'medicine men', 'priests', blacksmiths, carvers, and market traders; the unskilled was mainly agricultural labourers and, particularly during the eighteenth and early nineteenth century, slaves. The unskilled labourers worked seasonally in the food-, and, when these developed, in the palm oil-producing regions, re-turning home for the rest of the year; the skilled travelled abroad for longer periods. (1963:13)

It would be mistaken to assume that the present very high densities were in existence in the same magnitude during the nineteenth century.[3] There is no evidence that the population distribution has been static over long periods of time. Rather, one is faced with a long and dynamic process of population growth in which a general high density has long been a charac-teristic feature.

The next question, then, is the degree of political complexity among the Ibo. A survey of the literature reveals a general con-sensus that traditional Ibo society was "acephalous," "segmen-tary," and "stateless." Meek, the only one to date to attempt a survey of Ibo social and political institutions as a whole, may well be taken as prototypical in his pronouncements:

It may be said generally that the most characteristic feature of Ibo society is the almost complete absence of any higher political or social unit than the commune or small group of contiguous villages, whose customs and cults are identical, who in former times took common action against an external enemy (though they frequently also fought among themselves) , and whose sense of solidarity is so strong that they regard themselves as descendents of a common ancestor. (1937:3)

This impression is echoed by Green, who cites "social fragmentation" as the distinguishing mark of Ibo society:

This great people is broken up into hundreds of small, more or less independent, social units, the largest being, in many cases, what we may call the village-group. This is a collection of villages bound together by certain ties, but each one, at any rate in the district with which we are concerned, largely managing its own affairs. . . . It is not, I think, possible, at least among the Ibo people of the interior with whom I am concerned, to point to any territorial unit within which there is a sovereign governmental authority. (1947:3–5)

In the volume prepared for the International African Institute's *Ethnographic Survey of Africa,* Forde and Jones state rather succinctly that "Political authority was formerly widely dispersed among a large number of small territorial groups." (1950:9)

The preceding were all statements from the pens of British anthropologists. However, Ottenberg, the American most closely associated with Ibo studies, would seem to be in general agreement.

Before direct European contact the Ibo consisted of more than two hundred independent territorial groups, each composed of one or more villages or of dispersed residential groupings. The internal organization of these territorial groups was based on patrilineal clans and lineages. Though there was some trade and intermarriage, each group had its own government and was relatively independent of the others. Hostility and small-scale warfare between neighboring units was common. There were no large political groupings—no states or kingdoms—to unite these groupings and provide them with an over-all unity of social structure and culture. (1959:130) .[4]

Given this general consensus, it is not surprising that Eisenstadt (1959) in his overview and typology of African political systems

classifies the Ibo together with the neighboring Yakö and Ibibio
and some Yoruba groups as "Acephalous Autonomous Villages." (1959:209) [5]

This is not a problem only in terms of the relationship between population density and state formation but is recognized
as a major problem currently confronting Ibo specialists. In a
recent article assessing the present state of research on the Ibo,
Ottenberg lists five problems that he regards as of major theoretical significance not only for Ibo studies as such but for
anthropology as a whole. None of these he regards as fully
analyzed or adequately explained and understood. Paraphrased
here as questions, they are:

(1) What is the nature of the traditional Ibo system of
    leadership? [6]
(2) Why did not complex state systems develop in the re-
    gion?
(3) Why do the Ibo possess such personality characteristics
    as "aggressiveness," "frankness," the "desire to get
    ahead," and a "high receptivity to change" when these
    characteristics are by no means typical of all groups in
    Nigeria or Africa?
(4) Why did high population densities develop among the
    Ibo prior to direct contact with European culture?
(5) What is the reason for the variations-in-settlement pat-
    tern within the region, where compact nucleated settle-
    ments in some areas contrasted sharply with dispersed
    residential groupings in others? (Ottenberg 1961:218–
    19)

In the same article Ottenberg makes a rather pessimistic assessment as to just how much is actually known concerning the
Ibo.

Although the postwar literature on the Ibo seems voluminous there
is inadequacy of knowledge in almost every direction. Some research
and writing have been done here and some there, but the sum total

of writings does not add up to a very substantial body of knowl-edge. (1961:217)

Furthermore: "Accurate ethnographic data are lacking on vir-tually all Ibo groups; as Forde and Jones' study (1950) clearly indicates." (Ottenberg 1961:219) He also specifically notes that detailed studies are not available on such important topics as secret societies, age grades (both important in Ibo political organization), warfare, and traditional trading practices and organizations. Finally, there is one major lacuna which in terms of our indicated line of argument places us at special disadvan-tage. This concerns information on Aro Chuku.

There seems to have been one Ibo group . . . which acted as a major unifying factor in Ibo society, at least during the days of the European slave trade. This is the Aro group, consisting of the home villages at Aro Chuku and the many Aro settlements scattered through Ibo country. Despite the fact that this group is of great importance in Iboland there has been no real anthropological research carried out at Aro or with Aro settlements in other areas of Ibo country, and there is strong need for further historical analysis as well. (Ottenberg 1961:221)

The five theoretical problems presented by Ottenberg are far from being unrelated. I believe, in fact, that ultimately they can all be answered within a single explanatory context.[7] The crucial question, among the five, from this standpoint is the second—the alleged failure of the state to emerge in the Ibo area.

The fact is that in certain parts of Africa, both on the West Coast and in Southeast Africa, rather complex state systems developed apparently in response to the demands of the European slave trade, and in some cases the Arab slave trade as well. This did not occur in southeastern Nigeria despite intensive trading for many years in the area, though small chiefdoms did develop along the coast. It may be because there are some fundamental factors in the nature of tradi-tional Ibo society and values that prevented such a development. What these are, however, have never been fully worked out. In terms of theories of traditional state development in Africa, as well as elsewhere, the negative case of the Ibo is as significant as the positive cases of Dahomey and other states which did so develop. (Ottenberg 1961:218)

Whereas I believe values must be taken into account in any total explanation, I do not believe that values are the best starting point for inquiry. Certainly here any explanatory attempt which starts with special Ibo values as a base line is inadmissible. Not only were many cosmopolitan elements being infused into and fused within Ibo culture as far back as it can be traced (Dike 1956, Jones 1963), but the values themselves varied from subregion to subregion and underwent rapid change as the expanding trade network more and more dominated the subsistence economy.

The dynamic nature of the values as well as of the social structure of the Ibo can be seen in Meek's (1937) treatment of traditional authority. Meek begins with a discussion of the *Okpara* or lineage head.[8] At first sight we would seem to have a typical segmentary lineage model for the political system of the type advanced by Evans-Pritchard for the Nuer. As Meek proceeds, however, the exceptions loom larger and larger, and his emphasis shifts away from ascribed lineage status to achieved status in the assignment of political roles at the local level.

According to Meek's initial formulations, traditional leadership among the Ibo was vested in the *okpara* who was both head of the lineage (*onunne*) and ritual leader in the cult of lineage ancestors (*umunne*). The position was structurally relative— that is, each extended family had its *okpara* and the senior among these was *okpara* of the lineage segment. Where affairs of an entire lineage were involved, the *okpara* of the senior branch was regarded as *okpara*. In affairs involving more than one lineage in a given locality the *okpara* of the lineage longest resident was considered to have seniority, but the status of *okpara* in these wider contexts essentially was one of *primus inter pares* and the *okpara*'s real authority was largely limited either to his lineage segment or extended family. (1937:104–11) "It may be said generally that among the Ibo government is based on the family organization, and that the controlling authority is the general body of family heads, the senior *okpara* acting as ceremonial president." (Meek 1937:110–11) Thus far we have a rather close correspondence to the classical segmentary model.

It must be borne in mind while considering these statements, that much of the fieldwork during this period, Meek's included, was stimulated by and oriented around practical problems of colonial administration. Warrant Chiefs, backed by the British administration, had proven to be an ineffective method of rule. Thus a conscientious search was undertaken to ascertain just who the traditionally sanctioned leaders in the indigenous society really were, in the hopes of making practicable something analogous at least to Indirect Rule in the north.[9] In a relatively stable and homogenous society such an attempt might bear meaningful results; but in a society where rapidly developing trade and commerce was, and had for some long time been, creating wide differences in wealth, power, and status, traditionally sanctioned authority and de facto power are likely in practice to be widely divergent—even apart from postcolonial changes. Indeed, Meek himself, despite the pragmatic orientation of his research, was too thorough an investigator not to take note of this fact. "Even in the olden days the chief executive control of the *onunne* might have been vested in some rich, generous man rather than in the *okpara*." (1937:106) Then, in a section entitled "Other Leaders of Society," he makes the following very important general observation:

In all society the possession of wealth confers power, and so we find that, if in any group there was a personage of outstanding wealth, that personage obtained a measure of authority within the group which overshadowed that of the *okpara*. Such a personage could, if he were able and generous, obtain a position of chieftainship of his local group (*nchi*), and be styled the *Onyisi* or head of the group. He might even be regarded as the *Onyisi* of the whole village-group. (1937:111)

Such a person obtained his position for "obvious reasons." As
he was able to purchase firearms and powder, he was not only
able to protect his own lineage segment but others as well. He
held the power to decide whether to go to war or not, for only
he could provide the necessary means for waging war successfully. This placed the younger age sets under his control. By
supplying financial aid he constantly added to his freeborn followers, and by effectively claiming a major portion of the captives (in compensation for his outlay on arms) he constantly
added to the number of his slaves. Such men tended to become
principal judges and centers of authority in their localities;
and their families tended to become hereditary rulers, unless
their wealth subsequently diminished to the point where they
could no longer act effectively in this role. (Meek 1937:111)

Meek then proceeds to give several known examples from the
Owerri area. Sometimes offenders against local rules and customs [10] were handed over to such "big men" to be either sold
into slavery or kept under forced labor until compensation was
raised by their kin. The rich, influential men of one community
were well-known to those of others, and reciprocal safe-conduct
was offered in return for tolls or dues. Not only were they principal judges in their own groups, but they frequently arbitrated
disputes between groups as well; and the outcome of wars between groups often depended on the financial status of the local
big man, who could supplement his own military resources by
hiring specialized mercenaries.[11] As one proceeds through
Meek's monograph, the exceptions loom larger than the rule.
Gradually a picture of Ibo society emerges which more closely
resembles ancient Greece or feudal Europe than it does the
classical acephalous segmentary tribal society.

Nor was the existence of rich men of the type described exceptional.
They could be found in almost every village-group. In those
districts in which titles were in vogue, as for example among the
Isu, they were the leaders of the titled classes, who were the 'heaven-
born' of Iboland. (Meek 1937:113)

Meek continues to show other important variations in political organization within the region, including the rather well-defined kingship at Onitsha, a city-state on the Niger, as well as the practice of obtaining titles for graded payments in the various title societies. This institution served to implement the political rule of an oligarchy of the wealthy. Institutions of this type were reported by Meek from Owerri, Awgu, Nsukka (a high-density area in the extreme north of Iboland), Awka, and Onitsha. (1937:170–96) His final summary of Ibo political organization thus takes into consideration a rather wide range of political forms, most of them not encountered in the classical segmentary or acephalous tribes.

Of outstanding importance is the wide distribution of authority in the Ibo social group. Kings or priest-chiefs may have functioned in a few communities like Onitsha, Aguku, Oreri, or Bonny; and an individual of exceptional wealth and personality may occasionally in his own village have wielded autocratic powers; but normally a village was governed by the whole body of the people, the heads of families and rich or titled or able men forming a kind of senate in this miniature republic. (1937:335) [12]

It is to be noted that although the type of local political organization summarized by Meek is segmentary in the broadest sense of the word (that is, there are a number of separate and opposed segments),[13] there are rather profound differences between Ibo social and political organization and that of the truly classical segmentary societies such as the Nuer. This is true both at the local level and, as we shall see later, in terms of regional institutions as well. Leadership and political office among the Ibo seem even in the precolonial period to have been much more largely based on achievement and wealth as opposed to lineage ascription than was so in lineage-organized societies. Furthermore, unlike the Nuer and other typically acephalous societies, there was among the Ibo decided social stratification— on the one hand the division between slaves and free men and on the other the further cleavage between the wealthy slave owners and those who owned few or no slaves. In all Ibo regions Meek has indicated that such wealthy and powerful men often emerged as the de facto political leaders, and in certain cases assumed the powers of local autocrats. Such villages or village groups may be regarded as formally acephalous in that there were no regularized and institutionalized rules and procedures for succession and elevation to political office. But, during the periods when powerful leaders and their families were in actual control, these villages or village-groups must be regarded as having actual de facto political heads. In those areas where the Title societies were important, more formalized institutions of political control were in evidence. The prices of the titles of higher rank denied access to political office to all but the wealthy and in fact produced local oligarchies which again, in the strict sense of the word, were not acephalous.

It is worth noting here that when confronted with the A and B classification in *African Political Systems* both Meek and G. I. Jones explicitly deny the applicability of the "stateless" designation to the Ibo. Thus, in his review of *African Political Systems,* Meek specifically and directly challenged the state-stateless dichotomy from the standpoint of Ibo examples.

This can only be regarded as the roughest of working definitions since numerous societies, which the editors class as stateless, display some or many of the features of the so-called primitive states. A single independent village-group or canton of the Ibo of Nigeria, who would obviously be included among the 'stateless' societies, may be possessed of some form of central authority, administrative machinery, and judicial institutions, and among its members there may also be marked distinctions of rank and status, which are assumed to be characteristics of 'state' societies. (1941:42)

More recently G. I. Jones has faced the same problem of classification.

In my own case, and in attempting to classify and differentiate between political systems in Eastern Nigeria, I find it convenient to regard the two main divisions of *African Political Systems* as polar or extreme types rather than as exclusive categories. . . . In Nigeria the kingdoms of Benin and Idah would fall closer to the A pole, the political system of the Tiv closer to the B pole, while most of the societies of Eastern Nigeria would occupy a more central position. All Ibo, Ibibio, or Ijo societies that have been studied can be said to possess the requirements of a primitive state, in that they have some centralized administrative and judicial institutions and cleavages of wealth and status corresponding to the distribution of power and authority. They are also segmentary in Fortes' sense, in that power is ultimately resident in the segments not in the central government, which consists essentially of a federation of politically equivalent segments. In the case of Ibibio and Ijo these federations can be called villages and in that of Ibo, village groups. (1963:5)

It should be clear, then, that the "stateless" or "acephalous" label must be heavily qualified before it can rightfully be applied to the Ibo government. As yet, nothing has been said of wider than local political integration. Eisenstadt's classification, it should be remembered, combined the terms "acephalous" and "autonomous." It is to this second term, then, that I shall next address myself.

The term "autonomous" may legitimately be applied to the Ibo but only in a relative sense. In actuality, during the period of the slave trade and the palm-oil trade that succeeded it, specialized institutions developed in this region which served to link together local Ibo groups and reduce local autonomy. In some cases this reduction was only slight, while in others it was virtually complete. Such intergroup ties included wider than local ritual and religious linkages; political and military alliances between local units (villages or village-groups), which were relatively permanent or shifting, depending upon changes in population, land pressure, and trade opportunities; and, in some areas, rather extensive networks of secret and/or title societies. By far the highest degree of areal integration and political domination was attained by organizations associated with oracles, and of these the most influential and widespread was the Ibini Okpabe oracle of the Aro Chuku, which was known to the Europeans as the "Long Juju." (Ottenberg 1958:297–99) [14]

During the period of the European slave trade in the region (1650–1850) the Aro, an Ibo group of specialized traders, developed a combined economic-political and ritual organization which was able to dominate and control all of the major interior routes of trade as well as the major markets. The Aro "capital" was an independent village group of some nineteen communities located near the Cross River just above the major slave market at Bende. From this center the Aro were in a strategic position for trade contacts with Efik and Ibibio trading states at the mouths of the Cross and Calabar Rivers to the south and with Ibo to the west and to the north and on into the Igala region, where Aro trade routes linked with those of the Hausa-Fulani. Dike, who has written a most comprehensive study of the development and impact of trade in the Eastern Nigerian Region, has cited an unpublished manuscript by Sidney R. Smith to the effect that the Aro oracle was some 80 miles from Bonny, 60 miles from New Calabar (both important city-states and trading ports on the Delta) and 70 miles from the mainstream of the Niger above Aboh. This location gave the oracle the requisite remoteness for its purpose and yet placed the Aro in close touch with the dense Ibo population as well as the Ibibio, Ijo, Isokos, Jekiri, Sobos, and Benis of the Delta. (Dike 1956:39–40)

The political organization of the Aro home communities is not known in detail, but Forde and Jones (1950:56) have sketched its outlines. The nineteen Aro towns were derived from nine *otusi* (patrilineages) which were localized in nine parent towns. The other towns were the products of fissioning and accretion from these primary centers. Each of the nine was under a headman (*otusi*) and the others were each under an officer called *eze*. The *otusi* of the town of Oror was also head of the Aro chiefly lineage and was known as the *Eze-Aro*. He was the oldest freeborn male tracing patrilineal descent from *Oke-*

Nache, the traditional lineage founder, and was always regarded as the senior *otusi* no matter what his age was relative to other *otusi.* There was an Aro council which consisted of the nine *otusi* together with representatives from the ten other towns.[15]

It would appear that the number of Aro residing in Aro "colonies" away from Aro Chuku proper was much greater than those living in the parent towns. Talbot (using the 1921 census) gives a figure of 14,163 Aro dwelling in the home province of Calabar as contrasted to 41,861 in Owerri and Onitsha provinces. (1926,4:43) It was through these colony-settlements that the Aro were enabled to dominate the major overland trade routes and markets in the entire area between the Niger on the west and the Cross River on the east and from the borders of the Igala state in the north to the Delta in the south. Aro settlements were of three types, according to Ottenberg:

(1) Small settlements which interfered little in local affairs and were usually along Aro trade routes (as at Akaeze).

(2) Larger settlements around a central market which dominated the market but still permitted local autonomy outside of market affairs and trade.

(3) "Large scale settlements in which one or more village group was thoroughly dominated, Aro control extending over land, property, and religious rituals." (Ottenberg 1958:301)

There seems little doubt that, here at least, we are in the presence of a fairly well-defined state organization.

Ottenberg refers to Aro settlements at Bende (the major slave market of the region and where the Aro completely dominated the market), Uburu, Aba, as well as in the Owerri, Okigwi, Ohaffia, Ada, and Afikpo regions and elsewhere. Dike cites Umo's listing of over 25 Aro settlements. (Dike 1956:38 fn.2) Talbot, who is followed in this by Dike, indicates that the entire region was:

divided into spheres of influence, each placed under one of the Aro quarters. For instance the country between Aro Chuku and Awka belonged to the quarters of Utari, Amove and Ndizioggu. Their trade consisted chiefly of fowls, native cloths, at first of palm-fibre then of cotton, obtained from the Awhawzara etc., matchets and hoes from Bende, and slaves. (Talbot 1926,1:183)

This sort of control was gained, consolidated, and extended through exploitation of the oracle, superior economic resources, and through the control of tribes of specialized mercenary warriors. Aro ritual, economic, and military activities reciprocally interacted and reinforced each other. The oracle was not only universally feared and respected throughout Iboland but through all Eastern Nigeria. (Dike 1956:37) Pilgrimages were made to the oracle from all parts of the region, and the town (Aro Chuku) was invariably mentioned with a respect verging on veneration. Any male freeborn Aro (*amade*) was empowered to act as an agent for trade as well as for the oracle, and the Aro and their agents, who could travel freely and securely through any portion of the country, would both gather information for the further use of the oracle and suggest to local persons with either unsolved problems or with disputes to settle that they should go to the oracle for determination of these matters. These persons or their representatives would, upon payment of a fee, be escorted by the oracle agents to Aro Chuku and quartered in the compounds of relatives of the agents. These gathered further information which was passed on to the keepers of the oracles to make their determinations seem both miraculous and convincing. Dispute cases often involved the litigants in competitive gift-giving in the attempt to influence the oracle. This, of course, worked to the economic advantage of the agents. Those adjudged guilty in dispute cases were either fined, sacrificed, or, more often than not, sold into slavery.[16] Thus the oracle also fed the Aro supply of slaves. Types of cases decided by the oracle included land and inheritance disputes, persistent local warfare, stealing (which was regarded as an

extremely serious offense), witchcraft, sorcery, and murder.
(Ottenberg 1958:303) This is not to say that the oracle forced
its intervention in all or even most of these disputes. On the one
hand, Aro and Aro agents endeavoured to recruit cases and to
set up local shrines which would be under the overall oracle
organization. On the other, cases which could not be resolved at
the local level were referred upwards to it. "The oracle thus
acted as a final court, a supernatural judicial body." (Ottenberg
1958:303) Though this is not explicitly stated by Ottenberg or
others, it should be obvious that this oracle network enabled the
Aro to effect decisions at the local level which would benefit
their policy.

In addition to their oracle and trading activities, the Aro
were also the main financiers and moneylenders of the Ibo
country. Those unable to pay their debts either sold a relative
or were themselves sold as slaves. (Forde 1950:56) It seems
likely that borrowing from Aro moneylenders might often assist
one of the local "big men" (mentioned above p. 198) along the
pathway to local domination. This of course would place him to
a degree under subsequent obligation to the Aro. Furthermore,
control of the trade in slaves meant also control of the only
effective means of transportation along the bush paths of the
interior—human-head porterage. Thus control of the trade in
slaves was a lever for the control of other trade as well.[17]

When the prestige or fear induced by the oracle failed them,
and economic pressure was insufficient to achieve their objec-
tives, the Aro had recourse to the services of several specialized
mercenary groups. These were largely Eastern Ibo and included
the Abam, the Ada (or Edda), Ohaffia, and Abiriba, as well as
some Aba from southern Ibo country. Some were of Aro origin;
others were not.

The mercenaries would sack communities or villages for the Aro,
keeping as booty the heads of the dead (used for ceremonial and
prestige purposes) and whatever property they obtained, and selling

or turning over those captured to the Aro as slaves. . . . The relationship was mutually beneficial. In some areas the Aro, as traders or as agents of the oracle, would scout the villages to be attacked and would pass on the information to the mercenaries who would use it for a surprise engagement, usually in the early morning. If two villages were in conflict the Aro might obtain mercenaries for one of them for a fee. The warriors also attacked groups that were unwilling to cooperate with the Aro. The existence of mercenaries facilitated Aro trade and made it easier for the Aro to move about openly. (Ottenberg 1958:302)

Dike has summed up the Aro position as follows:

Acting as mediators between God and the clans and assuming themselves to be the spokesmen of the Almighty, they held a privileged position throughout the land, erecting what amounted to a theocratic state over eastern Nigeria. Aro colonies became the divinely ordained trade centres of the interior; Aro middlemen the economic dictators of the hinterland. During the time of the slave trade and in the period of legitimate commerce [palm oil trade -RFS] they acquire immense wealth through a monopoly believed to be divinely appointed, and with wealth came great political influence. (1956:38)

It seems clear, then, that the Aro organization was a type of state, and, indeed, Dike, in the passage quoted has gone as far as to call it just that. What has seemed to bemuse the anthropologists in this situation is that the Aro type of organization does not conform closely to the conventional centralized, monarchical model characteristic of most indigenous African states and termed by Oliver and Fage (1962) "the Sudanic State" and by Murdock (with Wittfogelian overtones) "African Despotism." (1959)

Clearcut and formalized legislative, executive, and judicial structures are not immediately visible, as the functions of rule making, rule application, and rule adjudication (Almond 1960:17) were embedded in the multifunctional economic, political, and ritual organization of the Aro. Strictly formal definitions of the state can block rather than advance analysis in situ-

ations such as this. A more analytic discussion of the state which
is cast in both developmental and functional terms has been
offered by Fried and, I feel, has considerable utility when applied to the Aro. Fried distinguishes between the primary and
secondary functions of the state. In discussing the former he
notes:

The emergent state, then, is the organization of the power of society
on a supra-kin basis. Among its earliest tasks is the maintenance of
general order but scarcely discernible from this is its need to
support the order of stratification. The defense of a complete system
of individual statuses is impossible so the early state concentrates on
a few key statuses (helping to explain the tendency to convert any
crime into either sacrilege or *lese majeste*) and on the basic principles of organization, e.g., the idea of hierarchy, property, and the
power of law. (1960:728)

If to this be added the observation that the early state will by
necessity have to concentrate first on key functions; and if the
further qualification be added that the greater the area which
must be controlled the fewer the functions the emergent state
can successfully carry out, we would seem to have a framework
into which, despite their rather special nature, the Aro can be
made to fit. By concentrating on the vital nerves (routes) and
nerve centers (major markets) the Aro were enabled to gain a
rather complete economic domination over a large region. Aro
further served to guarantee the necessary peace of the market
and safety of arteries of communication so that goods and labor
could flow from one region or subregion to another, thus permitting a higher density of population than would otherwise
have been possible, funnelling goods and services across a very
wide region, and, by raiding the high-density areas for slaves,
serving to redistribute the population as well.[18]

Furthermore, according to Fried: "The implementation of
these primary functions of the state gives rise to a number of
specific and characteristic secondary functions, each of which is
associated with one or more particular institutions of its own."

(1960:729) Here he makes the important observation that they may be made to appear in two's and three's within nonstate societies by "exaggeration and the neglect of known history" but in no nonstate society do a majority of them appear. These secondary functions are:

(1) Population control (fixing boundaries, establishment of membership categories, census).

(2) Disposal of trouble cases (civil and criminal laws moving toward the status of codes, regular legal procedure, regular officers of adjudication).

(3) The protection of sovereignty (maintenance of military forces, police forces and power; eminent domain).

(4) Fiscal support through taxation and conscription.

I shall discuss their presence or absence under the Aro organization in the same order.

(1) The establishment of boundaries can be seen in the division of the country into spheres of influence under the control of separate Aro quarters. The fixing of membership categories included the definition of the statuses slave and free and Aro and non-Aro, and there may have been finer subdivisions within these categories as well. Census is not reported.

(2) Within the markets there was a very definite procedure for the disposal of trouble cases, and according to Harris (1942b), the Aro slave-trading apparatus was often utilized for the disposal of chronic trouble cases at the local level. The evidence would also indicate that the spread of the Oracle organization and the proliferation of secondary oracles fashioned on the Aro model, and most often under Aro control or influence, were part of an important development in the direction of greater regularization and strengthening of legal procedure over the region under an adjudicative hierarchy centering upon Aro Chuku.

(3) Control of the mercenaries gave the Aro both military and police forces and power and hence an effective monopoly of physical force in the region. Attested was the ability of the Aro and their agents to move freely throughout the country without fear of attack and their right to establish settlements when and where they wanted them. (Ottenberg 1958:301) Basden (1938:385) observed that the spilling of Aro blood involved such large-scale reprisals that it was avoided whenever possible. All of these last observations would indicate rather wide recognition of Aro sovereignty.

(4) Through their control of the mercenaries and their monopolistic position in the hinterland slave trade, the Aro eminently possessed the power of conscription. Conscription here merges with taxation, and taxation was both predatory and direct. Instead of taxing a portion of the laborer's product or demanding a portion of the laborer's time in labor service, the Aro were removing a percentage of the total labor force permanently and delivering them at a profit into the slave trade. For the individuals thus taxed, taxation was total. Given the likelihood that population density in the region was above carrying capacity of the land, this was doubtlessly the most viable type of taxation and fiscal support for such a system. In addition, and by the same methods, the Aro could conscript their own labor requirements for porterage and other purposes, but the number required here would be but a small fraction of those exported. Besides, slaves being exported could themselves carry Aro exports, thereby further reducing Aro porterage requirements. Additional fiscal support and revenue were of course obtained from market and safe-conduct tolls.

In terms of Fried's criteria, then, the Aro organization would seem to constitute a state. The major distinction between the

Aro and a state like Dahomey would seem to lie in the Aro concentration on crucial nerve centers, trade routes, and markets rather than on a circumscribed and bounded region as such.

If one moves from the level of structure to that of process, perhaps an even more meaningful point can be made. That is, whether or not the term "state" is granted as applicable to the Aro organization, it should be clear that what would have to be termed a process of state formation was underway in Iboland in the period of the slave trade, even though incompletely realized. Seen in this light, the important theoretical point is not "Why did not the state emerge?" but "Why did not state formation proceed further?" The issues raised in both this and the preceding paragraph invite further comparison with Dahomey.

Unlike Dahomey, the Aro organization developed in a hinterland where there were no contending states already in existence. At this stage the city-states (which were primarily adapted to water-borne commerce) were not strong enough to extend into the interior and relied upon Aro ties for their supply of slaves. Thus in a very real sense the Aro organization was a highly adaptive institution that evolved to fill the vacuum created by the penetration of the slave trade into a region initially characterized by clan and lineage organization. During the same period the pressure from slave raids from the north was compressing populations into the forest refuge areas south of the Benue River (see p. 219) and the stimulation of growing trade percolating up from the Delta regions was simultaneously serving as a magnet inducing the movements of populations southward. The effects of both influences upon population density and the potential supply of slaves, and hence the success of the Aro, should be obvious. Dike has rather neatly expressed the result.

The numerous political units represented by the clans, admirable as organs of local government, proved inadequate for the handling of matters of common interest such as commerce and justice. A central organization was needed to facilitate inter-tribal trade and provide a 'pax' without which commerce could not flourish. It was this vacuum existing at the centre of the tribal organization that the Aros, working through the medium of their Oracle, filled. The trading settlements they established at the crossing of the rivers and at the intersection of the main routes became the 'free cities' to which all who wished to 'traffic and exchange' safely repaired, international courts where individuals and clans in conflict sought justice from the undisputed authority of the Oracle. (1956:38–39)

As to why the Aro organization did not develop further as a state, several factors must be taken into account. The first is time. States do not spring full-blown either from the head of Zeus or the maw of the slave trade. As we do not know the date of the emergence of the Aro or other oracles in the region except that it was during the period of the slave trade (Ottenberg 1958:301), we have no way of knowing whether Aro development was relatively slow or rapid. Second is the problem of controlling through a trade network an area over four times that of Dahomey. Third is the absence of proximate competing units which seemed an important catalyst to state formation in the Dahomey case (Fage 1962:93–94; Arnold 1957:157). Those who have written on the Aro (Dike 1956, Forde 1950, Jones 1963, Leonard 1906, Ottenberg 1958, Talbot 1926) seem agreed that Aro domination of the interior trade remained essentially unchallenged during the period when the prime commodity remained human beings. Fourth, given the Aro policy, which was to control the trade and not necessarily to "form a more perfect union," it can reasonably be asked if the process of Aro domination itself did not involve tendencies inhibitive of further centralization. In other words, it would seem likely, in the attempt to obtain more slaves and as a numerical minority to gain domination over a large, heavily populated region, the Aro may have deliberately played off one village-group against another, not only to gain captives from the result-

ing wars and fees from the leasing of their mercenaries, but also
to hold down the emergence of other and possibly contending
nuclei of power.

Here an important and perhaps crucial difference between
the Dahomean situation and that of the Aro must be noted.
Dahomey was raiding other tribes and states beyond its borders
for slaves while the Aro's major source of supply was internal—
within the Ibo region under their control. The extent to which
this difference in situation entailed important differences in
both political structure and policy must, however, await a more
complete answer to another problem in Aro research which,
judging by the statements of the experts, is still largely unresolved. This is the question as to whether the slaves were pro-
cured primarily through warfare and raids or through the
normal operations of the oracle itself. Ottenberg would seem to
lean toward the former position: "On the basis of only meager
evidence, it seems likely that most of the slaves who came into
Aro hands were from sources not directly associated with their
oracle, and those who became slaves following oracular consul-
tation formed a much smaller group." (1958:304) If it be taken
as the case that the majority of slaves were obtained through
raids and local warfare, then it seems a reasonable hypothesis
that the Aro would pursue a definite policy of stimulating inter-
village-group conflict in order to feed constantly the supply of
slaves. There seems to be no direct empirical evidence either to
confirm or deny this suggestion. There is certain logical support
in the observation that a policy of "divide and rule" is generally
a rational policy for any minority group bent on domination of
a large area and large population.

On the other hand, we have a rather contrary suggestion from
Udo. In arguing that both a high population density and a dispersed settlement pattern were present in the central Ibo region
(Mba Ise in Owerri and Afaha Obong in Abak are examples),
he has claimed that:

This was made possible by the fact that in the core areas of Eastern Nigeria slaves were recruited chiefly through the medium of the Long Juju of Arochuku, and not through tribal wars. Only victims of this deity and social undesirables were sold into slavery in these central areas. There was therefore little incentive for people to flock together for defense, as in the grassland areas farther north where intergroup warfare was the main source of slaves. (1965:62)

If the first alternative be accepted, then it should be argued that in this phase we have a process of state formation which in its very operation tends to inhibit further centralization and integration. If the second be accepted, then we are forced to ascribe greater powers, control, and centralization to the Aro Chuku state than most writers on the subject have been willing to admit. Probably the reality of the process fluctuated between these extremes depending on the circumstances and the degree of Aro power and control in the area (and at the time) involved. Dike would seem to take such a middle view:

The belief that the bulk of the slaves handled in the Atlantic trade were captives from tribal wars or that kidnapping and raids were the normal methods of obtaining the human victims is now seen to be but a half truth when applied to the tribes east of the Niger. The Oracle, directed by the Aros, was the medium through which the slaves exported from the Delta ports were largely recruited. . . . Only when the injunctions of the Oracle were defied did the Aros, in his name, turn their fierce mercenaries on the offending party. . . . But the dominant power of the Oracle was widely understood and rarely opposed, so that the slaves obtained by violence and kidnapping could not have greatly exceeded, and may even have been fewer than, those who surrendered to the dictates of the Oracle. (1956:41)

Finally, full consideration must be given to a major change in the trade which took place in the last two-thirds of the nineteenth century. As British naval squadrons in the Bights of Benin and Biafra succeeded finally in containing and drying up the external slave trade, the Delta Trading States, with characteristic adaptability, turned to a lucrative substitute, the trade in palm oil. During this period Nigeria became the world's leading producer of palm oil and the Eastern Region the major source area within Nigeria. It can also be reasonably argued that the development of the trade in palm oil served further to increase population densities in the producing regions by providing a demand for additional labor (to be supplied either by immigration, natural increase, or both) [19] and by making it possible through the proceeds of the sale of palm products to import foodstuffs from other areas where the pressure on the land was less. On the other hand, this same shift in the trade pattern seems to have weakened (though by no means ended) the Aro domination of the interior.

Jones, speaking both of the coastal city-states and the Aro, has noted that:

In the economic sphere these states had to adjust to a change over in the principal export from slaves to palm oil. This change meant among other things that the Aro people lost their monopoly of the hinterland trade. The internal slave trade remained in their hands as did the import trade in the more valuable imports, cloth, tobacco, gunpowder and muskets. But in the marketing of palm oil the Aro were at a disadvantage as against the local producers and their trading relatives. The oil could be produced by anyone who had access to the trees and traded in by anyone who could find the cash to buy it or could obtain it on credit. (1963:73)

This should not be taken as meaning that the process of state formation in the Ibo hinterland was terminated. Rather, it took a new and in many ways more important direction. As Dike has pointed out, Aro domination in the oil markets at least tended to be replaced by what he (Dike) has termed the "market governments," dominated mostly by the Delta Trading States.

The area from which the bulk of the oil was derived lay immediately within the Delta hinterland. The famous 'oil markets' which loomed so large in the consular reports of the last century were situated in the palm belt, at the heads of the creeks and rivers linking the interior to the coast. Each city-state had its own exclusive

markets in which it maintained trading posts and in which hundreds of its subjects lived for the greater part of each year. Over half
the oil handled in the Delta trade was sold at Bonny, all of which
came from the exclusive markets of Essene, Obunku, Imo, Akwete,
Urata, Azumiri, Ohambele, Ngwa (landing port, Aba), and Ndele.
In theory these tribal states which came under the Bonny sphere of
interest were politically independent but in practice they were
virtually the protectorates of the latter. (1956:51)

This indicates greater coastal involvement in the hinterland.
During the same period there is also evidence of a "hardening"
of the conditions of trade and a greater opposition and competition between the Delta Trading States, conditions which, in the
contrasting example cited by Ottenberg, led to the formation of
larger and more centralized states. At this point interpretation
and analysis of these processes might be assisted by more explicit
reference to the Dahomey case.

Dahomey arose under conditions where several small states
were apparently in existence before the Europeans first came to
trade on the Slave Coast. There were several small coastal city-
states of which the largest, Whydah and Jacquin, held coastlines
of only twenty miles each and extended back into the interior
about the same distance. The most important of all these states,
however, lay slightly inland, just to the north of Whydah. This
was the Fon state of Great Ardra. Initially the slave trade stimulated prosperity and expansion of almost all these small states,
and about 1620 scions of the Fon line established two further
states, one on the coast (Little Ardra) and one even further inland and about fifty miles to the north of Whydah at Abomey.
Abomey expanded by raiding the smaller tribes of the north for
slaves and selling them to Great Ardra for resale to Europeans
there or at Whydah or Jacquin. In the struggle which ensued
for the control of the trade routes and access to the sea, Abomey
emerged supreme, absorbing its smaller neighbors and establishing the state known to the Europeans as Dahomey. (Fage
1962:93–95; Labouret 1962:109) It is instructive to note that

by policy Dahomey remained an inland power, moving by force to take Whydah, for instance, only when its trade rights and crucial access to European slave-buyers were threatened. (Arnold 1957) Conflict, competition, and rather constant military involvement with the neighboring states of Oyo and later Ashanti might also be cited as external pressures fostering the centralization of Dahomey. It should also be borne in mind that estimates by Skertchly (1874) and Burton (1893) quoted in Herskovits (1938,I:8–10) would give the area of actual Abomey control as being in the neighborhood of 4,000 square miles only. Compared to the Niger Delta and its hinterland this is quite compact.

Now let us see how the situation differed in Nigeria. There were other geographical factors in addition to area that helped modify development in southeastern Nigeria along a course somewhat different from that in Dahomey. The low-lying Nigerian coastal plain stretches from Lagos in the west to Cameroons in the east, the greater part of this region being occupied by the Niger Delta, which covers an area of some 270 miles along the coast and 120 miles in depth. The two mouths of the Niger are known as the Forcados and the Nun, but a veritable maze of creeks and lagoons in this mangrove-covered area link these mouths with such streams as the Cross, Imo, Kwa-Ibo, Bonny, Brass, and Benin rivers. The ecology of creek, mangrove swamp, and interspersing fingers of land tended to insulate and isolate the coastal towns one from another as they developed, while at the same time affording natural links to the hinterland and to the entire Niger River system. The marked difference between this environment and that of the forest zone on the higher land back of the Delta also tended to foster and reinforce that marked separation of coastal and interior polities which Polanyi and others (Polanyi 1957) have noted to be a characteristic feature of all early Port-of-Trade development.

Dike (1956:21–28) has suggested that populations moved

into this broad region in three general waves. Actually the process was undoubtedly more complex, but what is important is the general pattern. The first wave is seen as that which brought the Ijaws to locations at or near the creek mouths and which has been associated by Jones with a development of trade that antedated the Portuguese period (1450–1550).

We can assume that the production of salt, the large canoes, and the trade with the interior antedated the Portuguese period, and this regular internal trade in salt and provisions would provide quite as good a reason for a movement into the delta as that of the overseas trade with Europeans, which must at that time have been very sporadic and uncertain. (1963:30) [20]

As trade developed further population was attracted to the region and the transfer of foodstuffs across different zones made possible the maintenance of larger populations. Dike sees the most important of the early movements as occurring between 1450 and 1800 and resulting in the conversion of what were originally small Ijaw fishing villages into trading city-states. (1956:24)

The next migratory wave saw the establishment of Bonny and Old Calabar, which grew to be important city-states in the slave and palm-oil periods. With the founding of the city-states fresh voluntary movements from hinterland to coast became virtually impossible; but the forced migrations of the slave trade kept population in the Delta advancing, and by 1848 it was estimated that only a minority of the population in Bonny, for example, was freeborn. With the strategic coastal ports occupied, the commercial highway of the Niger itself became increasingly attractive, and movements traditionally ascribed as from the Benin region moved into such Niger locations as Aboh and Onitsha. (1956:25) This eastward movement was paralleled by another movement from the north, which was a direct result of the slave trade and an indirect effect of state formation in the northern region.

The indigenous home of the Ibos, which lies mainly to the east of the Niger valley, is within the forest belt where the cavalry used by the Fulani in their annual slave-raids could not operate. These raids were conducted mainly in the plains north of the forest region, and were organized from Kano, Sokoto, Bida, and Ilorin. They inevitably led to the movement of tribes, south of the Benue, to inaccessible areas and places of safety such as the Ibo forest area provided. (Dike 1956:27) .[21]

We have seen that the shift from the trade in slaves to that in palm oil brought a weakening of the hinterland monopoly of the Aro Chuku and at the same time a growing involvement in the hinterland on the part of the Delta City-States—what Dike has called the rise of the market governments and the establishment of coastal protectorates in the interior. "Market laws were enacted to regulate the relations between the two communities and these were administered by equal numbers of the Bonny-men and the owners of the territory concerned." (Dike 1956:42) These market laws were quite severe. Fights in the market entailed heavy fines, and if they resulted in death the slayer was hanged from a special tree. If a man refused to accept the agreed upon currency he was sacrificed to the market juju.

It was on the ruthless enforcement of the market laws that the tranquility of the trading areas depended; the Delta states learnt from hard experience that commerce could not flourish in lawlessness and disorder. Anything, therefore, which disturbed the peace was quickly stamped out. It was not uncommon in time of crisis for a Bonny king to go to the tribal interior specifically to restore order in the markets. (Dike 1956:43) [22]

The palm-oil trade commenced with a boom, and apparently there was room for the Delta states to expand their volume of trade and hinterland spheres of influence without encroaching on each other's domains. This phase was brought to a close by 1862, when competition from mineral oil, among other factors, brought a fall in oil prices. There is also some indication that

Delta expansion into the interior was approaching the effective limits of waterway access to oil markets and producing areas.

Transport difficulties prevented much of the hinterland oil from reaching the delta, and prevented the delta states from increasing the volume of their trade to compensate for the fall in oil prices. The result of this in the Eastern Delta was competition between the different states to secure the control of the rival's principal oil markets which culminated in warfare between them, accompanied in the case of Bonny and Kalabari by a withdrawal from the coast to the northern margin of the delta to be closer to these markets. (Jones 1963:73)

This passage indicates two important, though related, changes in the intra-Delta and Delta-hinterland relationships. First, although there had been wars before (such as the Bonny-Andoni war of the early 1840s [Jones 1963:115]), these were part of the growth and expanding hegemony of separate city-states. In the latter half of the nineteenth century there now emerged that major contest for military and political domination in the trading zone, which in the Dahomey instance led to the reduction in the number of competing units and the emergence of a centralized state. Second, there was a progressive movement into the hinterland to control the trade at its source, a movement whose logical outcome would have been domination of the densely populated producing areas themselves. What limitations may have been placed on the realization of this trend by the essentially naval nature of the coastal military power (fleets of 60 or 70 foot canoes armed with cannon and manned by musketeers) is not clear.[23] In this event we are forced to speculate, for the operation of these factors—in fact the very struggle itself—was strongly circumscribed, held in bounds, and finally circumvented by the intervention of the British.

Whereas there had been no strong European presence to oppose the Dahomean occupation of Whydah there had been throughout the entire nineteenth century a growing British in-

volvement in the local politics of the Bights of Benin and Biafra. This has been admirably documented by Dike (1956) and
there is no need of recapitulating the entire sequence of events
here. It should be remembered that it was British naval power
that ended the coastal slave trade, that the British had intervened in the succession at Bonny in 1850, and that treaties imposed in 1850 and 1854 proscribed trading on the part of the
King of Bonny and in effect reduced the king's status to that of
being chief executive agent of the "court." This in turn became
the supreme authority on the Bonny River.

The 'court' was the assembly of 'kings and chiefs and masters
assembled,' referred to in article III of the 1850 treaty. Its venue
was the court house built by the European community, and its
personnel were the king and chiefs of the Bonny community and
the masters, supercargoes and other European traders of the British
community. (Jones 1963:121)

Both the king and the chiefs were made subordinate to the
court and responsible to carry out its decisions. The sovereign
power of Bonny was limited by a provision that the supercargoes should first be notified and all debts paid in advance of
initiating hostilities. As the entire trading apparatus and fiscal
strength of the Delta States rested on large advances of British
trade goods (known as "Trust"), this was in effect an economic stranglehold. This does not mean that in every instance
the British were able to bring an immediate cessation to hostilities; but their capacities in that direction, as well as their interest and involvement, were constantly growing.

The struggle in the Delta was further complicated by internal factions and civil war between groups of trading houses
within the city-states themselves. These factional disputes were
abetted and fanned by other factions within the British trading
community. In the entire process the necessity of moving into
the hinterland for ultimate control became even more manifest.

In 1869, under the blind of a major artillery duel between two house groups across the open square at Bonny, Jaja, the emergent slave-born leader of one faction, withdrew into the Andoni Country, where he established the new state of Opobo with himself as king. Here he was joined by the European traders from Brass, de Cardi, and McEachen. This move toward the hinterland placed Jaja and those trading with him in a position to dry up Bonny's trade. Naturally the traders at Bonny pressed for British intervention, but the British consul, Livingstone (quoted by Jones:1963) expressed the following view:

In 1872 Livingstone wrote "The Bonny Opobo difficulty may now be considered in fact practically settled. Jaja has all the Eboe and Qua markets and our five great English firms in the Opobo are doing an immense trade. Oko Jumbo has the Okrika markets and the eight firms in Bonny are doing a comparatively small trade. But the total of oil from the two rivers is probably as great." (Jones 1963:131–32)

Bonny and Opobo finally submitted to arbitration by Okrika and New Calabar, and attempted violations of the treaty were met with direct and abrupt trade embargo on the part of the British consul. As a result Opobo retained control over the Anang and Imo River oil trade and replaced Bonny as the wealthiest and most powerful state in the Eastern Delta.

Jaja was able to enjoy his triumph for a brief decade and then came into conflict with the British Government which had now taken over the country. Jaja, who had pioneered the inland movement of trade with Bonny to Opobo, now found himself trying to stop the British carrying this trade still further inland. (Jones 1963:132)

The upshot of this encounter was the deportation of Jaja to the West Indies and the final breakup of the monopolies of both Bonny and Opobo. The monopoly which replaced them was one administered by the British.

In New Calabar a similar secession upstream was attempted by a faction under the leadership of a Kalabari known to the

Europeans as Will Braid. The presence of H. M. S. *Dido* in the
river and the general reluctance of Bonny and Opobo to toler-
ate the emergence of yet another state brought Will Braid's
group to acceptance of a treaty by which they were to return to
New Calabar. The treaty was ignored and New Calabar constructed forts to contain those of Will Braid. This brought New
Calabar into war with Bonny. Finally in 1883 the British consul
intervened, ordering the Kalabari to dismantle their forts at
Degema and other places and Bonny to withdraw war canoes
from the New Calabar River. Bonny was adjudged the most
guilty and fined 200 puncheons of palm oil to 60 assessed from
New Calabar. This ended the war but resulted in a wholesale
move of the Kalabari from close proximity to Bonny and resettlement on the northern margins of the Delta.

The leapfrog movement into the interior continued apace,
but with the British becoming ever more dominant in the process. Technologically, the introduction of the shallow-draft
steamboat gave the British an access to the major streams not
available in the days of sail, while economically the formation
of trading monopolies enhanced the strength of British traders
vis-a-vis the Delta middlemen. An initial cleavage within British
ranks between the inland traders and the Liverpool coastal
traders disappeared as, in Dike's words, it became "a fight between the European merchants, on the one hand and the Niger
Delta middlemen on the other." In the 1870s the word "tap-
ping" came in vogue to describe the process by which trading
steamers passed above the Delta and intercepted produce that
formerly passed through the hands of the coastal middlemen,
thus sounding the death knell for the Delta States. British economic penetration was backed and supported by British arms.
H. M. S. *Pioneer* bombarded Onitsha for three days in 1879,
after first removing fifty thousand pounds worth of British trade
goods; and Yamaha on the Benue was shelled in the same year.
Idah and Aboh on the Niger were also bombarded. The process

of monopoly went forward with the formation of Sir George Goldie's National African Company, which established over one hundred trading posts employing more than 1,500 men. (Dike 1956:212) The Delta States were by this time largely bypassed and their further growth not only militarily and politically contained but economically without foundation. Out of this melee one state did finally emerge supreme over the region, but that state was British. An ironic postscript is provided by the fact that one of the first acts of pacification carried out by the British into the interior was the Aro Expeditionary force of 1901, which brought to a complete termination Aro domination of the interior.

In his article on the Aro and upon Ibo oracles Ottenberg has posed the following interesting question:

If the slave trade had continued for a longer period of time without European occupation of the country, it is problematical whether a political state or a large-scale political organization would have developed out of the Aro oracle system. We do not know because we cannot tell to what extent the system was still developing, or was stabilized just previous to European occupation. (1958:312)

This question should be further generalized to read: Given the tendencies operating in the periods of both the slave trade and subsequent palm-oil trade, would a more comprehensive state organization have emerged in the high-density hinterland of southeastern Nigeria had the British (or another external power) not intervened to establish their own? On the face of available evidence the answer would seem to be a likely "yes," but given the historical circumstances this can only be hypothesized and never validated. And given the apparent weakening of the Aro network due to the shift to palm oil, it is certainly problematical whether the Aro would have developed that state. It should be noted that a genuine Aro decline would have made possible and likely the further expansion and development of a small state like Onitsha, or one of the Delta States, or even the emergence of an entirely new center further developed from the local tendencies noted by Meek.

In terms of our own hypothesis, concerning the relationship between state formation (as a process) and population density (which, of course, dynamically viewed is also a process) the following points should be underscored.

(1) The densities which developed both in Iboland and the Delta during the slave trade were partly a response to the pressures from states and slave raiding to the north and partly the result of the stimulation of growing trade on the coast. The trade as it developed stimulated the development of city-states along the coast. At the same time it both induced and made possible higher densities in the interior.

(2) The growth of trade in the interior resulted in inequalities in wealth and the emergence of social classes and at least partial state formation (title-societies, wealthy big men with armed followers, and large holdings in slaves).

(3) Continued development of the trade is held to have been impossible without at least minimal state control of the major markets and routes of trade. At the same time the funnelling of goods and personnel in and out of the region and between subregions was necessary for the maintenance of the high densities. This trading pax was provided by the Aro organization, which was able to spread its control over a rather wide and previously stateless region by concentrating on the vital nerve centers and routes of trade. Concurrently, it seemed for a time, at least, to be further elaborating its oracle into a sort of international court of last resort. Further problems concerning the Aro cannot be answered because of the lack of information, but there seems some question as to whether the Aro's control of the region may not

have been greater than is usually supposed. On the other hand, there is also the strong likelihood that the very process of Aro domination involved a divide and rule policy that kept local units fragmented.

(4) As Aro control in the interior was apparently weakened and this line of development consequently blunted by the shift to the palm-oil trade, the Delta States which had been expanding in wealth and power then moved to establish larger trading "empires" and "protectorates," swallowing or dominating smaller units (for example, Bonny vs. Andoni) until they were thrown into conflict with each other. The British intervened with force to prevent the full development of this process.

(5) The struggle for control of the trade which was consistently moving in the direction of penetration and control of the interior was, as far as the coastal states were concerned, blocked by the British, and it was the British who brought the process to its logical termination by imposing its state over the region.

It seems clear, then, that throughout this period both the process of state formation and the development of higher densities were more or less consistently under way, although there was no neat unilinear progression of either. Rather there was variation depending on fluctuations in trade and the world market, shifts in British policy, relative military strength of various contenders, and others. Finally, I should want to make the qualifying observation that whereas in the long run there seems to have been a general increase in the development of states and a general upward rise in population density, in the short run, and also varying from locality to locality, density may have advanced ahead of and earlier than state formation and vice versa. In other words, the two processes were not perfectly synchronized; but given the indirect complex and mediated relationship between these two variables—a relationship which is further one

of reciprocal feedback—one has never supposed such close synchronization. In short, I feel that the Ibo, or rather the southeastern Nigerian case (for the region can only reasonably be
viewed as an interconnected whole), admirably displays the in-
tricacies and complexities of the positive relation between population density and state formation that I have proposed. I do
not feel that it in any way negates it.[24]

CHAPTER X. Conclusion

THE ANALYSIS of the southeastern Nigerian Region in the period of the slave and palm-oil trades has shown that trade, population density, and state formation were all interrelated in a developmental process. This brings this important region into the state column so that the two highest and largest density concentrations in sub-Saharan Africa, Ruanda-Urundi and Ibo, are both seen as associated with state formation. At the other extreme it has been noted that the very low densities of the Ba-Mbuti Pygmies and the South African Bushmen are associated with the most rudimentary degree of political specialization. Both extremes confirm the proposition with which this paper began, that average population density and state formation are generally positively correlated.

The full demonstration, however, has been somewhat more complicated, and I shall here recapitulate the steps which have been taken.

I began with a survey from other continents which gave strong general support to the empirical generalization that state formation and population density are positively related and then confronted it with the position stated in Section VI of the Introduction to *African Political Systems*—whose position seemed empirically to indicate a negative correlation but in fact merely asserted that the relationship was completely indeterminate. That is, there was no relationship at all! At this point I adopted the hypothesis that a careful scrutiny of the African data, including the cases in *African Political Systems*, would demonstrate that population density and state formation are positively related. I pointed out that I was not interested in solving every particular exceptional case, but rather in ascertaining the general pattern of the relationship. Specifically, I limited my argument to the area of sub-Saharan Africa, a continental area of rather open inter-communication and contact between societies. Here it was recognized that isolated societies or insular systems might display somewhat different characteristics. I further limited the inquiry to an assessment of the empirical relationship rather than to the development of theory, as this limitation was necessary in order to bound a rather extensive undertaking. My analysis then proceeded through three main stages.

(1) An analysis in historical depth of the six cases presented by *African Political Systems*.

(2) A general survey of the contemporary population pattern of Africa in relation to what it might show of the relationship between density and indigenous state formation.

(3) A detailed analysis in historical depth of an important apparent major exception—the southeastern Nigerian Region.

The findings in (1) have rather radically revised the impression conveyed by the sample of *African Political Systems*. The Tallensi were found to be historically part of the Mamprusi state system and hence ruled out. Tables were presented which compared density estimates for both the historic precolonial period and the "present" time of ethnographic study in the 1930s. Both sequences confirm rather than deny the proposition that state formation and average density are positively related. I feel that the sequence for the historical period is more meaningful than the present one, although the figures are, of course, less firm. On the other hand, census figures for the 1930s were more often than not in the nature of estimates and the densities were either inflated (markedly for the Logoli) or depressed

(Bemba) by the results of colonial rule. The historical sequence showed that the states were uniformly above the single
truly acephalous society (Nuer), with the Logoli in an anoma-
lously high position (see Table I p. 160). This anomaly was explained by the position of Logoli on the borders of an expansive
node of density and state formation extending from Busoga
down the eastward side of Lake Victoria along the recently
opened trade route to the coast. At the time of European penetration the process had advanced to the Wanga, who were functioning as a small state on the northern borders of the Logoli.
The Logoli in turn were tied into the regional trade network
and were showing tendencies toward greater stratification and
political specialization than is typical of segmentary or acephalous societies.

The table for the period of ethnographic study in the 1930s
(Table II) showed the Ngwato as unexpectedly low (2.5), but
this average for the entire reserve hides pronounced concentration along the railroad to the east and the settlement of the majority of the Ngwato in the large settlement (25,000) of Serowe.
The Bemba were low (6 per square mile) and overlapping with
the Nuer (5–10), but the anomaly was explained by the demonstrated collapse of the Bemba system as their monopoly of the
slave and ivory trades was broken with the coming of colonial
rule. The Logoli density in this latter sequence was even
higher, but this rise from a density of 50 to 70 per square mile
to one five times that figure was delineated as a product of the
coming of the railroad, the system of reserves, and the successful
institution of cash-cropping. In sum, the cases in *African Political Systems* themselves supported the hypothesis and not the
contention of Fortes and Evans-Pritchard. When to this rather
narrow range of what were not entirely typical examples were
added band societies at the lower end and major states at the
upper end there was a general upward progression from .25 per
square mile for the Bushmen to 187 per square mile for Ruanda-
Urundi (for the decade of the 1950s). Logoli was still higher in

the 1950s, with 700 per square mile, but this was demonstrated to be a localized nodal pocket of only 122 square miles in area, a node that could more than be matched by nodes of larger area within such systems as Ruanda.

Recognizing that this expanded sample was still limited, I next turned to a survey of the density pattern of tropical Africa as described and analyzed by Trewartha and Zelinsky. (1954a, b) Their Sudan regional band of high density was found to display a significant incidence of state formation, while their Guinea coast and Atlantic coast regional bands displayed both indigenous state formation and the influence of postcolonial commercial development. An exception as yet unexplained was noted here—the Ibo. The Interlacustrine zone of East Africa was also found to be associated with a high historic incidence of state formation. Here some exceptions were noted and explained as (1) densities induced along the borders of states showing definite signs of influence from the states as well as postcolonial inflation of density (Amba, Kiga), (2) artificially high densities created by wholesale alienation of lands to settlers and the establishment of Reserves (Kikuyu, Kamba, and to an extent Nandi), and (3) densities created by successful involvement in cash-cropping (Chagga). The operation of a number of these factors in conjunction had already been analyzed in considerable detail for Nyanza Province in western Kenya. The coastal zone on the East coast was seen to confirm the hypothesis, although in a less dramatic fashion. Finally, general confirmation was seen from the Central African Region, although inferences were made difficult because of the evident ravages of the slave trade in this region.

Finally, in a separate chapter, a historical analysis of the southeastern Nigerian region revealed that during the slave trade the main arteries of trade, the major markets, and the major sources of slave supply were dominated and controlled by the Aro organization, which in terms of the major functions it fulfilled must be considered a state. The reason this state has not hitherto been recognized as such is largely because of pre-occupation with the largely formal criteria of the "typical" African or "Sudanic" state. That the state was weakened and did not reach full maturation prior to British colonial rule can be attributed in large part to the shift from the trade in slaves to the trade in palm oil and the accentuated competition among the Delta city-states and between the Delta states and the British for control of both the trade and the sources of supply. Still, the position of the Aro seemed relatively strong in the interior to the end of the century, and further historical research may yet reveal greater strength and flexibility and even continued growth there than my analysis has indicated.

My research would indicate that the hypothesis should be modified to acknowledge that along the borders of states or within the interstices of states formally acephalous systems may develop or maintain quite high densities in small areas well in advance of the development of specialized political institutions of their own. Once this modification is made there is rather impressive support for the hypothesis. In short, analysis of the cases in *African Political Systems* and the picture of tropical Africa as a whole (viewed as a general pattern) shows a pronounced general conjunction between state formation and higher population density. In this sense, Africa is brought fully into line with the other continents cursorily surveyed in the Introduction. On the other hand, in the African cases the evidence would seem to indicate that, with the exception of militaristic states of the Zulu-Ngoni type, population density as such was not directly causative of the state formation process. Rather, in far the majority of cases the process involved at least a threeway nexus between developing trade and trade routes, developing political and economic organization, and higher population densities (both nucleations and average densities), all reciprocally interacting and feeding back upon each other.

NOTES

CHAPTER I. Introduction

1. This, of course, would exclude by definition those relativists who see the state as universal and present in some form at all levels of social evolution.

2. Some overlap is to be expected at the boundaries as, for instance, between developed chiefdoms and incipient states. Partially this is due to taxonomic difficulties.

3. It must be noted that the Table of Densities on p. 53 of the same volume shows a marked progression of densities, band-tribe-chiefdom-state with one noteworthy, anomalous exception. Northern Venezuela chiefdoms and Western Chaco hunters and gatherers are both given the same density—1.1 per square mile.

4. Noting that California and the Northwest Coast with smaller political units have higher densities than the Plains, Prairies, or even the East, Driver goes on to observe that the normal relationship is actually reversed in these areas of intermediate density. It is noteworthy that Service (1962:119–53) classifies the Plains societies as Tribes and the Northern California–Northwest Coast groups as Chiefdoms, yielding a sequence parallel to that of Steward and Faron. Driver's difficulties are further compounded by basing Plains political units on the entire tribes periodically assembled for the communal buffalo hunts. The relationship would seem to be more nearly perfect than Driver realized.

5. Sub-Saharan Africa is the single major areal exception.

6. The average rural density for the Tonking Delta is given by Gourou as 1,200 per square mile with densities in excess of 2,500 over wide areas.

7. Gourou notes one exception for Asia, the Igorot of the Philippines, with densities of 180 per square mile.

8. "The section on population-numbers (XI) stands still today as the most widely accepted estimate for the continent north of Mexico, but there are recent studies which indicated that a rather larger Indian population prevailed in California, and that the number for Mexico have been very much underestimated," Robert F. Heizer in the Foreword to the 1963 reprint edition of this work. Even with this underestimation the region of High Culture (states) in Mexico is given as 5 per cent of the continental area containing 70 per cent of the population or a density "fifty-five times as great as the average north of the Rio Grande." (Kroeber 1939:159)

9. The reasons for this are certainly worthy of a study in the sociology of knowledge but are beyond the scope of this paper.

10. "Some general assumptions have been made on the correlation between the development of the political system and population density and modes of subsistence (Fortes and Evans-Pritchard 1940; Lowie 1948; Schapera 1956), but they have not been systematically analyzed or subjected to rigorous examination." (Eisenstadt 1959:204) Note how this appreciation differs from that of Herskovits previously cited.

11. In Krader's consideration, what he calls "net density," i.e., permanent concentration of population in focal points and dispersion in the interstices is a more important index of political centralization than gross average density. Nonetheless, a general relationship is seen with average density as well: "Gross density is only a secondary consideration in political analysis. That is steppe herdsmen have a greater density as an order of magnitude than reindeer breeders (Tungus) or hunters (Ket) of the Siberian forest. If steppe herdsmen have densities of one to five per square km, hunters and reindeer breeders have less than one tenth of that. Concomitantly the political organization of the latter is neither complex nor centralized." (Krader 1955:323–24)

12. The Ottenbergs seem hesitant to join this issue directly. In another passage of the same Introduction they observe that "the variation in Africa's population density has never been fully explained." (1960:17)

13. See the discussion of the use of this term *adaptive* in Harris, 1960.

14. On the other hand, the formal typology and other aspects of *African Political Systems* have received considerable attention,

refinement, and criticism. (Almond and Coleman 1960; Brown 1951; Easton 1959; Eisenstadt 1959; Middleton and Tait 1958; Smith 1956)

15. See Meek (1937), Forde (1950), Green (1947), and Basden (1938).

16. Data from Oceania and, more recently, from fieldwork in New Guinea (Brookfield 1963; Vayda, personal communication) have indicated several cases of high average population density without the concomitant development of specialized or complex political institutions. These cases should receive important mention in addition to the other exceptions I have already noted. I shall not undertake, however, the analysis of cases outside the geographical limits of sub-Saharan Africa. Evidence from several world areas has been utilized in this introduction as background and to demonstrate the status of generalizations concerning the relationship between population density and state formation for those areas. An analysis of the relationship on a global basis is beyond both the scope and intent of this paper. My concern here is solely with an assessment of the evidence from sub-Saharan Africa.

17. Researches by Ember (1963), Harris (1959), Naroll (1956), and Sanders (1962) have given growing theoretical as well as empirical support to the concept of a systematic interrelationship involving feedback between economic productivity, the growth of redistributive centers, population nucleation around these centers, average population density in the areas served, and the development of more complex and specialized political institutions. For Africa, the findings of Meillassoux (1962) as well as the summarized observations of the Fourth International African Seminar of 1961 (Vansina 1964) are important in their indications of a triple relationship between density (both average and nucleations), trade centers, and political organization.

CHAPTER II. Functionalist Demography

1. This general empirical relationship has been noted as holding for nearly 70 African societies coded in the *Ethnographic Atlas.* Furthermore, the Dinka population of 900,000 is small compared to 2.5 million Rundi or 5 million Yoruba. The 5 million Ibo would seem the most convincing case for Doctorow; but as will be demon-

strated in Chapter IX, they are no more an argument for his case here than they are a case for the position of *African Political Systems* concerning population density.

2. But see also Chapter IX where the virtues of these criteria may be seen in its ability to analyze institutional types not conventionally associated with political organization.

3. Logically, there are two opposites: (1) Governmental institutions are found in those societies with the least density, such as BaMbuti Pygmies (0.66 per square mile) (Turnbull, personal communication) or 0.25 Bushmen (Schapera 1956:35) ; or (2) Governmental institutions are *not* found in those societies with the greatest density. The highest rural densities in sub-Saharan Africa are found in Ruanda, an indigenous state, and in southeastern Nigeria, conventionally associated with acephalous political organization. Our analysis of this latter case in Chapter IX will show that it in no way contradicts the proposition that population density and state formation are positively related.

4. The relationship between degree of centralization and population density both in terms of nucleations (capital centers, urbanization) and average density is a somewhat different and more complex question than the question we are arguing here as to a general relationship between population density and state formation and organization. I believe the latter problem must be settled first and the former is beyond the scope of this paper.

5. See Kuczynski. (1948:252)

6. One example of several may be cited in the select bibliography in Fried (1964:190). "More conventional anthropological approaches may be found in Hoebel (1954), Schapera (1956), the now classic *African Political Systems* edited by Fortes and Evans-Pritchard (1940), and the recent paperback by Mair (1962) ."

7. It is to be noted that Krader's careful appraisal is strictly limited to an acceptance of just these six cases. (1955:323, quoted p. 5 above)

8. With the rather inconsistent exception of the Zulu, whose density estimate is for the decade of the 1850s, all of the density figures are for the decade of the 1930s.

9. One has only to read such as the district reports of the period to learn that the densities of the Tallensi and the Logoli (both classified as acephalous) had been decidedly influenced by the presence of colonial state power.

10. Obviously, it is impossible to proceed in depth, case by case, through all African societies.

11. The discussion here is based primarily upon the concepts introduced and explained in Finch, Trewartha, Robinson, and Hammond: *Elements of Geography* (1957).

12. Even here one is forced to use rather arbitrary boundaries (colonial districts, locations, and reserves) which only very roughly and—sometimes not at all—reflect the actual reality of native life.

13. Our survey would indicate that states of the Zulu type are the most important exception to this generalization.

CHAPTER III. Low-Density States I: The Zulu

1. On Christmas Day of 1497 the ships of Da Gama's squadron passed near the site of modern Durban and hence named the area the "Land of the Nativity" or "Natal," a name it has borne to this day.

2. Schapera has noted that the Bantu "tribes" of Natal and Zululand had only a few hundred or thousand members, as compared to some of the Xosa groups with membership of more than ten thousand at certain periods and some of the more important Tswana with memberships averaging between ten and twenty thousand. (1934:5)

3. This is essentially the same as the reconstruction given by Gluckman (1940:25–26, 1958:28–29) except that Gluckman in his earlier account employs the term "patrilineal clans" where Barnes uses "agnatic lineages." And Gluckman includes cattle raids within the early warfare pattern. Both reconstructions are admittedly indebted to Bryant (1929). Both Gluckman and Barnes express high admiration for Bryant's account, terming it "magnificent" and "masterly" respectively.

4. Those students concerned with contemporary economic and ecological theories of chiefdom formation will be interested in the following observation by Shepstone: "Then, as now, the seasons favoured the high lands one year, and the low the next, and interchange of commodities for food went on, as it still continues to do, between inhabitants of the two different classes of country." (1875:192)

5. Zwangendaba moved north again and crossed the Zambesi in

1835. This was the parent group for the Fort Jameson Ngoni studied by Barnes (1954).

6. These events in Bechuanaland have an important bearing on the development of our next topic of analysis, the Ngwato or Bamangwato.

7. All subjects were organized into age groups that cut across kin and local lines. These were placed under rigid discipline from the capital. Special royal villages were established as mobilization centers, and military outposts were set up as positions for attack upon independent nations.

8. Circa 1825, when Shaka was visited by the trading parties of Messrs. Farewell, Fynn, Isaacs, Lt. King and their assistants. Fynn and Isaacs have provided us with our only contemporary eyewitness accounts of Shaka and his court.

9. Bryant points to the distance involved to the nearest European settlements to the south, the fact that Shepstone confuses "white person" in the legend with "white *people*," and that all other indications are that Dingiswayo went north.

10. Gluckman, personal communication.

11. Certainly 15,000 square miles should be the maximum area that could be allowed. At the coast the Tugela River roughly bisects modern Natal (which includes Zululand) but bends sharply to the north as it enters the interior. Standard reference sources differ slightly as to the exact area of Natal—the *Columbia Encylopedia* (Third edition) giving 35,284 square miles while the *Encyclopaedia Britannica* gives 33,578 square miles. Using the figure 15,000 square miles for Zululand, we would get a density of 14.

12. For the use of this phrase by social anthropologists, see Radcliffe-Brown. (1923, 1952:3)

13. There are some further criticisms of the idea of large area of Zulu control or influence which are better reserved until discussing density at the time of Shaka.

14. In any case, Hattersley (1950:13) gives the Tongaat River, some 30 miles south of the Tugela River, as the southern boundary of Zululand in 1824. Depending on how far the area of control extended into the interior, this might add another 3,000 square miles to Zululand. This would probably be compensated by the general depopulation of northern Zululand noted by Gluckman. (1958:32, 36)

15. A shifting referent for density should be noted here. Natal is

equally densely populated but only in occupied areas. The average density for the total area of Natal is much lower than that of Zululand.

16. This would be particularly likely in regiments of village head men.

17. If the figure of 50,000 accepted by Hattersley is used we get (still using a factor of 8) a total population of 400,000 and a density of 40.

18. This pattern was noted by Ferguson for the Zulu and by Barnes for the Ngoni.

19. "Such was the condition of perhaps a million souls in what is now the colony of Natal up to the year of 1812." (1875:193)

20. Bryant's estimates (100,000 for Natal, 78,000 for Zululand), when divided by approximately 25,000 square miles for the former and 10,000 square miles for the latter, yield densities of 4 per square mile and 8 per square mile respectively—a ration of 2–1.

21. One feature of the "cul-de-sac" explanation that has consistently puzzled me is that whereas the freezing of the frontier took place at the line of the Fish River (c. 32° S.) the explosion took place not here but in Zululand (c. 29° S.). It is for this reason that I spent a considerable period of unsuccessful research in the attempt to demonstrate more northern derivation of this phenomenon in terms of trade and acculturation with Delagoa Bay. There may still be instructive clues in this region if one scrutinizes both topographical and vegetation maps. The area of the Mthethwa chiefdom on Bryant's map is close to the point where the coastal plain suddenly narrows and nearly disappears. Although this effect is not so marked on vegetation maps there is nonetheless a narrowing of the "Coastal Forest-Savannah Mosiac" as well as a progressive narrowing of the parallel, somewhat wider, interior and adjacent zone listed as "undifferentiated, relatively dry types." Just to the south of the Mthethwa area and well within the Qwabe region a tongue of the latter zone extends some distance into the interior, penetrating the next zone to the west, the "Temperate and Subtropical Grassland" of higher elevation. (Association pour l'Etude Taxonomique de la Flore d'Afrique, 1959) I would suggest, then, as a fruitful hypothesis for further research that it is not simply a matter of the clash of the Boer and Bantu frontiers along the Fish River, but that what is more important is a consideration of (1) the close proximity of different ecological zones running parallel east to west in the

Zululand area which could be considered to be important in the development of exchanges across zones and the formation of redistributive centers with implications for the development of more centralized political control and (2) the more rapid rise in population density in this more favored coastal region so that both political centralization and population pressure on the land would tend to approach critical thresholds in advance of those on the Fish River frontier. In short, I am suggesting a secondary and largely ecological "cul-de-sac" derivative in part, probably from the stiffening of the Fish River frontier. When to this is added probable tendencies in the direction of attrition among the tribes directly along the Boer-Bantu frontier, including such effects as the smallpox epidemic among the Xosa reported by Lichtenstein (1928), the situation becomes less problematical. I do not consider that this supersedes Gluckman's explanation but rather that it complements and supplements it and is rather intellectually in its debt.

22. This is the same as the Zulu pattern. Ferguson observes of Shaka: "Those that could not escape he plundered and harried unmercifully so that eventually he surrounded his enlarged nation with a wide depopulated tract as a sort of protecting ring-wall." (1918:221)

23. One additional postscript might also be added, though this point will become even clearer in terms of the Ngwato in the next chapter. This is that the simple dichotomy between state and nonstate tends to obscure the considerable difference in development and complexity between groups like the Zulu, the Tswana, and even the Bemba on the one hand and systems like Buganda or Hausa-Fulani on the other. This is not to deny the applicability of the designation "state" to any of these.

CHAPTER IV. Low-Density States II: The Ngwato

1. "Bechuana" is, of course, a corruption of BaTswana.

2. Schapera also noted that "The Proclamations have therefore become binding upon the Ngwato, and Tshekedi has now begun to apply them." (1940:68) In 1950 the Crown exercised its power in a situation that made world headlines. Seretse Khama was relieved of the Bamangwato chiefship and temporarily exiled because of his marriage to a white Englishwoman.

3. Some Tswana settlements *c.* 1813 have been estimated by Stow (Theal 1905:547) to run as high as 30,000 inhabitants. The 10,000 to 15,000 figure would seem to be closer to the norm. This may be compared to a figure of 15,000 for contemporary Cape Town. (Sillery 1952:2) The density of these single large settlements, which comprise in most cases practically the entire tribe, should not be confused with a high *average* population density for the area actually controlled and in use. Modern data exaggerate to the other extreme because of arbitrary boundaries, but Serowe, the Ngwato capital, had a population of 25,000 about 1940 while the population density for the reserve was only 2.5. While Lichtenstein deliberately termed these settlements "towns" in opposition to "villages" there was apparently no greater specialization or division of labor involved than in the dispersed Nguni settlements of the same period.

4. For the mid-nineteenth century, Sillery makes the following observation: "Primarily it was a country of fear. The horror of the Mantatees had passed, but was replaced by the more enduring menace of the Matabele. . . . Then, as now, the people were predominantly cattle breeders, and hunted game with which their country teemed, making notable karosses from skins. The tribal structure was comparatively cohesive and the chiefs were powerful, as is natural in a country much harassed by external enemies, since power is most effective when concentrated. (1952:27–28)

5. This event is mentioned in the Ngwato traditions but not in those of the Kaa.

6. "This hiving off is a recurring phenomenon in Tswana political history and may have been due to some family quarrel, or as one story has it, to a dispute about the leadership of the section, which may also have been a family quarrel." (Sillery 1952:133) The Ngwaketse apparently split from the Kwena in the same general period as the Ngwato. Thus these splits account for the formation of the Kwena, Ngwato, Ngwaketse, and Tawana. Later three smaller but independent tribes entered Bechuanaland—Kgatla, the Lete, and the Tlokwa. The Rolong, of whom only 5,500 live in the Protectorate, is the eighth of the independent tribes but its main affiliations are with the southern Tswana. (Sillery 1952:xi)

7. Matsheng was the son of Kgari's second wife whereas Sekgoma was the son of the third wife.

8. He was backed in this by Tshukudu, his father-in-law, not so

much from Christian proclivities on the part of the latter but because it meant his daughter would have no rivals and hence his own influence would be stronger.

9. For an explicit application of Fried's criteria for the state to the Ngwato and other Tswana see pp. 80–81 below.

10. "Strategic resources are those things which, given the technological base and environmental setting of the culture, maintain subsistence." (Fried 1960:731, n.5)

11. British power in the Protectorate was early made manifest. In 1886 the British compelled arbitration of a boundary dispute between the Ngwato and the Kwena. In 1887 a detachment of Bechuanaland Border Police participated as "observers" in a Ngwato punitive expedition against the Seleka. In 1893 British forces with maxim guns and seven pounders were assisted by the Ngwato in the campaign that finally broke the Matabele power to the north and eliminated Kgama's main foe. In 1895 the entire Protectorate came perilously close to being handed over to Rhodes and the British South Africa Company, and three chiefs, Sebele, Bathoen, and Kgama, traveled to England to plead their cause. The abortive Jameson's Raid in December of that year served to discredit the Company at a crucial moment in these negotiations. (Sillery 1952:65, 78, 123–25)

12. The "negotiations" here were phrased somewhat abruptly. Sillery quotes the Blue Book C. 4588, p. 37 as follows: Sir Charles Warren—'I have been desired by the Queen's Government to give you the following notification. The Queen's Government has established a Protectorate over the part of Bechuanaland and the Kalahari west of the Transvaal, north of the Cape Colony and westward towards Namaqualand.' Sechele—'Has the Chief (i.e. Warren) nothing more to tell us?' Sir Charles Warren—'No.' (Sillery 1952: 56fn. 2)

13. This is a primary function of the state according to Fried. (1960:728)

14. Kgama and his successors grouped these large centers into districts based partly on geographical convenience and partly on an ethnic basis, placing special administrators over these districts.

15. These distinctions are discussed in detail and applied to the pastoral Fulani. (Stenning 1957)

16. I have counted a minimum of eight moves of the Ngwato center during the nineteenth century.

17. "arable land is initially portioned out among the wards, and since each ward receives a special holding for its people, their fields will obviously tend to be close together." (Schapera 1943:128)

18. Schapera's statements on which these projections are based are as follows: "The inhabitants of Mochudi, for instance, plough mostly at Talane, a broad belt commencing about seven miles south of the town, and extending, at an average depth of five to seven miles, for about fifteen miles east and west. They also have many fields at Seleme and Malotwana, between eight and twelve miles away to the north-west. The Molepolole fields lie in a crescent-shaped zone, beginning about twelve miles from the town, and extending around it for about thirty miles, from Mmamorobole in the north-east to Mosinki in the south-west. The Serowe people have most of their fields in some twenty to thirty blocks, radiating out in different directions from the town at distances of five to twenty-two miles, and the people of Kanye plough mainly in about fourteen blocks of the same kind, which are from fifteen to forty miles away from the town." (1943:128) As I have said, to get my initial areas (fields for cultivation) I used the map areas for Mochudi, the radius of 9.5 miles for Molepolole, the radius of 14 miles for Serowe, and the radius of 27 miles for Kanye. Because of the semi-circular nature of the Molepolole holdings, I took half the area of the resulting circle, and for the rest, the entire circle. The populations of these settlements are: Molepolole (14,000), Serowe 25,000), Mochudi (8,500), and Kanye (15,000). (Schapera 1943:24)

19. Ward headmen have the pick of land within the area allocated to the ward. They also occupy the best building sites. They may call out labor to build or repair the *kgotla* (assembly area) or the adjoining cattle *kraal*, but they cannot order tribesmen to do their own private work. Neither is there any recognizable tribute that must be paid to them. (Schapera 1938:92)

CHAPTER V. Low-Density States III: The Bemba

1. This refers to the population density–state formation relationship and to the economy–state relationship noted by Richards.

2. Bemba tradition maintains that Kaffir corn, finger millet, Kaffir beans, cow peas, pumpkins, and the cucumbers called *amankolobwe* were brought by Citi Muluba from the Luba country. Bemba assert that sweet potatoes were introduced by Swahili

traders at the end of the nineteenth century and that they learned to grow cassava from the Bisa.

3. By 1957 emigration of males had increased to an estimated 70 per cent of taxable males. A number of women without men to support them were living on the sale of beer. No viable cash crop had been found for the area, largely because of transport costs. (Richards 1961b:xiii–xiv)

4. As the total population of the Bemba is estimated at not in excess of 150,000 at the time of Richards' 1934 visit, one can get some inkling at least of the scale of these chiefdoms and sub-chiefdoms. That is, compared to such state systems as Hausa-Fulani, Buganda, etc. the Bemba chiefdoms are quite small. Also the time depth of the Bemba state formation process is comparatively shallow, i.e. 150 years or under. (Richards 1940:85–86)

5. Actually, most of the clues to the answer of the riddle can be found in Richards' own accounts. This in itself is a tribute to the general excellence of her work. However, since she wrote the general historical background and economic context of the region is becoming much clearer, thanks to the researches of Cunnison and others. It is important to avail ourselves as far as possible of what is actually known of this history before drawing the inferences which inevitably remain.

6. Citimuluba = Citi the Luban.

7. Interestingly enough, Oliver and Fage have suggested a Luba origin to the Kongo kingdom encountered by the Portuguese. It is noteworthy that the Kwango boundary of the Lunda marked the upper point of Portuguese penetration in Angola through the seventeenth century. (Oliver 1962:125–28)

8. Always the daughter of a former paramount, she did not marry, had her own court, and possessed independent territories for her support.

9. It would be interesting to know to what extent this type of arrangement could be regarded as typical of chiefdoms expanding rather rapidly out along lines of trade. Bemba also entered into similar arrangements with conquered Bisa and others. (Richards 1960:182)

10. Compare Verhulpen, who notes that Mwata Yamvo Naweji sent his relatives Kazembe Matunda, Kazembe ya Kaumba, Mukon-toto, Kazembe Mushidi, and Kazembe Munkinde to conquer and rule over the people to the south and east. It is thought that

Mushidi became the first Citimukulu and Munkinde the first Kazembe of the Lake Mweru region. (1936:152–54)

11. These traditions rather graphically recount how Nkuba and his followers approached various Bwilili ("chiefless" from kwilila "to eat on one's own") "Owners of the Land" with offerings of ivory as tribute. If the answer was "Give me meat, we do not eat ivory," it was decided that the area was a good one for colonization. (Cunnison 1959:38)

12. The Kazembe maintained an interest in Bemba internal politics and upon one occasion at least made his influence effective in the succession. Later the Kazembe received aid from the Mwamba in his struggle with the Yeke, while, reciprocally, Kazembe's aid helped build the Mwamba's power.

13. Compare Sir Harry Johnston: "In Livingstone's day (1867) they do not appear to have been a particularly warlike or aggressive race; but soon after they came under Arab influence and were supplied by the Arabs with guns and gunpowder, and thenceforth took to slave raiding with extraordinary zest." (1897:145) This was Citapankwa whose capital Livingstone visited in 1867. (Waller 1875:152 ff) At this time the previous Citimukulu had died but Citapankwa had not yet been installed.

14. The modern rendering of these names are the Senga, Bisa, Iwa, and Nyamwanga, in that order. (Murdock 1959)

15. In modern times this is the "only place in Bemba area which is big enough and rich enough to stand tribute and to attract a number of people." (Brelsford 1944:22–23)

16. Pirie also reported that considerable numbers of wild, hoofed herbivores were also lost to the epidemic. Surviving domesticates were rapidly consumed except some few reserved for the chiefs, he said. "This accounts for the small number of cattle to be found in the country today." (Pirie 1905:310)

17. Two stations or "bombas" had already been built, one at Ikawa called "Fife" and the other at Nyala called "Fort Hill."

18. This individual is entitled Shimwalule by Brelsford (1944:21) but Wini Maruli by Pirie (1905:143), who also calls the grove Maruli.

19. With all of the emphasis in the literature upon ritual and ideology as prime buttresses of Bemba chieftainship, it should also be remembered that torture, execution, mutilation, and the sale into slavery—in short, the monopolization of the means of terror—

also played an important role. Both the early European accounts and the oral autobiography of Bwenbya (Richards 1963) make this abundantly clear.

20. All of these events—war, civil war, the last rush to meet the demands for slaves, rinderpest, smallpox, sleeping sickness, the loss of important external resources—strongly imply depopulation. There is no confirming empirical evidence of a quantitative demographic nature. In the absence of contradictory evidence, the inference, however, seems clear.

21. This administration lasted until 1924, when the Colonial Office assumed control. (Richards 1940:113)

22. Modern density figures can of course be used as part of an analysis of a collapsed chiefdom, occupying a labor reserve under conditions of colonial indirect rule, but that is a different problem from the one we are investigating.

23. The area of Ireland is 32,408 square miles (*Columbia Encyclopedia,* Third Edition). In another source (1959:164), Richards uses the combined areas of Scotland and Wales. I do not wish to criticize this procedure as such. Richards was not engaged in a demographic survey. These statements are in the way of introductory remarks to a detailed study of the economy or the social structure. As such, "Ireland" or "Scotland and Wales" probably conjures up a more meaningful image to the British reader than does a statement of square miles. It would be helpful, however, if ethnographers would make a practise of supplementing such statements with as precise a determination as possible of actual area, and beyond this to note also such important features as areas of open water, sleeping sickness zones, uninhabitable marsh, area under cultivation, and others.

24. I have thought it advisable to go into some detail in this matter, as too often a reader is given the impression that a density figure carried to one or two decimal places represents something very definite and rather precisely measured.

25. Barnes (1954:103) has criticized Johnston's map, but for the Fort Jameson region further south: "Johnston, in his highly ambitious population density map, appears to have assumed a population of about 50,000, while an official estimate in 1898 was nearly 150,000. . . . Johnston implies, on his map, an inhabited area of 3,200 square miles, but again there is clear evidence that in fact

much of this was uninhabited." In this case at least, Johnston's errors would seem to lie far on the side of underestimation.

26. Richards reports that by 1957 the move toward decentralization had greatly accelerated due to a Government decision to group taxpayers in parishes in which they were free to move. This, in effect, ended the legal fixed minimum of ten taxpaying males per village, and Richards says it is no longer true to say that the average village numbers 30 to 50 huts.

27. The traditional explanation is that the latter chieftainships were created after entering the country.

28. I should like to make clear that whereas I feel that dense, permanent settlement can be an important contributing factor facilitating the development of the state, I do not believe that in and of itself it can be regarded as a sufficient cause.

29. The greater productivity of the Luapula Valley and the expansion of the fishing industry there has led to further population growth and prosperity during the colonial period. (Cunnison 1959)

CHAPTER VI. The Classical Segmentary Societies I:
            The Nuer and the Tallensi

1. The first census, in any real sense of the word, for this area was that undertaken by the Republic of the Sudan in 1955–1956 (Barbour 1961:101–4) and even this involved total enumeration only for the towns. Population for rural areas was calculated by sampling methods. Barbour attests fully to the difficulties faced in the demographic study of the nomadic and semi-nomadic groups in the Republic of the Sudan. (1961:110ff) It should also be remembered that these figures are simple averages obtained by dividing an estimated population by an estimated area. This in itself perforce glosses over the reality of Nuer life, which involves annual transhumance from dispersed wet-season settlements on unflooded ground to large dry-season camps. By way of comparison, it should be noted that under the more pacific conditions of the present, with a nation state over the entire area, an acephalous group similar to the Nuer has attained very high single-season density. This group is the Aweil Dinka. "The astonishingly high density of population of the Aweil Dinka is explained by the fact that for much of the

year the Dinka cattle are able to graze away from the villages on the flood-plains of the local rivers. In the rains they are driven to the limited areas near to the summer cultivations, and there their manure is used to fertilize the soil, which is cultivated very intensively and supports numerous villages. The resultant density of population—almost 100 persons to the square kilometre in the summer—seems very high for the Sudan, though it is nothing like equal to the densities of more than 500 to the square kilometre that are common in parts of south-east Asia." (Barbour 1961:98)

2. This inventory refers of course to the sample of *African Political Systems* alone. Actually there are several other formerly acephalous societies of high present densities which I shall take up in Chapters VIII and IX.

3. The use of density figures based upon colonial administrative districts introduces a certain inevitable distortion. The boundaries are often arbitrary, not conforming to indigenous socio-cultural configurations. Nor are such units alway commensurate. Again, the smaller the unit the more preponderant is the possible influence of such disturbing factors as epidemics, labor migration, game preserves, etc., which obscure rather than clarify the relation between state-formation and population density. This difficulty will be discussed more fully in Chapter VIII.

4. The ethnographic present indicates the time of Fortes' field work, January 1934 to April 1937.

5. This is usually ascribed as being the walled city of Nalerugu, capital of the Mamprusi state.

6. "*Talis* (sing. *Talis*) is used both as a substantive and as an adjective to refer to the 'real' Tallensi, as the natives call them, who live on and around the Tong Hills. They are usually contrasted with the *Namoos* (sing. and adj. *Namoo*) who are also Tallensi but a different section of the population. This nomenclature is artificial, though derived from native speech forms." (Fortes: 1949:2)

7. "Tale standards of wealth are extremely low. Except for a handful of chiefs and headmen—who have herds of cattle numbering from 20 to 50, and in at least one case, apparently over 100, as well as numbers of small stock—and with a dozen sheep, a few goats, and three or four head of cattle is considered to be wealthy (bondaan)." (Fortes 1949:82 fn)

This has drawn from E. R. Leach the comment: ". . . proportionally speaking, the rich men of a capitalist society are always only a handful of the total." (Leach 1950:21–22)

8. "Na'am brings Taleland into the political orbit of the Mamprusi. The prototype and fountain-head of all na'am is the Chief of Mampurugu. To be valid, the mystical attributes which constitute its essence must be ritually vested in the holder by him or by someone endowed with *na'am* by him. Na'am is also an ancestral heritage and therefore most appropriately held by those who belong to the same stock as the Chief of the Mampurugu, i.e. the Namoos. Accordingly, the elector of most Tale . . . Chiefships is one of his sub-chiefs, the Kuna 'aba." (Fortes 1940:251)

9. Actually, from at least the eighteenth century on, this entire region was crisscrossed by trade routes. (Wilks 1962; Barth 1857–1858, IV:556ff; Binger 1892, II; Skinner 1962) Here I stress only the trunk line passing closest to Taleland.

10. Of course the right to vagrant humans had a far different significance in the days of the slave trade.

11. On Rattray's map (1932, II) these were a people further to the west, but this name was also often a generic term applied by Mossi, Mamprusi, and Dagomba to all non-Namoos.

12. "This cleavage is given a symbolic formulation in myths of origin the historicity of which need not concern us." (Fortes 1945:27) It is instructive to compare the Mossi myths of origin in Skinner (1964:7–10) with the Mamprusi myths in Cardinall. (1925:3–9) The accounts are very similar.

CHAPTER VII. The Classical Segmentary Societies II: The Logoli

1. These administrative subdivisions of the North Kavirondo District are called "Chieftaincies" by Wagner. In the official British reports they are referred to as "locations." I will use the latter term as it is less prejudicial to the argument.

2. The table in Wagner (1949:21) gives a figure of 1,137.26 per square mile. In the light of the rather shaky basis of Kavirondo demography at the time, the carrying to two decimal places would seem to connote an exaggerated accuracy.

3. A further word should be said concerning the reliability of the raw statistics. Although Wagner refers to the "census" of 1932

(1940:199; 1949:17), it was really an estimate based upon hut counts, tax figures, and samples. Actual counts were taken in Nairobi and Mombasa only. Nothing approaching a real census was even projected before 1946. (Kuczynski 1948, 2:132–33) The figures are sufficiently accurate for our purposes, and the error is likely to lie on the side of underestimation.

4. Debate concerning this case continues (see Easton 1959:215–17). Though the theoretical points raised by Easton remain unaltered by this result, Radcliffe-Brown's suggestions concerning the facts would seem vindicated by the findings of the 1930 Committee on Native Land Tenure. (Kenya 1931) (See pp. 135–36 and fn 7 infra.)

5. This Report is listed in the bibliography under Kenya Colony and Protectorate 1931, but for economy of citation is referred to above as Kenya 1931. The actual investigations were carried out in 1930.

6. Wagner's accounts are based primarily on the Logoli in the south and the Vugusu in the north.

7. It is interesting to note that the official government sources report a recurrent native complaint to the effect that difficulties encountered in exiling habitual offenders since the establishment of British rule have resulted in the erosion of tribal authority and discipline. In the light of this and the above and in re Radcliffe-Brown's discussion of the legitimacy of "lynch" mobs, it may well be that they were either legitimate "survivals" or, on the other hand ad hoc emergency groups endeavoring to cope with situations formerly handled by legitimate and definitely structured institutions.

8. "The Political Organization of the Bantu of Kavirondo." His monograph is entitled *The Bantu of North Kavirondo,* Vol. I 1949; Vol. II (edited posthumously by L. P. Mair) 1956.

9. A total of 2½ years of field study carried out between 1934 and 1938.

10. "The Vugusu lived in walled villages, the construction and maintenance of which demanded the co-operation of a large number of people, while the Logoli, like most of the other tribes, lived in isolated homesteads that were scattered over the whole countryside." (Wagner 1940:198) "In pre-European days, the Vugusu, Kabras, Tsotso, Marama and Wanga lived in walled and fortified villages." (Wagner 1956:6) Hobley (1902:13) reports that in Kaka-

mega and the southeastern Bantu section the pattern was one of isolated, dispersed homesteads—Ithako, Isukha, Lakoli (Logoli), Mangali, and Tiriki tribes. The Nilotic Luo again lived in villages walled by mud, stone, or euphorbia hedges. Jackson, in 1889, encountered a village with moat and double walls on the south bank of the Yala River, but he does not record the tribe. (1930:220) This may have been a Wanga intrusion in the Nyole-Logoli region. After British pacification and the cessation of intertribal warfare the walled village pattern was generally abandoned and the people moved out in dispersed homesteads.

11. Alternatively rendered: Wanga, Wa-Wanga, Awa-Wanga, Hanga, Bahanga.

12. "These burial customs have been described by K. Dundas (1913, pp. 28–29), but as I have done no fieldwork among the Wanga I cannot expand his account." (Wagner 1949:476 fn 1)

13. Many of the sources use the title "king" while others prefer "chief." I shall use the native term "Nabongo" to refer to the paramount, reserving the term "chief" for district chiefs.

14. Also rendered Sundu or Khyiundu.

15. According to Stam, the Wanga before Shiundu were at war with most of the neighboring tribes and at times were invaded by several at once. On the accession of Shiundu they are described in serious plight, having suffered famine and the loss of many cattle in raids. Further cattle were given in "tribute" to a colony of Masai in their midst in return for the assistance of the latter in warfare. This role of the Masai pastoralists should prove of some interest to students of the Oppenheimer "Conquest Theory" of the origin of the state. This was not an isolated case. There was a Masai settlement in Marama a few miles south of Mumias, another at Nduis about seven miles west, one at Ugema between Kitosh and Elgumi country, and a few odd settlements in Nandi and near the Eldama Ravine. These were Uasin-gishu Masai driven west by the Laikipia Masai and who "resettled among the Kavirondo and Nandi people and hired themselves out as mercenaries in the various intertribal wars." (Hobley 1902:9) They are reported to have amassed considerable livestock as a result.

16. The Europeans named villages after the reigning chiefs.

17. Stam interprets this move by the British as attributable to an erroneous overrating of Mumia's position. That is, he leans toward the view, previously criticized, that the Wanga chiefdom and the

position of the Wahkitsetse (ruling clan) were largely products of British rule.

18. The Kitosh also possessed considerable quantities of firearms, having traded cattle for each gun they could obtain from deserters of the British-led forces. The desertion business was apparently profitable, and Hobley also noted that each chief in the region liked to have a few gunners in his entourage as it "gave them prestige with their rivals." (Hobley 1929:81)

19. The names of these chiefs and the locations over which they were placed are as follows: Mulama—Marama; Katima—Samia; Murunga—N. Kitosh and Wamia; and Were—Waholo. (Stam 1929:147)

20. Although the Anti-Wanga movement seems to have been the major focus for discontent, this entire period was marked by disputes in other locations involving other tribes and chiefs. There was also a general popular demand for a paramount chief, or series of paramounts, in order to gain a greater native voice in the colonial administration.

21. This was neither the earliest nor (until the British penetration) the major route to the interior. Southall cites the roundabout southern route that went south of Lake Victoria from Bagamayo through Unyamwezi and Karagwe as the main track to Buganda, and Buganda tradition recounts that trade goods were coming in via Karagwe by the end of the eighteenth century. More northerly and more direct ones from Mombasa through Mau and Nandi to Kisumu, Kakamega, and Kitosh were in use by at least 1870. Major obstacles to the use of this route were the depredations of the Masai and Nandi. (Southall 1961:163–65) "Nandi" is itself a Swahili word meaning "cormorant." The Nandi's own word for themselves is "Chemwal" which means "to raid" (cattle). (Huntingford 1950)

22. ". . . enormous quantities of flour were brought in for sale, and the cheap rate at which it is obtainable proves that this country produces a very large surplus of food beyond the wants of its population, and being well watered and with rich soil, it is capable of producing very much more, since (along our route at least) there were very large areas as yet unreclaimed." (Lugard, quoted in Hill 1949:42) "At Sakwa's village 25,000 lbs. of flour had been bought and packed in bags made by the porters." (Hill 1949:79) This last refers to a survey party in May, 1892.

23. "The maximum extension of the district from north to south is 64.6 miles and the maximum distance from east to west 64.0 miles, its total area comprising 2,684 square miles." (Wagner 1949:4) This is the modern limit of North Kavirondo. Excluded is Nilotic Central Kavirondo and the area around Kisumu and the Nyando Valley.

24. Itawkho hunters were entitled to receive a bullock.

25. There was no rule of primogeniture, though the successor had to be one of the Nabongo's sons. As the Nabongo had up to eighty wives, this left a large field of contenders. Traditionally the reigning Nabongo conveyed his choice to the Wakhalivu elders during his lifetime. Should they reveal the choice prematurely the chosen successor would automatically die.

26. There may have been some compensations in prestige. Their ideological rank (as opposed to objective position) is not given, but it is noteworthy that they shared with the Wakhalivu and Wachero positions of prestige at royal circumcisions. (Dundas 1913:26,29)

27. Part of Wagner's problem in delineating the political structure and arriving at the political unit would seem to have been that more traditional channels of authority through primogeniture and clan position were often upset by the emergence of "big men" whose status was largely achieved and based upon wealth. This is a rather common phenomenon in contact situations where trade is involved and has also been reported for the late nineteenth-century Kamba and Kikuyu. (Low 163:311–12)

28. Wagner also mentions precontact specialists—iron workers, basketmakers, etc. "From the evidence I have been able to gather it seems that in pre-contact days specialists mainly worked 'to order' (as many of them still do), while the 'wholesale' manufacture of objects and their subsequent marketing seems to have been limited to those areas where a certain amount of intertribal trading had already developed, e.g. along the main caravan route to Uganda which crossed the district from east to west. . . ." (Wagner 1956:161)

29. As the area "under control" was given as 3,000 square miles, this would give an average density of 67 per square mile.

30. Capital village of Nabongo Shiundu, referred to in other sources as Sundu's, Sundus, Shiundus.

31. Even after the construction of the direct rail line to Uganda,

Kisumu continued to hold importance as one of the major inter-mittent landing stations on the Cairo-Capetown air route. The gold strike in Kakamega and the "steady economic progress of the native reserves in the three Kavirondo Districts have given its development new vigorous impulse." (Wagner 1949:7)

32. The outstanding reliability of rainfall in Bunyole resulted in its chief's being regarded as the major rainmaker of the entire district. Tribute was rendered to him on a tribal scale by the Logoli, in return for his services. (Wagner 1949:211) The Wanga also availed themselves of his services. (Hobley 1902:349–50)

33. Fried (1960) has distinguished between conditions of pristine state formation, where the state arises *sui generis* (such as the hydraulic states of Mesopotamia, Peru, etc.) and secondary state formation which is stimulated by trade or acculturation with already existent states. In the context of trade, most African states would be considered "secondary states" but not in the sense of ongoing acculturation as such.

34. Compare Wagner: "As the result of a variety of influences (agricultural instruction, taxation, the opening up of the District by roads and railways, the organization of marketing facilities, the creation of new wants that can only be satisfied by means of money, &c.) Africans now produce a steadily increasing quantity of cash crops. . . . The production of these extra crops was made possible partly by increasing the acreage under cultivation (in 1932 esti-mated at 77.45% of all arable land in the southern locations) and partly by improving the quality of the produce and the yield per acre (1956:93).

CHAPTER VIII. State Formation and the Population Pattern

1. The figure for the Ngwato in Table I is my own estimate based upon a projection backward from current land-use patterns allowing for differences in the aboriginal pattern as well as possible environmental differences as explained in Chapter IV. The figure for the Zulu is my projection from higher and more recent density figures (Schapera 1956:35, *Columbia Encyclopedia*) in order to bring the Zulu more realistically into alignment with the 1930 time horizon used for the others.

2. I should hasten to point out that the single inclusion of the Ibo of southeastern Nigeria would upset the neatness of this

sequence as surely as the inclusion of Ankole and Nupe would upset the neatness of the sample in *African Political Systems*. The Ibo are conventionally classified as acephalous but maintain densities quite commensurate with those of Ruanda-Urundi over nearly commensurate areas. My reasons for not including Ibo here will become clear in Chapter IX, wherein I challenge the validity of the acephalous or stateless label.

3. Actually, as I have shown on page 16, this statement is limited to the threefold relationship between size of population, density of population, and high centralization in the political sphere. Given the total context of the paragraph the implications mentioned above would still seem to have force.

4. Trewartha (1954a) contains a bibliography of statistical sources, maps and studies as of that time. Barbour (1961) contains an excellent series of articles of more recent vintage by a group of specialists, and a map (66–67) showing the extent of postwar population mapping. Porter (1966) has constructed a distribution map (scale 1:2,000,000) together with detailed tables of areas, total population, and density for administrative subdivisions in the East African nations of Kenya, Uganda, and Tanzania. Allan (1965), while utilizing somewhat earlier census materials, contains much important comparative material and analysis of population distributions in relation to resources and agricultural systems.

5. It should be noted that within this excluded area we have also discussed Bechuanaland in some detail and have dealt at least briefly with the Nuer and Aweil Dinka of the Sudan.

6. I have altered their order of presentation but not the substance of their divisions. Also I have revised the names of former colonies to conform to the names of the new independent nations.

7. Boahen (1962) has noted the effect of this upon the size of Timbuctu.

8. This corresponds to the analysis of the comparison between Ruanda-Urundi and Bunyore-Maragoli on pp. 161–62 above.

9. This is partly because of admnistrative segregation of Alur. (Southall 1953:267)

10. To illustrate this principle let us take the extreme and hypothetical example of two societies each with densities of 10 per square mile. (A) is only 100 square miles in area and (B) is 100,000 square miles in area. This gives (A) a population of 1,000 and (B) a population of 1,000,000. Now, if an immigration stream of 1,000 is

introduced into each, the population density of (A) becomes doubled, while the density of (B) rises to only 10.01.

11. Murdock also notes that Mwata Yamvo reduced the Chokwe, Luchazi, Luvale, Mbangala, Ndembu, and Yaka tribes to vassalage during the seventeenth century and that the Yaka, in turn, had "destroyed" the Kongo in 1569. The Portuguese and the slave trade probably played an even greater role in the dismemberment of Kongo.

12. Murdock further lists complex social stratification, including universal slavery, and the prominent role of intergroup trade and regular markets with conventional media of exchange (cowrie shells, salt, raffia cloth, brass rods, iron bars) as distinctive characteristics of this region. (1959:296)

13. "It can be accepted as certain that the spearhead, and indeed more than the spearhead, of the early southward immigrations crossed the Somerset Nile, between Lake Albert and Lake Kyoga, into the southern or Bantu-speaking half of Uganda. There they settled in considerable strength, adopting the Bantu speech of the country, while their leaders, having ousted the previous rulers, founded a number of related Bito dynasties, some of which survive to this day, including, notably, those of Bunyoro and Buganda. It is from the genealogical evidence of these dynasties that the arrival of the first Lwo can be roughly dated, for a large number of distinct and collateral lines show between eighteen and twenty generations from the foundation of these dynasties to the present day. At even twenty-five years to the generation, this is a period which must extend to the very beginning of the sixteenth century and is likely to have started a little earlier still." (Oliver 1963:172) These same traditions also indicate the pre-existence of states in the region. Bunyoro traditions, for example, indicate two previous dynasties, the Tembuzi and the Chwezi. (Beattie 1960:13)

14. The phrase "arbitrary pattern" refers to Kimble's directly preceding analysis of the influence of such factors as climate, soil, topography, rainfall, sleeping sickness or other disease, in which he concludes that "over large sections man's presence, or absence, is more readily accounted for in cultural and historical terms than in physical ones." (Kimble 1960, 1:103) For West Africa he notes military patterns and slave raiding and the different policies of the colonial powers as important, then—"History and politics, between them, have probably had an even bigger hand in the making of the

population map of Central Africa." (1:104) In terms of cultural regularities, the twin and related processes of developing trade and state formation could be substituted for historical and cultural factors.

15. The alternative would seem to be to insist that the population pattern of this area has been too disrupted by these conditions to be usable. This would then throw us back on our analysis of the other major areas.

16. The major concentration in the Shire Highlands of southern Nyasaland is especially noteworthy since it appears that despite its excellent resources, the area began to attract population only after European planters began its development during the twentieth century. (Trewartha 1954a:143)

17. Floyd (1962:566) has reported that as of 1958 an African population numbering 2,550,000 had 41,950,000 acres of land for agrarian settlement while 207,000 Europeans had almost 48,000,000 acres.

18. The reader may legitimately inquire why the data in this chapter was not more systematically ordered. An attempt was made, in fact, to establish a statistical correlation by testing against some 75 sub-Saharan societies published by Murdock and his associates in the *Ethnographic Atlas*. (Ethnology 1962–1964) The results of this test, however, were inconclusive. It should be pointed out that there are special difficulties encountered in the use of this cross-cultural sample for density comparisons which are quite apart from and in addition to other criticisms that might be or have been directed against the sample. The atlas itself provides neither density nor areal information. Total population figures are given in the majority but by no means all of the instances; but, unfortunately, these totals are from time periods ranging from 1890 down to the present. It was only possible to obtain anything approximating reliable areas, total populations, and average densities on some 64 cases. I endeavored as far as possible to obtain these figures within a decade (plus or minus) of 1950, but in some cases monographic or census sources which could be used to estimate tribal areas or population were only available for the 1930s or even the 1920s. Furthermore, areas of the sample societies varied over a rather wide range. The range extends all the way from Gure, a single village, through Amba (164 square miles) up to the 55,000 square miles of Bambara. This often meant that nucleation peaks were being

compared to broad averages. Several cases in the two classes of lower political integration were among those discussed in this chapter— i.e. Kikuyu, Amba, Luo, Chagga; whereas a third of those in the category of highest political complexity were of the Zulu type or region—i.e. Zulu, Swazi, Pondo, Sotho. Some four cases were doubly classified as nonstate and also as formerly part of a state; and at least one, the Tallensi, should be reclassified.

CHAPTER IX. High Density and State Formation in
Southeastern Nigeria: The Ibo Problem

1. This case was not specifically cited by Fortes and Evans-Pritchard, although it is likely that it is one they had in mind when they expressed confidence that data from other African societies would strongly support their position. (Fortes 1940:8)

2. Leonard's estimate of between 5 and 6 million Ibo (1906:31) must be regarded as excessively high, as it closely matches current figures—5 million (Ottenberg 1959:130), 5.5 million (*Columbia Encyclopedia*, Third Edition 1963:999). Leonard's estimate can reasonably be taken qualitatively as reflecting the impression of a man closely acquainted with a region that contained a dense population at the turn of the century.

3. Something like this, nonetheless, would seem to be the implication of Ottenberg's statement quoted above.

4. This gives a rather different impression of the overall relationship between local groups than that conveyed by an earlier article by Ottenberg on the important political and economic utilization of oracles for regional domination of the trade routes and important markets. (Ottenberg 1958) This is discussed at length below.

5. This classification has been adopted by works of standard reference. The *Columbia Encyclopedia*, Third Edition, carries the statement: "Originally divided into a large number of autonomous villages, the Ibo had little of tribal unity before the British occupation." (p. 999)

6. The society is described as a "nonstate organization in which both unilineal descent and association groupings play strong roles in government" and leadership, both traditional and emerging is described as "not simple, not strictly hierarchical or centralized" and largely based on rather informally cast political roles." (Ottenberg 1961:218)

7. Points (1) and (2) are obviously related, and, if our hypotheses

concerning the relationship of population density and state formation are as true of the Ibo as they are of other societies, then
explanations of (1), (2), and (4) should reinforce each other. Udo
has quite recently argued that the dispersed settlement pattern is a
breakdown from the nucleated form under conditions of peace on
the one hand and high density on the other. (Udo 1965) Finally,
the pronounced development of trade and class stratification which
seems true of Ibo society from the days of the slave trade onwards
would seem to encourage such personality patterns as aggressiveness,
the desire to get ahead, as well as receptivity to change.

8. Strictly speaking, the senior male member of the extended
family, lineage segment, or lineage as the case may be. Meek rather
confusingly applies the term "kindred" to what are clearly patrilineages and lineage segments.

9. Green (1947:4) has termed this the "search for 'natural
rulers'." Green also expresses the double-sided nature of the then-
current research. "The social anthropologist has the problem of dis-
covering how, with so little, apparently, in the way of authority or
of familiar forms, public business gets done. And in the search a
number of interesting social devices appear. The Government
official has to ask himself how indigenous institutions can not only
be found and defined but also adapted to the task of indirect rule."
(1947:3)

10. Meek does not specify here the types of offenses, but a listing
of those noted by other authorities affords further evidence of the
degree to which Ibo society had developed away from a typical
tribal situation. For the region around Bende, Harris has noted
such offenses as chronic adultery, failure to return bridewealth
of a divorced woman, theft (particularly theft from the father)
where the thief refused to return the stolen goods, and sale, rental,
or alienation of communal land without the consent of the land-
owning group. (1942b) Market rules tended to be quite stringent
and were stringently enforced. Fights resulting in death or failure
to accept the standard currency were regarded as capital offenses.
(Dike 1956:42–43)

11. The hiring of mercenaries brought these local "big men" into
dependence upon the Aro (see page 296) who controlled the
mercenaries.

12. This is a type of summation which is apparently designed to
confound all classifiers.

13. It is well to consider in this connection M. G. Smith's conten-

tion that power itself and hence politics is inherently segmentary. (1956)

14. Ottenberg has performed a valuable service by bringing together much of the rather fragmentary information concerning the Aro organization in the article cited. (1958:295–317) What follows in my account here is largely based upon material in that article, with other sources as cited below.

15. The same source indicates that Aro Chuku was founded after a successful revolt of Ibo slaves against Ibibio masters in which Akpa mercenaries were involved. A cosmopolitan origin would be indicated by the following: "Of the present patrilineages in Aro Chuku, six claim to be of Akpa, five of Ada Ibo, three of Amaseri Ibo, two of Ibibio and three of other regions." (Forde 1950:56)

16. According to De Cardi (1899) the "sacrifices" were actually staged illusions and the alleged victims were in fact sold as slaves. De Cardi actually interviewed several such sacrificial victims who could never return to their own villages as they were very much believed to be dead.

17. It is noteworthy that the Aro restricted their trading and major political endeavors to the interior and did not attempt to compete for control of the creeks and rivers leading to the Delta coast, nor for control of the traffic along such major arteries as the Cross or Niger rivers. Here the large canoe fleets of the Delta and river city-states such as Bonny, Calabar, or Aboh retained an interlocking control.

18. Horton (1954:311–12) observes just this process among the Nike group, whom he characterizes as "northern agents of the Aro." "From a study of past trading arrangements in this area it seems probable that one of the major determinants of the enormous number of slaves in Ibo-land before the advent of the British administration was the close juxtaposition of areas of exhausted, barren land with areas of great agricultural fertility; in such cases an exchange of men for yams was the quickest method of securing a more equitable distribution both of population and of food."

19. Forde (1937, 1938) describes this process for the Yakö, a non-Ibo group on the eastern side of the Cross River. The Yakö were coming increasingly under the influence of the palm-oil trade when Forde was there in 1935.

20. In relation to the later elaboration of the trade in foodstuffs, Jones notes: "The bulk of the protein imported by the hinterland

was in the form of smoke-dried fish from the delta, which also originally provided most of their salt. The bulk foodstuffs which fed the delta came from the food-producing areas most accessible to the delta and remote from the over-populated areas. Those closer to the over-populated areas exported food to those areas." (Jones 1963:14)

21. But compare Armstrong (1955:82–83), who claims Fulani raided all the way into the Delta. The following remark by Dike is pertinent to the problem of density and its antiquity: "The density of population which was and still is a main feature of the Ibo country was due in part at least to this accession of new blood from the west and north. The Ibos might be, as has often been asserted, a prolific race, but there can be little doubt that the migrants from the seventeenth century onwards added not a little to the existing population and occupied lands the original tribe could ill afford to lose." (1956:28) Here it should be noted that population inputs from the north were compensated in part at least by the outputs into the export slave trade, and what was increased pressure on the land from the standpoint of the subsistence farmer was increased supply of potential slaves for the Aro.

22. Talbot reported a similar process among the Kalabari (the Coastal City-State known to the Europeans as New Calabar). "Since the stoppage of the slave trade the Kalabari have devoted themselves almost exclusively to fishing and trading. By means of colonies, placed in the upper reaches of the rivers, they control the greater part of the inland trade and act as middlemen between European merchants and Ibo producers. In this they are greatly helped by their almost entire control of the fishing grounds; for dried fish here, as throughout West Africa, is one of the most highly prized articles of food. (Talbot 1932:9)

23. The possibility of the resurgence of a hinterland power is not to be ruled out. Indeed, the Aro, although allegedly having declined from their earlier position, were still a potent factor in the hinterland, and Leonard (1898) reported that at that time they were still strong enough to blockade the major roads and temporarily stop much of the trade with the British. This same account of Leonard's journey up to Bende to negotiate with the Aro reveals, on the other hand, a number of cleavages and dissident factions within the Aro network.

24. As an added observation, it would seem that in general this rather sizeable development of trade through an entire region

tended to foster the development of oligarchic states (Meek and Dike both call them "republics") rather than centralized monarchies on the model of Dahomey. Aro was ruled by an aristocratic council and the Title Societies in the Onitsha and other regions seem to follow the same principle. In Old Calabar the wealthy traders ruled through the Ekpe society, a combined chamber of commerce, city council, and fraternal and ritual organization (secret society). Bonny, which began as a monarchy, was transformed into a constitutional monarchy by British intervention, although indigenous tendencies were also present, reducing the relative strength of the crown; and G. I. Jones has observed of the New Calabar state after its move to the northern Delta fringe: "The Kalabari state had assumed its modern form, its king reduced to a nonentity, its government an oligarchy of chiefs, the heads of houses who had brought their war canoes from Elem Kalabari [New Calabar]. (Jones 1963:155)

BIBLIOGRAPHY

* Abraham, D. P. (1964). Ethno-history of the empire of Mutapa. Problems and methods. In *The historian in tropical Africa*. J. Vansina, R. Maury, and L. V. Thomas, eds. London: Oxford University Press.

Adams, Capt. John (1801). *Sketches taken during ten voyages to Africa between the years 1786 and 1800*. London: Hurst, Robinson and Co.

Alexandre, P., and J. Binet (1958). Le groupe dit Pahouin. *Monographies ethnologiques africaines*. L'Institut International Africain. Paris: Presses Universitaires de France.

* Allan, William (1949). *Studies in African land usage in Northern Rhodesia*. Rhodes-Livingstone Papers No. 15. London: Oxford University Press.

——— (1965). *The African Husbandman*. New York: Barnes and Noble.

Allen, Capt. Wm., and Dr. T. R. H. Thomson (1848). *A narrative of the expedition sent by Her Majesty's government to the River Niger in 1841 under the command of Capt. H. D. Trotter*. 2 vols. London: Richard Bentley.

* Almond, Gabriel A., and James S. Coleman, eds. (1960). *The politics of the developing areas*. Princeton: Princeton University Press.

* Alsop, M. H. (1952). *The population of Natal*. Natal Regional Survey 2. London: Oxford University Press.

Anene, J. C. (1956). The Protectorate Government of Southern Nigeria and the Aros, 1900–1902. *Journal of the Historical Society of Nigeria* 1:20–26.

* Apter, David E. (1961). *The political kingdom in Uganda, a*

* Works cited.

study in bureaucratic nationalism. Princeton: Princeton University Press.

Ardener, E. W. (1954). The kinship terminology of a group of southern Ibo. *Africa* 24:85–99.

* Armillas, Pedro (1961). Land use in pre-Columbian America. In *A history of land use in arid regions.* L. Dudley Stamp, ed. Paris: UNESCO.

* Armstrong, Robert G. (1955). The Igala. In *Peoples of the Niger-Benue confluence.* Daryll Forde, Paula Brown, and Robert G. Armstrong. Ethnographic Survey of Africa. London: International African Institute.

* Arnold, Rosemary (1957). A port of trade: Wyhdah on the Guinea Coast. In *Trade and market in the early empires.* Karl Polanyi, Conrad Arensberg, and Harry Pearson, eds. Glencoe: The Free Press.

* Association pour l'Etude Taxonomique de la Flore d'Afrique Tropicale, L' (1959). *Vegetation map of Africa* (with explanatory text by R. W. J. Keay). London: Oxford University Press.

* Baker, S. J. K. (1937). The distribution of native population over East Africa. *Africa* 10:37–54.

* Barbour, K. M. (1961). *The Republic of the Sudan, a regional geography.* London: University of London Press.

* Barbour, K. M., and R. M. Prothero, eds. (1961). *Essays on African population.* London: Routledge and Kegan Paul.

* Barnes, J. A. (1954). *Politics in a changing society: a political history of the Fort Jameson Ngoni.* Cape Town: Oxford University Press.

* Barrow, John (1806). *A voyage to Cochinchina in the years 1792 and 1793 . . . to which is annexed an account of a journey made in the years 1801 and 1802 to the residence of the chief of the Booshuana Nation.* London: T. Cadell and Davies.

* Barth, Heinrich (1857–1858). *Travels and discoveries in North and Central Africa (Journal of expedition 1849–55).* 2nd ed. London: Longmans, Brown, Green, Longmans and Roberts.

* Bartholomew, G. A., and Joseph B. Birdsell (1954). Ecology and the protohominids. *American Anthropologist* 55:481–98.

Bascom, W. (1948). West Africa and the complexity of primitive culture. *American Anthropologist* 50:18–22.

* Bascom, William R., and Melville J. Herskovits, eds. (1959).

Continuity and change in African cultures. Chicago: University of Chicago Press.

* Basden, G. T. (1938). *Niger Ibos.* London: Seeley Service.

Bates, Marston (1955). *The prevalence of people.* New York: Scribners.

Baxter, P. T. W., and Audrey Butt (1953). *The Azande, and related peoples of the Anglo-Egyptian Sudan and Belgian Congo.* Ethnographic Survey of Africa. London: International African Institute.

Beachey, R. W. (1962). Arms trade in East Africa in the late 19th century. *Journal of African History* 3:451–67.

* Beattie, John (1960). *Bunyoro, an African kingdom.* New York: Holt, Rinehart and Winston.

Becker, Peter (1962). *Path of blood. The rise and conquests of Mzilikazi, founder of the Matabele tribe of Southern Africa.* London: Longmans, Green and Co.

Beemer, Hilda (1937). The development of the military organization in Swaziland. *Africa* 10:55–74, 176–205.

Benson, Mary (1960). *Tshekedi Khama.* London: Faber and Faber.

Biebuyck, Daniel, ed. (1963). *African agrarian systems.* London: Oxford University Press.

Bindloss, Harold (1898). *In the Niger country.* Edinburgh and London: Wm. Blackwood and Sons.

* Binger, Lt. Gustave (1892). *Du Niger au Golfe de Guinée, 1887–1889.* 2 vols. Paris: Librairie Hachette et Cie.

* Boahen, A. Adu (1962). Caravan trade in the nineteenth century. *Journal of African History* 3:349–59.

* Boateng, E. A. (1960). *A geography of Ghana.* Cambridge: Cambridge University Press.

* Bohannan, Laura (1958). Political aspects of Tiv social organization. In *Tribes without rulers.* John Middleton and David Tait, eds. London: Routledge and Kegan Paul.

Bohannan, Paul (1954). The migration and expansion of the Tiv. *Africa* 24:2–16.

—— (1964). *Africa and Africans.* Garden City: The Natural History Press.

* Bohannan, Paul, and George Dalton, eds. (1962). *Markets in Africa.* Northwestern University African Studies 9. Evanston: Northwestern University Press.

Boissevain, Ethel, ed. (1962). Anthropology and Africa today. *Annals of the New York Academy of Sciences* 96:491–680.

Bosman, Wm. (1705). *A new and accurate description of the coast of Guinea*. London: James Knapton.

Boston, J. S. (1960). Notes on contact between the Igala and the Ibo. *Journal of the Nigerian Historical Society* 2:52–58.

* Bourret, F. M. (1952). *The Gold Coast*. Stanford: Stanford University Press.

——— (1960). *Ghana: the road to independence, 1919–1957*. Stanford: Stanford University Press.

Boxer, C. R. (1963). *Race relations in the Portuguese colonial empire, 1415–1825*. Oxford: Clarendon Press.

Boxer, C. R., ed. and trans. (1959). *Tragic history of the sea: 1589, 1593, 1622*. (Translations of Portuguese accounts of shipwrecks on south-east coast of Africa.) Hakluyt Society. Cambridge: Cambridge University Press.

Bradbury, R. E. (1957). *The Benin kingdom and the Edo-speaking peoples of South-western Nigeria*. Ethnographic Survey of Africa. London: International African Institute.

Braidwood, Robert J., and Gordon Willey, eds. (1962). *Courses toward urban life*. Chicago: Aldine Publishing Co.

Brantz, Mayer (1854). *Captain Canot; or twenty years of an African slaver*. New York: D. Appleton Co.

* Brelsford, W. V. (1944). *Aspects of Bemba chieftainship*. Livingstone; Rhodes-Livingstone Institute Communications 2.

Brookes, Edgar H., and N. Hurwitz (1957). *The native reserves of Natal*. Natal Regional Survey 7. Cape Town: Oxford University Press.

* Brookfield, H. C., and Paula Brown (1963). *Struggle for land: agriculture and group territories among the Chimbu of the New Guinea highlands*. London: Oxford University Press.

Brooks, Henry (1876). *Natal; a history and description of the colony*. London: L. Reeve and Co.

Brown, G. Gordon (1932). Bridewealth among the Hehe. *Africa* 5:145–58.

* Brown, Paula (1951). Patterns of authority in West Africa. *Africa* 21:261–78.

Bruk, S. E., and V. S. Apyenchyenko (1964). *Atlas Naradov mira*. Moscow: Soviet Academy of Sciences.

* Bryant, Rev. A. T. (1929). *Olden times in Zululand and Natal.* London: Longmans, Green and Co.

Buchanan, Keith (1953). The northern region of Nigeria: the geographical background of its political duality. *Geographical Review* 43:451–73.

* Buchanan, K. M., and J. C. Pugh (1958). *Land and people in Nigeria: the human geography of Nigeria and its environmental background.* London: University of London Press.

Buell, Raymond Leslie (1928). *The native problem in Africa.* New York: Macmillan Co.

Burton, Richard F. (1864). *A mission to Gelele, king of Dahome.* 2 vols. London: Tinsley Bros.

—— (1961). *The lake regions of Central Africa.* 2 vols. New York: Horizon Press.

Burton, Richard F. (translator and annotator) (1873). *The lands of Cazembe.* London: Royal Geographical Society.

Butt, Audrey (1952). *The Nilotes of the Anglo-Egyptian Sudan and Uganda.* Ethnographic Survey of Africa. London: International African Institute.

* Buxton, M. Aline (1927). *Kenya days.* London: Edward Arnold and Co.

* Cardinall, A. W. (1925). *Natives of the Northern Territories of the Gold Coast.* London: George Routledge.

* —— (1932). *The Gold Coast, 1931.* Accra: Government Printer.

Central African Statistical Office (1951). *Report on the demographic sample survey of the African population of Southern Rhodesia* (1948). Salisbury.

* —— (1952). *Report on the 1950 demographic survey sample of the African population of Northern Rhodesia.* Salisbury.

* —— (1959). *The 1953–1955 demographic sample survey of the indigenous African population of Southern Rhodesia.* Salisbury.

* Childe, V. Gordon (1936). *Man makes himself.* London: Watts and Co.

* —— (1942). *What happened in history.* Middlesex: Penguin.

Childs, Gladwyn Murray (1949). *Umbundu kinship and character.* London: Oxford University Press.

* Church, R. J. Harrison (1961). *West Africa: a study of the environment and of man's use of it.* 3rd ed. London: Longmans, Green and Co.

Cipolla, Carlo (1962). *The economic history of world population.* Baltimore: Penguin.

* Colson, Elizabeth, and Max Gluckman, eds. (1959). *Seven tribes of British Central Africa.* Manchester: Manchester University Press.

* *Columbia Encyclopedia* (1963). 3rd ed. New York: Columbia University Press.

Coontz, Sydney H. (1961). *Population theories and the economic interpretation.* London: Routledge and Kegan Paul.

* Cory, H. (1953). *Sukuma law and custom.* London: Oxford University Press.

Cottrell, Fred (1955). *Energy and society.* New York: McGraw-Hill.

Coulborn, Rushton, ed. (1959). *Feudalism in history.* Princeton: Princeton University Press.

Cowan, Alex A. (1935). Early trading conditions in the Bight of Biafra. *Journal of the Royal African Society* 24:37.

* Coxhead, J. C. C. (1914). *The native tribes of north-eastern Rhodesia: their laws and customs.* Royal Anthropological Institute Occasional Papers No. 5.

Crow, Capt. Hugh (1830). *Memoirs of the late Captain Hugh Crow, of Liverpool.* London: Longmans, Rees, Orme, Brown and Green.

Cunnison, Ian (1951). *History on the Luapula.* Rhodes-Livingstone Papers 21. London: Oxford University Press.

* ——— (1959). *The Luapula peoples of Northern Rhodesia: custom and history in tribal politics.* Manchester: Manchester University Press.

——— (1960). Review of *Historical notes on the Bisa tribe of Northern Rhodesia.* (F. M. Thomas, Rhodes-Livingstone Communication 8, Lusaka, 1958). *Journal of African History* 1:339.

——— (1961). Kazembe and the Portuguese, 1798–1832. *Journal of African History* 2:61–76.

Czekanowski, J. (1924). *Forschungen im Nil-Kongo-Zwischengebeit* 2:257–81. Leipzig.

* D'Azevado, Warren (1962). Some historical problems in the delineation of a Central West Atlantic region. (Anthropology and Africa today.) *Annals of the New York Academy of Sciences* 96:512–38.

* De Cardi, M. le Comte C. N. (1899). A short description of the natives of the Niger Coast Protectorate with some account of their customs, religion, trade, etc. In *West African Studies.* Mary H. Kingsley. London: Macmillan and Co.

De Cleene, N. (1937). La structure de la société Yombe. *Bulletin Séances Institut Royal Colonial Belge* 8:44–51.

———— (1957). *Introduction à l'ethnographie du Congo Belge et du Rwanda-Burundi.* 2ième ed. Anvers: Editions de Sikkel, S. A.

De Kiewiet, C. W. (1941). *A history of South Africa, social and economic.* London: Oxford University Press.

Denham, Edward B. (1926). *Tours in the native reserves and native development in Kenya.* London: His Majesty's Stationery Office.

De Schlippe, Pierre (1956). *Shifting cultivation in Africa. The Zande system of agriculture.* London: Routledge and Kegan Paul.

Deshler, Walter (1963). Cattle in Africa: distribution, types and problems. *Geographical Review* 53:52–58.

* Dike, K. Onwuka (1956). *Trade and politics in the Niger Delta, 1830–1885.* Oxford: Clarendon Press.

Dilley, Marjorie Ruth (1937). *British policy in Kenya Colony.* New York: Thomas Nelson and Sons.

Dixey, F. (1928). The distribution of population in Nyasaland. *Geographical Review* 18:274–90.

* Doctorow, O. (1963). Group structure and authority. *American Anthropologist* 65:312–22.

Dorjahn, Vernon R. (1959). The factor of polygyny in African demography. In *Continuity and change in African culture.* W. R. Bascom and Melville Herskovits, eds. Chicago: University of Chicago Press.

Douglass, Arthur (1881). *Ostrich farming in South Africa.* London: Cassell, Petter, Galpin and Co.

Driberg, J. H. (1923). *The Lango, a Nilotic tribe of Uganda.* London: T. Fisher Unwin.

* Driver, Harold (1961). *Indians of North America.* Chicago: University of Chicago Press.

* Duffy, James (1959). *Portuguese Africa.* Cambridge: Harvard University Press.

* Dundas, Kenneth R. (1913). The Wawanga and other tribes of the Elgon District, British East Africa. *Journal of the Royal Anthropological Institute* 43:19–75.

East African High Commission. East African Statistical Department (1950a). African population of Kenya Colony and Protectorate. *Geographical and tribal studies.* Nairobi.

* —— (1950b). African population of Tanganyika Territory. *Geographical and tribal studies.* Nairobi.

* —— (1950c). African population of Uganda Protectorate. *Geographical and tribal studies.* Nairobi.

* Easton, David (1959). Political anthropology. In *Biennial Review of Anthropology 1959.* Bernard J. Siegel, ed. Stanford: Stanford University Press.

Egharevba, Jacob (1953). *A short history of Benin.* Ibadan: Ibadan University Press.

Eisenstadt, S. N. (1954). African age groups, a comparative study. *Africa* 24:100–112.

—— (1956). *From generation to generation.* Glencoe: The Free Press.

* —— (1959). Primitive political systems: a preliminary analysis. *American Anthropologist* 61:200–220.

* Ember, Melvin (1963). The relationship between economic and political development in nonindustrialized societies. *Ethnology* 2:228–48.

* Encyclopaedia Britannica (1963). Encyclopaedia Britannica. A new survey of universal knowledge. Chicago.

* Evans-Pritchard, E. E. (1940a). *The Nuer.* Oxford: Clarendon Press.

—— (1940b). The Nuer of the Southern Sudan. In *African political systems.* Meyer Fortes and E. E. Evans-Pritchard, eds. London: Oxford University Press.

—— (1940c). The political structure of the Nandi-speaking peoples of Kenya. *Africa* 13:250.

—— (1940d). *The political system of the Anuak of the Anglo-Egyptian Sudan.* Monographs on Social Anthropology 4. London: London School of Economics.

—— (1948). *The divine kingship of the Shilluk of the Nilotic Sudan.* The Frazier Lecture 1948. Cambridge: Cambridge University Press.

* Fage, J. D. (1959). *Ghana, a historical interpretation*. Madison: University of Wisconsin Press.

———— (1961). Anthropology, botany, and the history of Africa. *Journal of African History* 2:299–309.

* ———— (1962). *An introduction to the history of West Africa*. 3rd ed. Cambridge: Cambridge University Press.

Fair, T. J. D. (1955). *The distribution of population in Natal*. Natal Regional Survey 3. London: Oxford University Press.

* Fallers, Margaret Chave (1960). *The Eastern Lacustrine Bantu*. Ethnographic Survey of Africa. London: International African Institute.

Fawcett, C. B. (1935). Population maps, a discussion. *Geographic Journal* 85:142–59.

* Ferguson, W. S. (1918). *The Zulus and the Spartans: a comparison of their military systems*. Varia Africana II, Harvard African Studies II. Cambridge: Harvard University Press.

* Finch, Vernor C., Glenn T. Trewartha, et al. (1957). *Elements of geography*. New York: McGraw-Hill.

Firth, Raymond (1951). Review of *Web of kinship among the Tallensi* (Meyer Fortes, London, Oxford University Press, 1949). *Africa* 21:155–59.

* Fitzgerald, Walter (1942). *Africa: a social, economic and political geography of its major regions*. London: Methuen and Co. (1st ed., 1934).

* Floyd, Barry (1962). Land apportionment in Southern Rhodesia. *Geographical Review* 52:566–82.

Forbes, Robert (1933). The black man's industries. *Geographical Review* 23:230–47.

* Forde, Daryll (1937). Land and labor in a Cross River village. *Geographical Journal* 90:24–51.

* ———— (1938). Fission and accretion in the patrilineal clans of a semi-Bantu community in Southern Nigeria. *Journal of the Royal Anthropological Institute* 68:311–38.

———— (1947). The anthropological approach to social science. *The Advancement of Science* 4:213–24.

———— (1951). *The Yoruba-speaking peoples of Southwestern Nigeria*. Ethnographic Survey of Africa. London: International African Institute.

* ———— (1964). *Yakö studies*. London: Oxford University Press.

Forde, Daryll, and Richenda Scott (1945). *The native economies of Nigeria.* M. Perham, ed. Vol. 1. London: Faber and Faber.

* Forde, Daryll, and G. I. Jones (1950). *The Ibo and Ibibio-speaking peoples of Southeastern Nigeria.* Ethnographic Survey of Africa. London: International African Institute.

* Forde, Daryll, Paula Brown, and Robert G. Armstrong (1955). *Peoples of the Niger-Benue confluence.* Ethnographic Survey of Africa. London: International African Institute.

Forde, Daryll, ed. (1954). *African worlds.* London: Oxford University Press.

———— (1956). *Efik traders of Old Calabar.* London: Oxford University Press.

* Fortes, Meyer (1940). The political system of the Tallensi of the northern territories of the Gold Coast. In *African political systems.* London: Oxford University Press.

* ———— (1945). *The dynamics of clanship among the Tallensi.* London: Oxford University Press.

* ———— (1949). *The web of kinship among the Tallensi.* London: Oxford University Press.

* Fortes, M., and E. E. Evans-Pritchard, eds. (1940). *African political systems.* London: Oxford University Press.

Frantz, C. (1958). Review of *Government and politics in tribal society.* (I. Schapera, London, Watts, 1956). *American Anthropologist* 60:182.

Freeman-Grenville, G. S. P. (1963). The coast, 1498–1840. In *History of East Africa,* Vol. 1. Roland Oliver and Gervase Mathew, eds. Oxford: Clarendon Press.

* Fried, Morton H. (1957). The classification of corporate unilineal descent groups. *Journal of the Royal Anthropological Institute* 87:1–29.

* ———— (1960). On the evolution of social stratification and the state. In *Culture in history: essays in honor of Paul Radin.* Stanley Diamond, ed. New York: Columbia University Press.

* ———— (1964). Anthropology and the study of politics. In *Horizons of anthropology.* Sol Tax, ed. Chicago: Aldine Publishing Co.

Fuller, Charles Edward (1959). Ethnohistory in the study of culture change in southeast Africa. In *Continuity and change in African cultures.* W. R. Bascom and Melville J. Herskovits, eds. Chicago: University of Chicago Press.

Gabatshwane, S. M. (1957). *Introduction to the Bechuanaland Protectorate history and administration.* Kanye: S. M. Gabatshwane.

* Gamitto, Major A. C. P. (1854). *O Muata Cazembe e os povos Maraves, Chévas, Muembas, Lundas e outros da Africa Austral.* Lisbon: Imprensa Nacional.

* Gann, Lewis (1954). *The end of the slave trade in British Central Africa, 1889–1912.* Rhodes-Livingstone Journal 16 (Human Problems in British Central Africa) :27–51.

Gann, L. H. (1958). *The birth of a plural society: the development of Northern Rhodesia under the British South Africa Company, 1894–1914.* Manchester: Manchester University Press.

———— (1964). *A history of Northern Rhodesia: early days to 1953.* London: Chatto and Windus.

Gelfand, Michael (1961). *Northern Rhodesia in the days of the charter.* Oxford: Basil Blackwell.

* Gibson, J. Y. (1903). *The story of the Zulus.* Pietermaritzburg: P. Davis and Sons.

Gillman, Clement (1927). Southwest Tanganyika. *Geographical Journal* 69:97–131.

———— (1936). Population map of the Tanganyika territory (1: 3,000,000 with explanatory text). *Geographical Review* 26: 353–75.

———— (1949). A vegetation-types map of Tanganyika territory (1:2,000,000 with explanatory text). *Geographical Review* 39: 7–37.

* Giraud, Victor (1890). *Les lacs de l'Afrique Equatoriale, voyage d'exploration éxecuté de 1883 à 1885.* Paris: Librairie Hachette et Cie.

Girling, F. K. (1960). The Acholi of Uganda. *Colonial Research Studies.* London: Her Majesty's Stationery Office.

* Gluckman, Max (1940). The kingdom of the Zulu of South Africa. In *African political systems.* Meyer Fortes and E. E. Evans-Pritchard, eds. London: Oxford University Press.

———— (1941). *The economy of the central Barotse Plain.* Rhodes-Livingstone Papers 7. London: Oxford University Press.

———— (1943). *Essays on Lozi land and royal property.* Rhodes-Livingstone Papers 10. London: Oxford University Press.

———— (1954). *Succession and civil war among the Bemba: an*

exercise in anthropological theory. The Rhodes-Livingstone Journal 16. Manchester: Manchester University Press.

* Gluckman, Max (1958). *Analysis of a social situation in modern Zululand.* Rhodes-Livingstone Papers 28. Manchester: Manchester University Press.

Goodwin, A. J. H. (1937). Habitat. In *The Bantu-speaking tribes of South Africa.* I. Schapera, ed. London: Routledge and Kegan Paul.

Goody, Jack (1962). *Death, property and the ancestors.* Stanford: Stanford University Press.

* Gouldsbury, Cullen, and Hubert Sheane (1911). *The great plateau of Northern Rhodesia.* London: Edward Arnold.

Gourou, Pierre (1947). Geographie du peuplement en Nigeria méridionale. *Bulletin de la Société Belge d'Etudes Géographiques* 42:58–64.

———— (1953). *La densité de la population au Ruanda-Urundi; esquisse d'une étude géographique.* Appended map, "Densité de la population au Ruanda-Urundi, 1:750,000." Institut Royal Colonial Belge, Section des Sciences Naturelles et Médicales. Mémoires, Tome 21. fasc. 6. Brussels.

* ———— (1961). *The tropical world.* 3rd ed. London: Longmans, Green and Co.

Great Britain—Parliament (1933). *Parliamentary debates, official report, fifth series,* Vol. 86. Second session of the 36th Parliament of the United Kingdom of Great Britain and Northern Ireland. London: His Majesty's Stationery Office.

Green, M. (1941). *Ibo land tenure.* London School of Economics, Monographs in Social Anthropology 6. London: P. Lund Humphrey.

* ———— (1947). *Ibo village affairs.* London: Sidgwick and Jackson.

Greenberg, J. (1949). The Negro kingdoms of the Sudan. *New York Academy of Sciences,* Series 2, 11:126–35.

* Gulliver, Pamela, and P. H. Gulliver (1953). *The Central Nilo-Hamites.* Ethnographic Survey of Africa. London: International African Institute.

Gulliver, P. H. (1955). A history of the Songea Ngoni. *Tanganyika Notes and Records* 41:16–30.

* ———— (1958). *Land tenure and social change among the Nyakyusa.* East African Studies 11. East African Institute of Social Research. Kampala: Uganda.

———— (1960). *The population of Arusha Chiefdom.* Rhodes-Livingstone Journal 28. Manchester: Manchester University Press.

* ———— (1962). The evolution of Arusha trade. In *Markets in Africa.* Paul Bohannan and George Dalton, eds. Evanston: Northwestern University Press.

Gunn, Harold D. (1956). *Pagan peoples of the central area of Northern Nigeria.* Ethnographic Survey of Africa. London: International African Institute.

Gunn, Harold D., and F. P. Conant (1960). *Peoples of the middle Niger region, Northern Nigeria.* Ethnographic Survey of Africa. London: International African Institute.

Hahn, C. H. L. (1928). The Ovambo. In *The native tribes of South West Africa.* Cape Town: Cape Times, Ltd.

* Hambly, Wilfred Dyson (1940). Review of *African political systems* (Meyer Fortes and E. E. Evans-Pritchard, eds., London, Oxford University Press, 1940). American Sociological Review 5:796–98.

* Hance, William A. (1964). *The geography of modern Africa.* New York: Columbia University Press.

Hancock, W. K. (1942). *Survey of British Commonwealth Affairs.* Vol. 2, part 2. Royal Institute of International Affairs. London: Oxford University Press.

Hanna, A. J. (1956). *The beginnings of Nyasaland and North-eastern Rhodesia, 1859–95.* Oxford: Clarendon Press.

———— (1960). *The story of the Rhodesias and Nyasaland.* London: Faber and Faber.

Harris, Jack S. (1942a). Human relationship to the land in Southern Nigeria. *Rural Sociology* 7:89–92.

* ———— (1942b). Some aspects of slavery in Southeastern Nigeria. *Journal of Negro History* 28:37–54.

———— (1943). Papers on the economic aspect of life among the Ozuitem Ibo. *Africa* 14:12–23.

* Harris, Marvin (1959). The economy has no surplus? *American Anthropologist* 61:185–99.

* ———— (1960). Adaptation in biological and cultural science. *Transactions of the New York Academy of Sciences,* new series 2. 23:59–65.

Harris, Rosemary (1962). The influence of ecological factors and external relations on the Mbembe tribes of South-east Nigeria. *Africa,* 32:38–52.

* Hattersley, Alan F. (1950). *The British settlement of Natal: a study in imperial migration*. Cambridge: Cambridge University Press.

* Herrman, Louis, ed. (1936). *Travels and adventures in Eastern Africa. Nathaniel Isaacs*. Vol. 1. Cape Town: The Van Riebeeck Society.

* Herskovits, Melville J. (1938). *Dahomey, an ancient West African Kingdom*. 2 vols. New York: J. J. Augustin.

* —— (1941). Review of *African political systems* (Meyer Fortes and E. E. Evans-Pritchard, eds., London, Oxford University Press, 1940). *American Anthropologist* 43:465–67.

—— (1962). *The human factor in changing Africa*. New York: Alfred A. Knopf.

* Hill, M. F. (1949). *Permanent way, the story of the Kenya and Uganda railway*. Nairobi: East African Railways and Harbours.

Hilton, T. E. (1960). *Ghana population atlas*. Edinburgh: T. Nelson.

Hinderling, P. (1955). Versuch einer analyse der sozialen struktur der Matakam. *Africa* 25:405–26.

* Hobley, C. W. (1898). Kavirondo. *The Geographical Journal* Vol. 12.

* —— (1902). *Eastern Uganda: an ethnological survey*. Royal Anthropological Institute Occasional Papers, 1.

—— (1903). British East Africa: anthropological studies in Kavirondo and Nandi. *Journal of the Royal Anthropological Institute*, Vol. 33.

* —— (1929). *Kenya, from chartered company to Crown Colony. Thirty years of exploration and administration in British East Africa*. London: H. F. and G. Witherby.

Hodgkin, Thomas, ed. (1960). *Nigerian perspectives: an historical anthology*. London: Oxford University Press.

Hollis, A. C. (1905). *The Masai*. London: Oxford University Press.

* Horton, W. R. G. (1954). The Ohu system of slavery in a northern Ibo village-group. *Africa* 24:311–35.

Houis, Maurice (1953). *La Guinée Française*. Pays Africains 3. Collection publiée sous la direction de Georges Spitz, Gouverneur Honoraire des Colonies. Paris: Editions Maritimes et Coloniales.

Howard, C., ed. (1951). *West African explorers*. London: Oxford University Press.

Hoyle, B. S. (1963). The economic expansion of Jinja, Uganda. *Geographical Review* 53:377–88.

Hubbard, Rev. John Waddington (1948). *The Sobo of the Niger Delta.* Zaria: Gaskiya Corporation.

* Hughes, A. J. B. (1956). *Kin, caste and nation among the Rhodesian Ndebele.* Rhodes-Livingstone Papers 25. Manchester: Manchester University Press.

* Humphrey, Norman (1947). *The Liguru and the land: sociological aspects of some agricultural problems of North Kavirondo.* Nairobi: Government Printer.

Hunter, Monica (1961). *Reaction to conquest: effects of contact with Europeans on the Pondo of South Africa.* 2nd ed. London: Oxford University Press.

Huntingford, G. W. B. (1930). Tribal names in the Nyanza and Kerio Provinces, Kenya Colony. *Man,* Vol. 96.

* ——— (1950). *Nandi work and culture.* Colonial Research Studies 4. London: His Majesty's Stationery Office.

——— (1953a). *The Northern Nilo-Hamites.* Ethnographic Survey of Africa. London: International African Institute.

——— (1953b). *The Southern Nilo-Hamites.* Ethnographic Survey of Africa. London: International African Institute.

——— (1953c). *The Nandi of Kenya; tribal control in a pastoral society.* London: Routledge and Kegan Paul.

Hurault, J. (1962). La structure sociale des Bamiléké. Ecole Pratique des Hautes-Etudes. *Le Monde d'Outre-Mer Passé et Présent,* deuxième série. Paris: Mouton et Co.

Huxley, Elspeth, and Margery Perham (1956). *Race and politics in Kenya.* 2nd rev. ed. London: Faber and Faber.

Ingham, Kenneth (1962). *A history of East Africa.* London: Longmans, Green and Co.

* Jackson, Sir Frederick (1930). *Early days in East Africa.* London: Edward Arnold and Co.

Jarrett, H. Reginald (1948). Population and settlement in Gambia. *Geographical Review* 38:633–36.

Jaspan, M. A. (1953). *The Ila-Tonga peoples of Northwestern Rhodesia.* Ethnographic Survey of Africa. London: International African Institute.

Jeffreys, M. D. W. (1935). The divine Umundri king. *Africa* 8:346–53.

* Jennings, J. H. (1957). A population distribution-map of the eastern region of Nigeria. *Geographical Journal* 123:416–17.

Johnston, Bruce F. (1958). *The staple food economies of Western Tropical Africa.* Stanford: Stanford University Press.

* Johnston, Sir Harry H. (1897). *British Central Africa. An attempt to give some account of a portion of the territories under British influence north of the Zambezi.* London: Methuen and Co.

* ———— (1902). *The Uganda Protectorate.* Vol. 1. New York: Dodd, Mead and Co.

Jones, G. I. (1939). Who are the Aro? *Nigerian Field,* Vol. 8.

———— (1949). Ibo land tenure. *Africa* 19:309–23.

———— (1958). Native and trade currencies in Southern Nigeria during the Eighteenth and Nineteenth Centuries. *Africa* 28:43–54.

———— (1961). Ecology and social structure among the North Eastern Ibo. *Africa* 31:117–34.

* ———— (1963). *The trading states of the oil rivers.* London: Oxford University Press.

Joshi, N. R., E. A. McLaughlin, and Ralph W. Phillips (1957). *Types and breeds of African cattle.* FAO Agricultural Studies No. 37. Rome: Food and Agricultural Organization.

Junod, Henri Alexander (1914). The conditions of the natives of South Africa in the 16th century: report to the South African Association for the Advancement of Science. *South African Journal of Science,* Vol. 10.

Kaberry, Phyllis (1957). Primitive states. *British Journal of Sociology* 8:224–34.

Kagwa, Apolo (1934). *The customs of the Baganda* (translated by Ernest B. Kalibala). New York: Columbia University Press.

Kenya, African Affairs Department (1939/45–53). *Report.* Nairobi: Government Printer.

* Kenya Colony and Protectorate (1927–1934). *Native Affairs Department Annual Reports (NADAR).* Nairobi: Government Printer.

* ———— (1930). *Report of the Agricultural Commission, October 1929.* Nairobi: Government Printer.

* ———— (1931). *Report of the Committee on Native Land Tenure in the North Kavirondo District, October 1930.* Nairobi: Government Printer.

Kenya Land Commission (1934). *Report of the Kenya Land Commission, September 1933.* London: His Majesty's Stationery Office.

Kenyatta, Jomo (1962). *Facing Mount Kenya*. New York: Random House.

Kilson, Martin L., Jr. (1955). Land and the Kikuyu: a study of the relationship between land and the Kikuyu political movements. *The Journal of Negro History* 40:103–53.

* Kimble, George H. T. (1960). *Tropical Africa*. 2 vols. New York: The Twentieth Century Fund, Inc.

Kingsley, Mary H. (1899). *West African studies*. London: Macmillan and Co.

Kirchhoff, Paul (1955). The principles of clanship in human society. In *Readings in anthropology*, Vol. II. Morton H. Fried, ed. New York: Thomas Y. Crowell Company.

* Kitchen, Helen (1964). *A Handbook of African Affairs*. The African-Amercian Institute. New York: Frederick Praeger.

* Krader, Lawrence (1955). Ecology of Central Asian pastoralism. *Southwestern Journal of Anthropology* 11:301–25.

Kraeling, Carl H., and Robert M. Adams, eds. (1960). *City invincible*. Chicago: University of Chicago Press.

* Krige, Eileen Jensen (1936). *The social system of the Zulus*. 3rd ed. Pietermaritzburg: Shuter and Shooter.

Krige, Eileen Jensen, and J. D. Krige (1943). *The realm of the Rain Queen*. London: Oxford University Press.

Kroeber, A. L. (1923). *Anthropology*. New York: Harcourt Brace and Co.

* ――― (1939). *Cultural and natural areas of native North America*. University of California Publications in American Archaeology and Ethnology No. 38.

* Kuczynski, R. R. (1948). *Demographic survey of the British colonial empire*. Vol. 1, *West Africa*. Vol. 2, *East Africa*. Royal Institute of International Affairs. London: Oxford University Press.

* Kuper, Hilda (1947). *An African aristocracy: rank among the Swazi*. London: Oxford University Press.

――― (1952). *The Swazi*. Ethnographic Survey of Africa. London: International African Institute.

Kuper, Hilda, A. J. B. Hughes, and J. van Velsen (1955). *The Shona and Ndebele of Southern Rhodesia*. Ethnographic Survey of Africa. London: International African Institute.

Kuper, Hilda (1963). *The Swazi: a South African kingdom*. New York: Holt, Rinehart and Winston.

Labouret, Henri (1941). *Paysans d'Afrique Occidentale.* Paris: Librairie Gallimard.

—— (1958). *Nouvelles notes sur les tribus du rameau Lobi.* Mémoires de l'Institut Français d'Afrique Noire No. 54.

* —— (1962). *Africa before the white man.* New York: Walker and Co. (First published in 1946 as *L'Afrique précoloniale,* Presses Universitaires de France.)

Lambert, H. E. (1956). *Kikuyu social and political institutions.* London: Oxford University Press.

Lander, Richard, and John Lander (1832). *Journal of an expedition to explore the course and termination of the Niger.* 2 vols. New York: J. and J. Harper.

* Leach, E. R. (1950). Review of *The web of kinship among the Tallensi* (Meyer Fortes, London: Oxford University Press, 1949). *Man,* Vol. 50.

Lebon, J. H. G. (1956). Recent contributions to the geography of the Sudan. *Geographical Review* 46:246–52.

Leith-Ross, S. (1937). Notes on the Osu System among the Ibo of Owerri Province, Nigeria. *Africa* 10:207–20.

Lembezat, Bertrand (1961). *Les Populations païennes du Nord-Cameroun et de l'Adamaoua.* Monographies Ethnologiques Africaines publiées sous le patronage de l'Institut International Africain. Paris: Presses Universitaires de France.

* Leonard, A. G. (1898). Notes of a journey to Bende. *Journal of the Manchester Geographical Society* 14:190–207.

* —— (1906). *The lower Niger and its tribes.* London: Macmillan and Co.

Leys, Norman (1925). *Kenya.* 2nd ed. London: Hogarth Press.

* Lichtenstein, Henry (1928). *Travels in Southern Africa in the years 1803, 1804, and 1806.* (A reprint of the translation from the original German by Anne Plumptre.) Cape Town: Van Riebeeck Society. Vol. 2.

Light, Richard, and Mary Upjohn (1938). Contrasts in African farming: aerial views from the Cape to Cairo. *Geographical Review* 28:529–53.

Little, K. L. (1951). *The Mende of Sierra Leone: a West African people in transition.* London: Routledge and Kegan Paul.

Lorimer, Frank (1961). *Demographic information on tropical Africa.* Boston: Boston University Press.

Lorimer, Frank, and Mark Karp, eds. (1960). *Population in Af-*

rica: report of a seminar held at Boston University. Boston: Boston University Press.

* Low, D. A. (1963). The northern interior, 1840–1884. In *History of East Africa,* Vol. 1. Roland Oliver and Gervase Mathew, eds. Oxford: Clarendon Press.

* Lowie, Robert H. (1948). *Social organization.* New York: Rinehart and Co.

McArthur, Norma (1961). *Introducing population statistics.* London: Oxford University Press.

McCulloch, Merran (1951). *The Southern Lunda and related peoples.* Ethnographic Survey of Africa. London: International African Institute.

———— (1952). *The Ovimbundu of Angola.* Ethnographic Survey of Africa. London: International African Institute.

McCulloch, Merran, M. Littlewood, and I. Dugast (1954). *Peoples of the Central Cameroons.* Ethnographic Survey of Africa. London: International African Institute.

Mabogunje, Akin (1962). The growth of residential districts in Ibadan. *Geographical Review* 52:56–77.

MacDonald, J. R. L. (1900). Notes on the ethnology of tribes met with during progress of the Juba Expedition of 1897–1899. *Journal of the Royal Anthropological Institute* 29:226–50.

* Mair, Lucy (1962). *Primitive government.* Baltimore: Penguin Books.

Malcolm, D. W. (1953). *Sukumaland: an African people and their country.* London: Oxford University Press.

* Manoukian, Madeline (1952). *Tribes of the Northern Territories of the Gold Coast.* Ethnographic Survey of Africa. London: International African Institute.

Martin, C. J. (1954). Some estimates of the general age distribution, fertility and rate of natural increase of the African population of British East Africa. *Population Studies* 7:181–99.

Mayer, Philip (1949). *The lineage principle in Gusii society.* International African Institute Memorandum No. 24. London: Oxford University Press.

* Meek, C. K. (1937). *Law and authority in a Nigerian tribe: a study in indirect rule.* London: Oxford University Press.

* ———— (1941). Review of *African political systems* (Meyer Fortes and E. E. Evans-Pritchard, eds., London: Oxford University Press, 1940). *Man* (March–April): 41–42.

* Meillassoux, Claude (1962). Social and economic factors affecting markets in Guro Land. In *Markets in Africa*. Paul Bohannan and George Dalton, eds. Evanston: Northwestern University Press.

Middleton, John (1953). *The Kikuyu and Kamba of Kenya*. Ethnographic Survey of Africa. London: International African Institute.

———— (1958). The political system of the Lugbara of the Nile-Congo divide. In *Tribes without rulers*. John Middleton and David Tait, eds. London: Routledge and Kegan Paul.

* Middleton, John, and David Tait, eds. (1958). *Tribes without rulers: studies in African segmentary systems*. London: Routledge and Kegan Paul.

Mitchell, J. C. (1951). *The Yao village*. Manchester: Manchester University Press.

Mitchell, J. C., and J. A. Barnes (1950). *The Lamba village: report of a social survey*. Communications from the School of African Studies (New Series) No. 24. Cape Town: University of Cape Town.

Moçambique. Repartição de Estatística (1953). *Recenseamento geral da população em 1950*. Vol. 1. População civilizada. Vol. 3. População não civilizada. Lourenço Marques: Imprensa Nacional de Moçambique.

Mockford, Julian (1931). *Khama: king of the Bamangwato*. London: Jonathan Cape.

———— (1950). *Seretse Khama*. London: Staples Press.

Morgan, W. B. (1955a). Farming practice, settlement pattern and population density in Southeastern Nigeria. *Geographical Journal* 121:320–33.

———— (1955b). The Nigerian oil palm industry. *The Scottish Geographical Magazine* 71:174–77.

———— (1957). Some comments on shifting cultivation in Africa. *Research notes, Department of Geography* 9:1–10. Ibadan: University College.

———— (1959). Agriculture in Southern Nigeria. *Economic Geography* 35:138–50.

Mumford, W. B. (1934). The Hehe-Bena-Sangu peoples. *American Anthropologist* 36:203–22.

* Murdock, George Peter (1951). British social anthropology. *American Anthropologist* 53:465–73.

* ———— (1958). African Summaries, HRAF Press.

* ———— (1959). *Africa: its people and their culture history.* New York: McGraw-Hill.

* Murdock, George Peter, ed. (1962–1964). Ethnographic atlas. *Ethnology* 1–3.

Nadel, S. F. (1935). Nupe state and community. *Africa* 8:257–303.

———— (1942). *A black Byzantium.* London: Oxford University Press.

———— (1947). *The Nuba: an anthropological study of the hill tribes in Kordofan.* London: Oxford University Press.

* ———— (1951). *The foundations of social anthropology.* Glencoe: The Free Press.

* Naroll, Raoul (1956). Preliminary index of social development. *American Anthropologist* 58:687–713.

* New, Charles (1873). *Life, wanderings and labours in Eastern Africa.* London: Hodder and Stoughton.

Nigeria. Department of Statistics. (1951). *Population census of Lagos, 1950.* Lagos: Government Printer.

———— (1952). *Population census of the Northern Region of Nigeria, 1952.* Lagos: Census Superintendent.

———— (1953). *Population census of the Eastern Region of Nigeria. 1953.* Lagos: Census Superintendent.

———— (1956). *Population census of the Western Region of Nigeria, 1952.* Lagos: Census Superintendent.

Niven, C. R. (1935). Some Nigerian population problems. *Geographical Journal* 85:54–58.

Notcutt, H. Clement, ed. (1935). *Selections from Travels in Southern Africa,* by William J. Burchell. London: Oxford University Press.

Oliver, Captain Pasfield, ed. (1890). *Madagascar; or Robert Drury's journal, during fifteen years' captivity on that island.* London: T. F. Unwin.

Oliver, Roland (1955). The traditional histories of Buganda, Bunyoro and Ankole. *Journal of the Royal Anthropological Institute* 85:111–17.

* Oliver, Roland, and Gervase Mathew (1963). *History of East Africa,* Vol. 1. London: Oxford University Press.

* Oliver, Roland, and J. D. Fage (1962). *A short history of Africa.* Baltimore: Penguin Books.

Ottenberg, Phoebe V. (1959). The changing economic position of women among the Afikpo Ibo. In *Continuity and change in African cultures.* William R. Bascom and Melville J. Herskovits, eds. Chicago: University of Chicago Press.

* Ottenberg, Simon (1958). Ibo oracles and intergroup relations. *Southwestern Journal of Anthropology* 14:295–317.

* ———— (1959). Ibo receptivity to change. In *Continuity and change in African cultures.* William R. Bascom and Melville J. Herskovits, eds. Chicago: University of Chicago Press.

* ———— (1961). The present state of Ibo studies. *Journal of the Historical Society of Nigeria* 2:211–30.

Ottenberg, Simon, and Phoebe Ottenberg (1962). Afikpo markets, 1900–1960. In *Markets in Africa.* Paul Bohannan and George Dalton, eds. Evanston: Northwestern University Press.

* Ottenberg, Simon, and Phoebe Ottenberg, eds. (1960). *Cultures and societies of Africa.* New York: Random House.

Palerm, Angel, Eric R. Wolf, et al. (1957). *Studies in human ecology.* Social Science Monographs No. 3. Washington, D.C.: Anthropological Society of Washington and the Pan-American Union.

Palmer, H. R. (1908). The Kano chronicle. *Journal of the Royal Anthropological Institute* 38:58–98.

Paques, Viviana (1954). *Les Bambara.* Monographies ethnologiques africaines. L'Institut International Africain. Paris: Presses Universitaires de France.

Parkinson, John (1907). A note on the Efik and Ekoi tribes of the Eastern Province of Southern Nigeria, W. C. A. *Journal of the Royal Anthropological Institute* 37:261–67.

Patridge, Charles (1905). *Cross River natives.* London: Hutchinson and Co.

Paulme, Denise (1954). *Les gens du riz, Kissi de Haute Guinée Française.* Paris: Librairie Plon.

Perham, Margery (1937). *Native administration in Nigeria.* London: Oxford University Press. (Reprinted 1962.)

* Perham, Margery, ed. (1959). *The diaries of Lord Lugard.* London: Faber and Faber.

* Pim, A. W., and S. Milligan (1938). *Report of the commission appointed to enquire into the financial and economic position of Northern Rhodesia.* Issued by the Colonial Office (Great Britain). London: His Majesty's Stationery Office.

Pineau, H. (1949). *Mgr. Dupont, evêque-roi des brigands.* 3rd ed. Quebec: Les Pères Blancs.

* Pirie, George (1905–1906). North-eastern Rhodesia, its people and products. *Journal of the African Society,* Vol. 5, part 1 (October) 1905, part 2 (July) 1906.

* Polanyi, Karl, Conrad M. Arensberg, and Harry W. Pearson, eds. (1957). *Trade and market in the early empires. Economics in history and theory.* Glencoe: The Free Press.

Porter, Philip W. East Africa—population distribution as of August 1962. Map supplement number 6. *Annals of the Association of American Geographers,* Vol. 56 no. 1 March 1966.

Prescott, J. R. V. (1959). Nigeria's regional boundary problems. *Geographical Review* 49:485–505.

* ———— (1962). Population distribution in Southern Rhodesia, *Geographical Review* 52:559–65.

* Prins, A. H. J. (1953). *East African age-class systems: an inquiry into the social order of the Galla, Kipsigis, and Kikuyu.* Djakarta: J. B. Wolters.

* Prothero, R. Mansell (1955). The population of Eastern Nigeria. *The Scottish Geographical Magazine* 71:165–70.

*———— (1956). The population census of Northern Nigeria 1952: problems and results. *Population Studies* 10:166–73.

———— (1960a). Problems of population mapping in underdeveloped territory. *Nigerian Geographic Journal* 3:1–7.

* Purseglove, J. W. (1951a). Resettlement in Kigezi, Uganda. *Journal of African Administration* 3:13–21.

———— (1951b). *A survey of shifting cultivation in the Western Province.* Uganda Government Agricultural Department Report.

Quesnes, J. S. (1823). *Memoires du Capitaine Landolphe contenant l'histoire de ses voyages pendant trente-six ans, aux côtes d'Afrique et aux deux Amériques.* Tomes premier et second. Paris: Betrand.

Quiggin, A. H. (1950). *Trade routes, trade and currency in East Africa.* Rhodes-Livingstone Museum Occasional Papers 5:3–16.

* Radcliffe-Brown, A. R. (1923). The methods of ethnology and social anthropology. *South African Journal of Science* 20:124–47. Reprinted in *Method in social anthropology.* M. N. Srinivas, ed. Chicago: The University of Chicago Press. 1958.

* Radcliffe-Brown, A. R. (1952). *Structure and function in primitive society*. Glencoe: The Free Press.

Rattray, J. M. (1960). *The grass cover of Africa* (including color foldmap 1:10,000,000). FAO Agricultural Studies No. 49. Rome: Food and Agricultural Organization.

* Rattray, R. S. (1932). *The tribes of the Ashanti hinterland*. 2 vols. Oxford: The Clarendon Press.

Richards, Audrey I. (1932). *Hunger and work in a savage tribe*. London: George Routledge and Sons.

——— (1940a). *Bemba marriage and modern economic conditions*. Rhodes-Livingstone Institute Papers No. 4.

* ——— (1940b). The political system of the Bemba tribe—Northeastern Rhodesia. In *African political systems*. Meyer Fortes and E. E. Evans-Pritchard, eds. London: Oxford University Press.

——— (1952). *Economic development and tribal change—a study of immigrant labour in Buganda*. The East African Institute of Social Research. Cambridge: W. Heffer.

* Richards, Audrey I. (1959). The Bemba of North-eastern Rhodesia. In *Seven tribes of British Central Africa*. E. Colson and Max Gluckman, eds. Manchester: Manchester University Press.

* ——— (1960). Social mechanisms for the transfer of political rights in some African tribes. *Journal of the Royal Anthropological Institute* 90:175–90.

* ——— (1961a). African kings and their royal relatives. *Journal of the Royal Anthropological Institute* 91:135–50.

* ——— (1961b). *Land, labour and diet in Northern Rhodesia*. London: Oxford University Press.

* Richards, Audrey I. (recorder) (1963). The story of Bwembya of the Bemba Tribe, Northern Rhodesia. In *Ten Africans*. Margery Perham, ed. 2nd ed. Evanston: Northwestern University Press.

* Richards, Audrey I., ed. (1960). *East African chiefs*. New York: Frederick Praeger.

Ritter, E. A. (1955). *Shaka Zulu: the rise of the Zulu empire*. London: Longmans, Green and Co.

Robertson, W. Govan (1904). Kasembe and the Bemba (Awemba) Nation. *Journal of the African Society* 3:183–93.

Roscoe, John (1921). *Twenty-five years in East Africa*. Cambridge: Cambridge University Press.

* Sanders, William T. (1962). Cultural ecology of nuclear Meso-america. *American Anthropologist* 64, 1:34–44.

Schapera, I. (1930). *The Khoisan peoples of South Africa.* London: Routledge and Kegan Paul.

* ———— (1938). *A handbook of Tswana law and custom.* London: Oxford University Press.

* ———— (1940). The political organization of the Ngwato of Bechuanaland Protectorate. In *African political systems.* Meyer Fortes and E. E. Evans-Pritchard, eds. London: Oxford University Press.

* ———— (1943). *Native land tenure in the Bechuanaland Protectorate.* Cape Town: The Lovedale Press.

* ———— (1953). *The Tswana.* Ethnographic Survey of Africa. London: International African Institute.

* ———— (1956). *Government and politics in tribal societies.* London: Watts.

* Schapera, I., ed. (1934). *Western civilization and the natives of South Africa.* London: George Routledge and Sons.

* ———— (1937). *The Bantu-speaking tribes of South Africa.* London: Routledge and Kegan Paul.

Seaver, George (1957). *David Livingstone: his life and letters.* New York: Harper and Brothers.

Secord, Arthur W. (1961). *Robert Drury's journal and other studies.* Urbana: University of Illinois Press.

Segal, Ronald (1962). *African profiles.* Baltimore: Penguin Books.

Seligman, C. G., and B. Z. Seligman (1932). *Pagan tribes of the Nilotic Sudan.* London: George Routledge and Sons.

* Service, Elman R. (1962). *Primitive social organization: an evolutionary perspective.* New York: Random House.

* Sheane, J. H. West (1911). Wemba warpaths. *Journal of the African Society* 11:21–34.

Sheddick, V. G. J. (1953). *The Southern Sotho.* Ethnographic Survey of Africa. London: International African Institute.

* Shepstone, Theophilus (1875). The early history of the Zulu-Kafir race of South-eastern Africa. *Journal of the Royal Society of Arts,* Vol. 23.

Siegel, B. J. (1945). Some methodological considerations for the comparative study of slavery. *American Anthropologist* 47:357–92.

* Sillery, A. (1952). *The Bechuanaland Protectorate.* London: Oxford University Press.

———— (1954). *Sechele: the story of an African chief.* Oxford: George Ronald.

* Skinner, Elliott P. (1962). Trade and markets among the Mossi people. In *Markets in Africa.* Paul Bohannan and George Dalton, eds. Evanston: Northwestern University Press.

* ———— (1964). *The Mossi of the Upper Volta: the political development of a Sudanese people.* Stanford: Stanford University Press.

Smith, Michael G. (1955). *The economy of the Hausa communities of Zaria.* London: Her Majesty's Stationery Office.

* ———— (1956). On segmentary lineage systems. *Journal of the Royal Anthropological Institute* 86:39–79.

* ———— (1962). Exchange and marketing among the Hausa. In *Markets in Africa.* Paul Bohannan and George Dalton, eds. Evanston: Northwestern University Press.

* Southall, A. W. (1953). *Alur society.* Cambridge: W. Heffer and Sons.

* ———— (1961). Population movements in East Africa. In *Essays on African population.* K. M. Barbour and R. M. Prothero, eds. London: Routledge and Kegan Paul.

Southall, A. W., and Peter C. W. Gutkind (1956). *Townsmen in the making: Kampala and its suburbs.* Kampala: East African Institute of Social Research.

Spengler, Joseph J. (1956). *Population theory and policy.* Glencoe: The Free Press.

Spengler, Joseph J., and Otis D. Duncan, eds. (1956). *Demographic analysis: selected readings.* Glencoe: The Free Press.

* Stam, Rev. Father N. (1920). The Kavirondo of Mumias District. *Anthropos* 14–15:968–80.

* ———— (1929). The Bahanga. *Catholic Anthropological Conference Publications* 1:143–79.

Stamp, Lawrence Dudley (1938). Land utilization in Nigeria. *Geographical Review* 28:32–45.

———— (1953). *Africa, a study in tropical development.* New York: John Wiley.

Stayt, Hugh A. (1931). *The Bavenda.* London: Oxford University Press.

Steel, R. W. (1948). The population of Ashanti, a geographical analysis. *Geographical Journal* 112:64–77.

Steel, R. W., and T. E. Hilton (1952). *The distribution and density of population in the Gold Coast Colony and Southern Togoland.* International Geographic Union 17. Geographical Congress Abstract of Papers, Publication No. 6. Washington, D. C.

* Stenning, Derrick J. (1957). Transhumance, migratory drift, migration: patterns of pastoral Fulani nomadism. *Journal of the Royal Anthropological Institute* 87:57–73.

* Steward, Julian H. (1936). The economic and social basis of primitive bands. In *Essays in honor of A. L. Kroeber.* Berkeley: University of California Press.

* ———— (1937). Ecological aspects of Southwestern society. *Anthropos* 32:87–104.

* ———— (1955). *Theory of culture change: the methodology of multilinear evolution.* Urbana: University of Illinois Press.

* Steward, Julian H., and Louis C. Faron (1959). *Native peoples of South America.* New York: McGraw-Hill.

Steward, Julian H., Robert M. Adams, *et al.* (1960). *Irrigation civilizations; a comparative study.* Social Science Monographs No. 1. Washington, D. C.: Pan American Union.

Stewart, J. Q. (1947). Empirical mathematical rules concerning the distribution and equilibrium of population. *Geographic Review* 38:461–85.

* Stuart, James, and D. McK. Malcolm (1950). *The diary of Henry Francis Fynn.* Pietermaritzburg: Shuter and Shooter.

Talbot, P. Amaury (1923). *Life in Southern Nigeria: the magic, beliefs, and customs of the Ibibio tribe.* London: Macmillan and Co.

* ———— (1926). *The people of Southern Nigeria. A sketch of their history, ethnology and languages with an account of the 1921 census.* 4 vols. London: Oxford University Press.

———— (1927). *Some Nigerian fertility cults.* London: Oxford University Press.

———— (1932). *Tribes of the Niger Delta: their religions and customs.* London: The Sheldon Press.

Tauxier, Louis (1924). *Le noir du Soudan, pays mossi et gourounsi, documents et analyses.* Paris: Larose.

* Taylor, Brian (1962). *The Western Lacustrine Bantu.* Ethnographic Survey of Africa. London: International African Institute.

Theal, George McCall (1888). *History of South Africa (1795–1834)*, Vol. 3. London: Swan, Sonnenschein and Co.

* ——— (1898–1902). *Records of South Eastern Africa.* 9 vols. Cape Town: Cape Colony Government.

* ——— (1905). *The native races of South Africa.* George W. Stow, ed. London: Swan Sonnenschein.

——— (1916). *History of Africa south of the Zambesi.* Vol. 1. *The Portuguese in South Africa from 1505 to 1795.* 3rd ed. London: George Allen and Unwin.

——— (1919). *Ethnography and condition of South Africa before* A.D. *1505.* 2nd ed. London: George Allen and Unwin.

——— (1922). *History of Africa south of the Zambesi.* Vol. 3. *The Cape Colony to 1795, the Koranas, Bantu, and Portuguese in South Africa to 1800.* 3rd ed. London: George Allen and Unwin.

Thomas, H. B., and Robert Scott (1935). *Uganda.* London: Oxford University Press.

* Thomson, Joseph (1885). *Through Masai land.* 2nd ed. London: Sampson Low, Marston, Searle and Rivington.

Trapnell, C. G. (1953). *The soils, vegetation and agriculture of Northeastern Rhodesia.* Report of the Ecological Survey. Lusaka: Government Printer.

Turnbull, Colin (1961). *The forest people.* New York: Simon and Schuster.

Turner, V. W. (1952). *The Lozi peoples of Northwestern Rhodesia.* Ethnographic Survey of Africa. London: International African Institute.

——— (1957). *Schism and continuity in an African society.* Manchester: Manchester University Press.

* Trewartha, Glenn T., and Wilbur Zelinsky (1954a). Population patterns in Tropical Africa. *Annals of the Association of American Geographers* 44:135–62.

* ——— (1954b). The population geography of Belgian Africa. *Annals of the Association of American Geographers* 44:163–93.

* ——— (1957). New population maps of Uganda, Kenya, Nyasaland, and Gold Coast. *Annals of the Association of American Geographers* 47:41.

Udo, R. K. (1964). The migrant tenant farmer of Eastern Nigeria. *Africa* 34:326–39.

* —— (1965). Disintegration of nucleated settlement in Eastern Nigeria. *Geographical Review* 60:53–67.

United Nations (1963). *United Nations Statistical Yearbook, 1962.* New York: United Nations.

UNESCO (1963). *A review of the natural resources of the African continent.* Paris.

Urvoy, I. (1942). *Petit atlas ethno-démographique du Soudan entre Sénégal et Tchad.* Paris: Librairie Larose.

Van der Kerken, G. (1944). *L'ethnie mongo.* Brussels: Institut Royal Colonial Belge, Classe de sciences morales et politiques. Mémoires, old series 12, 1–2.

Vansina, J. (1960). Recording the oral history of the Bakuba. II. Results. *Journal of African History* 1:257–70.

—— (1962). Long distance trade-routes in Central Africa. *Journal of African History* 3:375–90.

* Vansina, Jr., R. Maury, and L. V. Thomas (1964). *The historian in tropical Africa.* London: Oxford University Press.

Varley, W. J., and H. P. White (1958). *The geography of Ghana.* London: Longmans, Green and Co.

Vaughn, James H., Jr. (1964). Culture, history, and grass-roots politics in a Northern Cameroon kingdom. *American Anthropologist* 66:1078–95.

Vedder, H. (1928). The Herero. In *The native tribes of South West Africa.* Cape Town: Cape Times, Ltd.

Venour, Capt. W. J., D. S. O. (1902). The Aro country in Southern Nigeria. *Geographical Journal,* 20.

* Verhulpen, Edmond (1936). *Baluba et Balubaises du Katanga.* Anvers: Les Editions de l'Avenir Belge 8.

Vilakazi, Absolom (1962). *Zulu transformation.* Pietermaritzburg: University of Natal Press.

Waddell, Rev. Hope M. (1863). *Twenty-nine years in the West Indies and Central Africa.* London: T. Nelson.

* Wagner, Gunter (1939). *The changing family among the Bantu Kavirondo.* Supplement to Africa, Vol. 12.

* Wagner, Gunter (1940). The political organization of the Bantu of Kavirondo. In *African political systems*. Meyer Fortes and E. E. Evans-Pritchard, eds. London: Oxford University Press.

* Wagner, Gunter (1949). *The Bantu of North Kavirondo*. Vol. 1. London: Oxford University Press. Vol. 2, 1956, ed. Lucy Mair.

* Wakefield, T. (1870). Routes of the native caravans from the coast to the interior of Eastern Africa. *Journal of the Royal Geographical Society* 40:303–38.

* Waller, Horace (1875). *The last journals of David Livingstone in Central Africa from eighteen hundred and sixty-five to his death.* . . . New York: Harper and Bros.

Wallerstein, Immanuel (1961). *Africa: the politics of independence.* New York: Random House.

White, Leslie (1949). *The science of culture.* New York: Grove Press.

———— (1959). *The evolution of culture.* New York: McGraw-Hill.

White, William (1800). *Journal of a voyage performed in the Lion extra Indiaman from Madras to Colombo, and Da Lagoa Bay on the eastern coast of Africa (where the ship was condemned in the year 1798) with some account of the manners and customs of the inhabitants of Da Lagoa Bay and a vocabulary of the language.* London: J. Stockdale.

* Whiteley, Wilfred (1951). *Bemba and related peoples of Northern Rhodesia with contribution on the Ambo by B. Stefaniszyn, S.J.* Ethnographic Survey of Africa. London: International African Institute.

Whittlesey, Derwent (1937). Kano: a Sudanese metropolis. *Geographic Review* 27:177–99.

* Wiedner, Donald (1964). *A history of Africa south of the Sahara.* New York: Random House.

* Wilks, Ivor (1961). The northern factor in Ashanti history: Begho and the Mande. *Journal of African History* 2:25–34.

* ———— (1962). A medieval trade route from the Niger to the Gulf of Guinea. *Journal of African History* 3:337–41.

Wilson, Monica (1961). *Good company: a study of Nyakyusa age-villages.* Boston: Beacon Press.

Wing, J. Van, S.J. (1959). *Etudes Bakongo: sociologie—religion et magie.* 2ieme ed. Leopoldville: Desclee de Brouwer.

* Winter, Edward H. (1956). *Bwamba: a structural-functional* *analysis of a patrilineal society*. Cambridge: W. Heffer and Sons.

* ———— (1958). The aboriginal political structure of Bwamba. In *Tribes without rulers*. John Middleton and David Tait, eds. London: Routledge and Kegan Paul.

Wittfogel, K. A. (1957). *Oriental despotism*. New Haven: Yale University Press.

———— (1959). The theory of Oriental Society. In *Readings in anthropology*, Vol. 2. Morton Fried, ed. New York: Crowell.

Wolfson, Freda (1958). *Pageant of Ghana*. London: Oxford University Press.

Worsley, P. M. (1956). The kinship system of the Tallensi: a re-evaluation. *Journal of the Royal Anthropological Institute* 86: 37–75.

Wrong, Dennis H. (1961). *Population and society*. New York: Random House.

Zelinsky, Wilbur (1962). *A bibliographic guide to population geography*. Chicago: University of Chicago Press.

INDEX

Aba, 192, 204

Abak, 213

Abam, as mercenaries, 206

Abiriba, as mercenaries, 206

Aboh, 168, 218; bombardment by British, 223

Abomey, 169, 216

Accra, 128

Acculturation, in North Kavirondo, 152, 153

Acephalous societies, Eisenstadt on Ibo, Ibibio, Yäko, 8; ratio of present densities to precolonial, 21; Nuer, Tallensi, Logoli, 115; North Kavirondo, 134; label questioned for Kavirondo, 149, 151; Ibo classified as, 167, 188, 193; Tiv, 172; East Africa, 176; Kiga, 177; Amba, 177

Ada (Edda), 204; as mercenaries, 206

Adjudication, among Aro, 205, 206; hierarchy, 209

Afikpo, 204

African-American Institute, 56; summary of Bechuanaland Protectorate, 57

African Political Systems (Fortes-Evans-Pritchard), formulation on relation between population density and political complexity, 4; reviews of, 4, 5; criticisms by P. Brown, S. Eisenstadt, M. Smith, J. Middleton, 19; Meek on classification, 201; Jones on classification, 201

Age grades, Ibo, 196

Age sets, Zulu, 32; Ibo, 199

Aguku, 200

Akan, 169

Akwamu, 169

Alladah, 169

Alsop, M., population profile, Zulu, 44, 45

Alur, parallels with Mamprusi, 126, 127; segmentary state, 175

Amba, 177; peasant cultivators, 178; immigration from Toro, 178; 181

Anderson, the missionary, 59

Andoni, 222, 226

Angola, 180, 185

Ankole, density of, 19, 174, 175

Arabs, trade with Bemba, 29, 99; invasion of Lake Mweru region, 99; Bemba-Arab attack on Ngoni, 99, 100; Bemba-Arab defeat by British, 102; influence on Bemba, 113; relationship with Kazembe, 113; slave trade, 184, 185

Ardra, Great, 216

Ardra, Little, 216

Aro Chuku, 190; as unifying factor, 196; oracle, 202, 203, 205; trade, 203; patrilineages and political organization, 203, 204; colonies, 204, 207; domination of trade routes, 204; Aro trade routes, 204; military activities, 205; use of the oracle, 205; financiers to Ibo, 206; use of mercenaries in trade, 207; monopoly of trade, 207; analysis of state, 207, 208; influence of area on emergent state, 208; Fried's secondary functions of state as applied to, 209; widespread recognition of Aro sovereignty, 210; date of emergence unknown, 212; domination of interior, 212; weakened by palm-oil trade, 215, 219; Expeditionary Force of 1901, 224; trading pax, 225; policy of divide and rule, 226

Ashanti, 169, 217

Atlantic Coastal Belt, 171

Aweil Dinka, 247n1

Awgu, 200

Awka, 192, 200

Azande, 180

Babatu, 130

Babwa, 181

Badintlha, 77

Bafaladi, 71, 77, 80

Bagakolodi, 76, 77

Bagamayo, 179

Baganda, 140

Bailie, A., 68

Bakabilo, 92

BaMbuti pygmies, 161; density of, 162

Bantu, population in Zulu and Natal, 46, 47; Tswana as Bantu-speaking, 54; 142

Bantu Kavirondo, 132

Bari, 128
Barkly, Sir Henry, 68
Barnes, J. A., on Nguni chiefdoms, 32
Barotse Kingdom, 186
Barrow, John, 60
Basutoland, 36
Bathoen, Chief of Ngwaketse, 56
Batlokoa, 36
Bawku, 125
Bechuanaland Protectorate, tribes of, 54; administration of, 54, 55; powers of British, 55, 56; environment, 58; reasons for establishment, 68, 69; German influence on establishment, 69; boundaries, 69, 70; settlement size, 71
Belgian Congo, 180, 185
Bemba, affected by Portuguese penetration into Zambesi, 27; trade with Arabs, 29, 99; population density, 88, 91; dispersed settlements, 88; coming of British, 88; shifting cultivation, 89; citemene, 89; crop yields, 91; crops, 91; cash crops, 91; copper belt influence on, 91; political organization, 92; Bemba chiefs, 92, 103; counsellor-priests, 92; matrilineal descent, 92; ranking, 92; royal women, 93; tribute, 93, 100, 111; migrations of, 97; trade and warfare, 99; expansion, 99; influence of trade in development of state, 99; boundaries at peak, 100; state and trade routes, 100; elephant-hunter specialists, 100; salt sources and trade, 101; cattle, 101; power basis broken by British, 101; defeat by British, 102, 103; population density analyzed, 104, 105; estimate of population, 105; modern boundaries, 105; shifting villages, 107, 108; communication with coast, 109; settlement size, 110; permanent villages, 110; tolls, 111; influence of stable and dense settlement, 111; development of state, 112, 114; destruction of, 114; density, 162; 181, 183; slave trade and depopulation, 184; shallow time depth, 186
Bende, 203, major slave market, 204
Benin, 168, 202; river, 217
Benis, 203
Benue, 223
Bida, 219
Bight of Benin, 214, 221

Bight of Biafra, 214, 221
Big Men, Tiv, 173; Kikuyu, Kamba, 179, 180; Ibo, 199, 259n11; assisted by Aro money, 206, 225; in Kavirondo, 253n27
Binger, G., 126; on caravan raiding, 128
Bira, 181
Bisa, middlemen, 96, 98
Boer, influence on Zulu, Ngwato, 27; conflict with Xosa, 30, 31; Boer advance, 30, 31; defeat of Zulu, 40; defeat of Matabele, 63; effect on Kgama III, 68; Boer-British tension, 69
Bohannan, L., on Tiv, 172
Bonny, 200; oil trade, 216; river, 217; establishment, 218, 220; war with Andoni, 220, 226; withdrawal of Jaja, 222; difficulties with Opobo, 222, 223
Bornu-Kanem, 170
Boundaries, Zulu, 43, 47, 48, 49; Bemba at peak, 100; Wanga, 139; Bunyole, Maragoli, 139
Braid, Will, 223
Brass River, 217
Brazil, slave trade, 184
Britain, influence on Zulu and Ngwato, 27; influence on Bemba, 88; breaking of basis of Bemba power, 101; intervention in Bemba succession, 102; effect of pacification on indigenous tariffs, Tallensi, 127; effect on Delta Trading States, 190, 221, 222, 223; Aro Expeditionary Force of 1901, 224; establishment of British state over southeastern Nigeria, 226
British Administration in North Kavirondo, 151; pacification, 151, 152
Bryant, A. T., 38, 40; pre-Shakan estimate of population, 42, 43; use of growth rates, 46
Buchanan, K. M., and Pugh, J. C., on Tiv economy, 172
Buffer zones, 178
Buganda, density of, 117; political communications with Kavirondo, 142, 143; 174, 182
Bulawayo, 36, 186
Bunyole, see Bunyore
Bunyore, inaccuracies of boundaries, 132; population density, 134, 161
Bunyore-Maragoli, density of, 162
Bunyoro, density of, 117, 175; 174; 178

Burton, R., estimates on effects of slave trade, 184, 185
Bushmen, 59, 66, 112, 161; density of, 162
Busoga, 139, 142, 143; depopulation, 175
Buye, 181
Bwamba forest, 177

Calabar, 191, 192; establishment of Old Calabar, 218; New Calabar, 220, 222; attempted secession by Will Braid, 223; intervention of British, 223
Cape Town, founding, 29; markets, 30; British entry, 31
Caravan routes, Wanga, 142; East Africa, 179; see also Trade routes
Cardinall, A. W., on density of Tallensi, 117, 118
Cash crops, Bemba, 91; coffee with Chagga, 176; coffee and cotton, Amba, 178
Central African zone, 180
Central Kavirondo, 152
Central Nyanza, 176
Cewa, 99
Chagga, density, 176; cash crops, 176
Chiefs, paramount, among Equatorial Bantu, 181
Chiefship among Wanga, 136; politically-loaded issue, 142; privileges of, 145
Childe, V. Gordon, on urban revolution, 2; Man Makes Himself, 4
Chokwe, 181
Church, R. J. H., on density of Zuarungu, 125; on estimate of Ibadan population, 168, 169
Citimene, 89
Citimukulu, 92, 93, 98, 99; competition with Mwamba, 102; description of capital, 109
Citimuluba, 94
City states, port-of-trade, 180; Onitsha, 200; Delta ties with Aro, 211; founding of, 218
Civil War, Bemba, 114
Clan, among Kavirondo, 135, 137; among Aro, 211
Colonialism, effects on population pattern, 164; on Atlantic Coastal Belt, 171
Communications, important condition for expansion of state, 16, 17; density bands and communication routes, 179
Congo estuary, 182; river, 182
Congo Free State, 185
Congress of Vienna, confirmed British position on Cape, 31
Conscription, Aro power of, 210
Copper belt, 89; influence on Bemba, 91
Cotonou, 169
Cross River, 192, 203, 217
Cul de sac theory of Zulu development, critique of, 239, 240n21

Dagomba, 118, 123; political ties with Mossi, Mamprusi, 123, 125; common origin with, 129
Dahomey, 169, 197; compared to Aro, 211, 212, 216, 220; important difference from Aro, 213; rise of state, 216, 217
Dakar, 171
Dande River, 182
Dar es Salaam, 179, 180
D'Azevado, W., on density and state, Atlantic Coastal Region, 171
Delagoa Bay, 35; trade with Dingiswayo, 47; as boundary of Zulu power, 48, 49
Delta Trading States, 190; trade in palm oil, 214, 215; markets, 219; law and order, 219; relationship with hinterland, 220; influence of British, 221
Depopulation, Northern Zululand, 41; Ngoni pattern, 51; among Bemba, 113, 114; Busoga, 175; in Central Africa, 181, 182, 183; from slave trade, 184, 185
Diachronic, perspective, utility of, 113; sequence, importance of, 156
Dike, K. O., on state among the Ibo, 207; on relation of oracle to slave trade, 214; on migrations to southeastern Nigeria, 218
Dikgosana, 77
Dingane, size of regiment under, 43; succession of, 49
Dingiswayo, began political centralization, 33; military tactics, 33; death of, 35; Portuguese, 47; trade with Delagoa Bay, 47
Dlamini, 37
Doctorow, O., on African Political Systems, 5, 10, 11, 15

Duffy, J., on effects of slave trade with Kongo, 183, 184
Dundas, K. R., on state among the Wanga, 138, 139; Wanga political organization described, 144; on ancestor sacrifices, 146; on law and penalties, 147
Dupuis Consul, on tribute of Dagomba, 123
Durban, founding, 38
Dutch East India Company, 29
Dutch West India Company, 29

Earth Cult, 121
East African Region, 174 ff.
Easton, D., on segmentation of support structure, 66; criteria of political development as applied to Tswana, 82, 83
Eisenstadt, S., on classification of Ibo, Ibibio, Yäko, 8, 195; on Nuer, Tallensi, Logoli, 115; on Tallensi chiefships, 118; on Bantu Kavirondo classification, 134
Emikuru, among Marama, 148
Equatorial Bantu, 181
Ethnographic Survey of Africa, 194
Europe, feudal, resemblances to Ibo, 199
European contact and trade, Ghana, 169; trade in Niger Delta, 218; traders in Niger Delta, 221
European settlers, relation to Bemba, 91
Evans-Pritchard, E. E., on density and political complexity, 4, 10, 11, quoted, 11-12; Group A, Group B dichotomy, 12, quoted, 12-13; population density-state correlation, 14, 15; on threefold relationship, 16, 17; criteria state and nonstate, 77; on shifting villages of Bemba, 107; generalization on stable vs. shifting settlements, 111; on Nuer, 116
Exchange, media of at Kwa-Sundu, 150
Export production, Tiv, 173
Eze-Aro, 203

Factionalism, among Kavirondo, 136
Fage, J. D., on reconstruction of Mamprusi-Dagomba history, 130; on Mamprusi, 131
Fang, 181

Fanti, 169
Farewell, Lt., 38; estimate of Shaka's army, 43
Ferguson, W., estimate of Zulu military strength, 44; composition of regiment, 45
"Feudal" institutions, among Karanga, 85
Finch, V., et al., on arithmetic density, 22; on economic density, 22, 23
Firearms, Ibo, 199
Fish River, 30
Fissioning among Zulu, 32, 34; among Tswana, 62, 73, 81; among Wanga, 140; Logoli, 148
Fokeng, see Kololo
Fon, hegemony, 169, 216; area of control, 217; see also Dahomey
Food-gathering bands, 161
Forde, D., and Jones, G. I., on Ibo political organization, 194; on Aro patrilineages, 203
Fortes, M., on density and political complexity, 4, 10, 11, quoted, 11-12; Group A, Group B dichotomy, 12, quoted, 12-13; population density-state correlation, 14, 15; on threefold relationship, 16, 17; criteria state and nonstate, 77; on shifting villages of Bemba, 107; generalization on stable vs. shifting settlements, 111; on cleavages Namoo and non-Namoo, 122; on powers of Namoo chiefs, 127; on oral tradition, Tallensi, 129
Fort Jameson, 186
Fort Victoria, 186
Fouta Djallon massif, 171
Freetown, 171
French Cameroons, 180
French Equatorial Africa, 180
Fried, M. H., ranking societies, 13; on social stratification, 66; on social stratification and relation to state, 80; primary and secondary functions of the state, 81, 208; ranking societies, 144; secondary functions of state applied to Aro, 209
Fulani process, 72, 73
Fulani, slave raids, extent of, 219
Fynn, 38, 47

Gamitto, 97
Gaseitsiwe, 68
German East Africa, 154

Ghana, Northern Territories, 117; Ancient Ghana, 170

Giraud, V., on Bemba settlement size and pattern, 109

Gluckman, M., on Zulu density figure, 39, 40; Zulu population estimate, 42, 47; on Zulu area of control, 48

Gold fields, 155

Goldie, Sir George, 224

Gold trade, Guinea Coast, 169

Goodwin, A., 58

Gourou, Pierre, population density, Asia, 2

Greece, ancient, resemblances to Ibo, 199

Green, M., on Ibo political organization, 194

Guinea Coastal Zone, density pattern analysis, 167 ff.

Hance, W., on Ibo density, 191

Hattersley, A., on Zulu military strength, 44; estimate on population, 46; Zulu area of control, 48, 49

Hausa-Fulani, 117, 161; density, 162, 170; trade routes, 203

Haya, 175, 179

Hilton, T. E., population density maps of Ghana, 169

History, conjectural, 130

Hobley, C. W., on regional trade network, 143; population estimate, North and Central Kavirondo, 149; estimate of Kavirondo density evaluated, 156

Hodgkin, T., 168

Humphrey, Norman, 132; on Bantu Kavirondo chiefships, 135

Hurutseland, 35

Hurutshe, 62

Ibadan, 168

Ibibio, 202; trading state, 203

Ibo, highly developed trade, 24; high density, 167; classified as acephalous, 167, 188; population density one of greatest, 190; antiquity of density, 192; trade network, 193, 197; political organization, 193, 194, 200, 201; social structure, 197; cult of ancestors, 197; traditional sanctions, 198; tolls, 199; resemblances to ancient Greece or feudal Europe, 199; title societies, 199, 201, 225; rule by wealthy, 200; social stratification,

achieved status, 200, 225; slavery, 200; Jones on political organization, 202, 203; indigenous home, forest area, 219

Idah, 202, bombardment by British, 223

Igala, 204

Igorot, 233n7

Ijaw (Ijo), 202, 203, 218

Ikot Ekpene, 192

Ilorin, 219

Imo River, 192, 217, 222

Indian Ocean trade, 174, 180

Indirect Rule, 114, 198

Interlacustrine Region, 174

Iron Age, B I, B II, in Rhodesia, 85

Isokos, 203

Itawkho, royal rank among Wanga, 144, 146

Ituri forest, 177

Ivory trade, Bemba, 29, 88, 109; Portuguese, 94, 95; Bemba interest in, 98; Lunda, 98; Bemba loss of control, 103; control by Mumia, 144; Central Africa, 183

Jackson, Sir Frederick, on Nzoia River-Wanga density, 150

Jaja, King of Opobo, 222; conflict with British, 222; deportation, 222

Jekiri, 203

Jennings, J. H., on Ibo density, 191

Johnston, B., on difficulties of determining physiological density, 23

Johnston, Sir Harry, on Bemba as cattle-raisers, 101; on density-estimate map of Bemba, 106, 107; density estimates along Luapula, 107; on rapid change in North Kavirondo, 152

Jones, G. I., on A-B classification in African Political Systems, 201

Jukun, 168

Kaa, as offshoots of Rolong, 59; attacked by Ngwato, 62

Kabaka, Suna, 142

Kabrai, 171

Kabrai Massif, high density, 170, 171

Kabras, trade, 144

Kaffir Wars, 33

Kakamega, trade, 144; gold rush in, 151

Kalabari, see Calabar, New

Kalobo, 186

Kalongo, 99

Kamba Reserves, 178; "big men," 179, 180; zoning for whites, 179; density band, 179
Kano, density, 170; 219
Kanye, population of, 75; population density of, 75
Kapandansaru, 102
Karanga, 84; metal work, 85; feudal-like institutions, 85
Kasai, 94, 180, 183
Kasama, 89
Katanga Province, 185
Kazembe, first, 95; trade with Mwata Yamvo, 96, 97; Kazembe II, III, 98; relationship with Arabs, 113; 183
Kede, 19
Kenya, 117, 132; Colony and Protectorate, 152
Kenya and Uganda Railway, Kisumu-Yala branch, 154
Kgalagadi, 59, 66, 78, 79
Kgama I, 62, 63
Kgama II, 63
Kgama III, 63, 64, 65, 67; missionary influence on, 68; reasons for wanting protection of British, 68, 69
Kgamane, 64, 65
Kgari, 63, 66
Kgatla, 54
Kgotla, 65, 77
Kiga, as acephalous, 177; possible clientship, 177
Kigezi District, Uganda, surrounded by states, 176; Purseglove on density, 176; density, 177; immigration from Ruanda, 177
Kikuyu Reserves, 178; "big men," 179, 180; zoning for whites, 179; density band, 179
Kilwa, 180
Kimberly diamond operations, recruitment among Ngwato, 68
Kimble, George, 181
Kimbundu, 181
Kirchhoff, P., on conical clan, 144
Kisumu, 152, 154, 179
Kisumu-Londiani, 152
Kitosh, 142
Kologo (Kurugu), 129
Kololo, effect of Zulu on, 27, 36; supported by sedentary populations, 52; effect on Ngwato, 66
Kongo, Kingdom, 180, 182; boundaries, 182; depopulation, 186

Konkomba, 118
Krader, L., on density and political complexity, 5, 15, 24
Krige, E., on breakup of Ndwandwe, 35; cited, 40
Kuba, 181
Kuczynski, R. R., cited, 117
Kumasi, density of, 117, 169
Kumba Kumba, 99
Kumu, 181
Kuna'aba, 123, 124
Kurugu, role in Tallensi chiefship, 124, 129
Kuruman River, 60
Kusasi, 118
Kwa-Ibo River, 217
Kwango, 94
Kwango River, 182
Kwa-Sundu, 150
Kwena, 54, 62

Labor, skilled and unskilled among Ibo, 193; migration, 193
Lacerda expedition, 97, 98, 112
Lacustrine Region, 161, 181
Lake Albert, 175
Lake Edward, 176
Lake Mweru, 97; Arab invasion of, 99
Lake Ngami, 58
Lake Victoria, 152, 179
Lala, 99
Lamba, 171
Land Tenure Committee, report, summary of Kavirondo political organization, 135; composite report, 137
Lengola, 181
Lete, 54
Levels of Socio-Cultural Integration (Elman Service), 1, 233n3
Lichtenstein, H., on Tswana, 60; estimate of tribe and settlement size, 61; powers of chief, 61; size of chief's house, 77
Lifiqane, 36
Liguru, 135
Limpopo River, 35, 36
Livingstone, David, 109
Logoli, density of, 18, 115, 132; compared to Zulu density, 50; high density, 117; Wagner study, 137; density analyzed, 150, 151; colonial factors influencing density, 150, 151, 155; economic factors influencing density, 154, 155; labor migration, 155; den-

Logoli (*Continued*)
sity a special condition, 158; tendencies toward state development, 158; corrected density, 159, 161
London Missionary Society, effect on Ngwato, 64
Long Juju, 203, 214; *see also* Oracles, Aro Chuku
Lourenço, Marques, 37
Low, D. A., on state among Wanga, 139; on "big men," 179
Lozi, slave trade and depopulation, 184
Luapula (tribes), 181
Luapula Valley, 94, 95, 107, 113, 183, 186
Luba, 94, 111
Lubaland, origins of Bemba, 94
Luba-Lunda, 180; satellites, 183
Lugard, Lord, on Nzoia-River-Wanga density, 150
Lugongo, 135
Luhya, 132
Lunda, relation to Bemba, 94, 111; trade with Portuguese, 94, 95; royal women, 95; Eastern Lunda, 95, 183; motives for expansion, 96; similarity to Tendaan-Namoo relationship, 96; population density and political complexity, 113, 181, 182; slave trade and depopulation, 184; shallow time depth, 186
Lungu, 99
Luo, 142; density, 176; immigration by, 182

Mackenzie, J., 64, 69; on Tswana "serfs," 79, 80
Mafeking, headquarters of Resident Commissioner, 54
Maize, as export crop, 154; production, North Kavirondo, 154
Makololo, *see* Kololo
Mali, ancient, 170
Malindi, 180
Malope, 62
Mamprusi, 118; relation to Tallensi, 118, 119, 122, 123, 124, 128, 129, 131; state, 120; Tri-Dominion, 123; political ties with Mossi and Dagomba, 123, 125; common origin with Mossi and Dagomba, 129
Mampurugu, role in Tallensi chiefship, 124
Mampurugnaba, 127, 128

Manikongo, 182
Manoukian, M., on investiture of Tallensi chief, 123, 124; on powers of Namoo chiefs, 127
Mantatisi, 36
Marama, 140, 148
Markets, Logoli, 148; control in, 149; southeast Nigeria and Aro control of, 209, 225; oil, 215, 216; in delta city states, 219; laws, 219; law and order, 219
Masai, mercenaries among Wanga, 140; density, 175
Masilo, 62
Matsheng, 64, 65
Matabele, effect of Zulu on, 27; defeat by Voortrekkers, 36; attacked by Dingane, 36; flight from Zulu, 48; supported by sedentary populations, 52; effects on Ngwato, 63, 66
Mavi, dominance, 148
Mbire, 85
Meek, C. K., on Ibo political organization, 193, 194, 200, 201; on Ibo social organization, 197, 198; on role of wealth, 198, 199; on A and B classification, *African Political Systems*, 201
Mercenaries, 199; use of by Aro, 205, 206, 210; influence on trade, 207
Metal, use of, by Karanga, 85; by Rozvi, 85, 86; brass wire, 143; copper bracelets, 146
Middleton, J., 115, 172
Migration, as used by Stenning, 72; water depletion as cause of, 73; frequent among Tswana, 73; southeastern Nigeria, 218
Migratory drift, 72
Militarism, in Zululand, 27; Bemba, 99, 103
Military activities, among Aro, 205, 210; among Delta Trading States, 220
Mituku, 181
Moçambique, 180, 186
Mochudi, population of, 75; population density of, 75
Mohurutshe, 62
Mole-Dagbane, linguistic distribution, 125
Molepolole, population of, 75; population density of, 75
Molopo River, 58

Mombasa, 179, 180
Mongu, 186
Monomotapa, *see* Mutapa
Monteiro, 97
Moshesh, 36
Mossi, 123; political ties with Dagomba and Mamprusi, 123, 125; caravan tolls, 127; common origin with Mamprusi, 129
Mosuor, 120, 124
Mpande, 40
Mpororo, 177
Mswati, 37
Mthethwa, 33, 34, 35, 37
Mumia, 140, 141, 144
Mumias, 140, 142, 151, 152, 155
Murdock, G. P., criticism of British Africanists, 19; on Naoudemba, Lamba, Kabrai, 171; on Equatorial Bantu, 181
Murunga, 142
Mutapa, Tswana origins, 84; Empire, 86; trade, 86
Mutesa, 142
Mutota Churuchamutapa, 85
Mwamba, 92, 93, 98, 99; competition with Citimukulu, 102
Mwata Yamvo, trade with Portuguese, 94, 96; 182, 183
Mzilikazi, 35, 63, 64, 66

Nabongo, 136, 139, 143; funeral, 145, 146; installation of, 146
Nadel, S. F., definition of state, 13
Nairobi, 155, 179
Nakuru, western, 152
Namoos, 96; Mamprusi origin, 119, 120, 121; monopoly of chiefships, 122; claim of common stock with others, 122; powers of chiefs, 127; loss of wealth, 128
Nandi, density, 175; analyzed, 176
Naoudemba, 171
Natal, Shaka's conquest of, 36, 37; Natal Republic, 40; boundaries, 43; population, 43; depopulation of, 45; estimates of population, 46, 47
Native Affairs Department Annual Report (NADAR), 141
Native Reserves, in Kavirondo, 152
Naval power, British, influence on Delta Trading States, 221
Navrongo, 118
Ndungunye, 37

Ndwandwe, 33, 34, 35
New, C., map of trade routes, East Africa, 142
New Juaben, 169
Ngoni, Zulu offshoot, 27; Fort Jameson Ngoni, 50; pattern of depopulation, 51; population density, 51; as a special type of state system, 52; dispute with Bemba, 99, 100; slave trade and depopulation, 184
Ngwaketse, 54, 62
Ngwane II, 37
Ngwato, product of penetration by Boer and Briton, 27; density, 53; largest of eight tribes, 54; founder, 62; as part of Kwena, 62; history of, 62-65; refugees among, 67; tributary relationship, 67; ward organization, 67; stratification, 70; population density in 1936, 70; reserve boundaries, 71; concentration of population to east, 71; territorial claims, 71, 72; cash crop influence on, 74; historical estimate of density, 75, 76; aboriginal political organization, 76; analysis of, 81; analysis of Ngwato as state, 82, 83; managerial role of chief, 84
Niger Delta, highly developed trade, 24; trade moving inland, 211; palm oil in hinterlands, 215; oil trade, 216; area of, 217; effects of ecology on state formation, 217; struggle for control of, 221
Niger River, 168, 192; system, 217; commercial highway, 218; introduction of steamboats, 223
North Kavirondo, 132; acephalous society, 134, 137; 140; British administration at, 151
North Kitosh, 140
North Maragoli, population density, 132
Nsukka, 192, 200
Nuer, density of, 18, 115; analyzed, 116; density, 162; Ibo compared, 200
Nyamwezi, 141
Nyanza province, 117, 132, 152
Nyoro, 177
Nzoia River, strategic position, 140; density node, 150

Ogoja, 191
Ohaffia, 204; as mercenaries, 206
Oil markets, 215, 216

Okavango Marshes, 59
Okigwi Division, 192, 204
Okpara, 197, 198
Oligarchy, of the wealthy in Iboland, 200; local, 201
Oliver R., on Bito, 182
Onitsha, 168, 191, 192; kingship at, 200; 218; bombarded by British, 223
Opobo, establishment of, 222; difficulties with Bonny, 222, 223
Oracles, and political organization, Tallensi, 128; Ibini Okpabe, Aro Oracle (Long Juju), 202, 203; univeral fear of, 205; use in slave trade, 205, 207; types of cases decided, 205; use with mercenaries, 207; development of theocratic state, 207; spread of organization, 209; facilitated trade, 212; as a major source of slaves, 214; Ottenberg on Aro oracle, 224; as court of last resort, 225
Orange River, 30
Oreri, 200
Orlu, 191, 192
Oror, 203
Ottenberg, S., on density of African states, 5; on Ibo density as precontact, 192; on Ibo political organization, 194; on major Ibo problems, 195
Ouagadougou, 125, 126
Owerri, 191, 192, 199, 200, 204, 213
Oyo, 217

Palm-oil trade, 169, 193; Aro as middle men, 207; influence on population density, 215; importance to Old Calabar, 218; expansion, 219; slump, 219; difficulties of, 220
Petauke, 186
Phaleng, 62, 66
Pim, A. W., estimate of Bemba density, 106
Polanyi, K., 217
Political Centralization, in Zululand, 27; Bemba, 99
Political Organization, southeastern Nigeria, 261, 262n24
Pombeiros, 96, 97
Pondo, 36
Pongola River, 34, 35, 37
Population, pressure on Xosa, 31; of Molepolole, Serowe, Mochudi, Kanye, 75; effect of epidemics on Bemba,

103; estimate of Bemba, 105; Taleland, 120; estimates insufficient, 163; colonial effects on population pattern, 164; Congo, 182; precolonial, 188; redistribution of by Aro, 208
Population Density, relation to political complexity, aboriginal South America, 1; aboriginal North America, 2; V. Gordon Childe on, 2; modern tropical Asia, 2; Fortes and Evans-Pritchard on, 4; L. Krader on Inner Asia, 5, 15, 24; Ottenbergs on density of African states, 5; Stevenson, 7; total population in states generally larger, 11; Fortes and Evans-Pritchard on correlation, 14, 15; Fortes and Evans-Pritchard on threefold relationship, 16, 17; arithmetic density, 21; economic density, 22; physiological density, 23; agricultural density, 23; types of density, utility of, 23, 24, 25; density and state formation not unicausal, 25; Zulu density, 39; analyzed, 40; necessity for single time level, 41, 42; pre-Shakan estimate, 42, 43; estimates of Zulu density, 46, 47, 49; Ngwato density in 1936, 70; historical estimate, Ngwato, 75, 76; densities of Molepolole, Serowe, Mochudi, Kanye, 75; Bemba, 88, 91; analyzed, 104, 105; Lunda, 113; Nuer, Tallensi, Logoli, 115, 132; Nuer analyzed, 116; densities of Zuarungu, Zaria, Sokoto, Kumasi, Buganda, Bunyoro, 117; Zuarungu, 118; Taleland, 118, 120; Trewartha on Tallensi, 125; Tallensi excluded, 131; South Maragoli, 132; North Maragoli, 132; Bunyore, 134; Nzoia River-Wanga, 150; Bunyole-Maragoli, factors influencing density, 154; Hobley's estimate of Kavirondo density evaluated, 156; Logoli density a special condition, 158; corrected density, Logoli, 159; Table I, 160; Table II, 161; Table III, 162; Areal-relative aspect of, 162, 170; positive relationship with state, 163; relative and absolute, 164; Yoruba, 169; peak density, average density, 170; nodal quality of, 170; Kano, 170; Kabrai Massif, 170, 171; Tiv, 172; Bunyoro, 175; Ankole, 175; Toro, 175; Busoga,

depopulation, 175; Sukuma, 175; Masai, Turkana, Nandi, 175; Nandi density analyzed, 176; Logoli, 176; Luo, 176; Chagga, 176; Moshi district, Chagga, 176; Kikuyu, Kamba, zoning for whites, 179; density bands and communication routes, 179; Central African zone, 180; Congo, 182; general correlation with state formation, 188; Ibo density, 191, 225; compared to Ruanda-Urundi, 191; Ibo, nineteenth century, 193; effects of Delta trade and refuge areas on, 211; influence of palm-oil trade, 215; relation to trade, 226; reciprocal relation to political organization and trade, 232; Aweil Dinka density, 247n1

Population geographers, surveys made by, 164

Porter, P., density map and population tables, 176

Porterage, Aro control of, 206, 210

Port-of-trade, 180, 217

Porto Novo, 169

Portuguese, trade with Mwata Yamvo, 94; slave trade, 95; ivory trade, 95, 98; 182, 183, 218

Primogeniture, among Kavirondo, 135

Privilege, presence among Wanga, 144; of Wanga chiefs, 145

Prothero, R., on Ibo density, 192

Purseglove, J. W., on Kigezi density, 176, 177

Quelimane, 180

Qwabe, 33, 35

Radcliffe-Brown, A. R., on Kavirondo political organization, 134

Railroad route, East Africa, 179

Rattray, R. S., 119; on Tallensi chiefship, 124; classes among Tallensi, 125

Refuge areas, south of Benue, 211

Rega, 181

Rhodes, C., 69

Rhodesia, 180

Richards, Audrey, on puzzling aspects of Bemba, 88; field studies, 89; on Bemba political organization, 92; estimates of Bemba population, 106

Ritual friendship, among Logoli, 148

Rolong, 59, 61

Royal women, among Wanga, 146, 147

Rozvi, 85; Iron Age B I, II culture, 85;

use of metals, 85, 86; trade with orient, 86

Ruanda-Urundi, high density, 161; density of, 162, 175, 191; density pile, 178; Ibo density compared to, 191

Sacrifice, to ancestors, Wanga, 146; Mavi, 148

Sakwa, 140

Sakwas, 140, 142

Salaga, 125, 126, 128

Salisbury, 186

Samia, 140

Samory, 130

Sanctions, traditional, Ibo, 198

Sarwa, 78, 79

Schapera, I., 54; on political organization of Tswana, 76, 77

Sebitwane, 36, 63, 66

Secret societies, Ibo, 196

Sedimo, 63

Segmentary societies, 115; Ibo, 188, 193

Segregation, enforced territorial, 186

Sekgoma, 63, 64, 65, 66

Sena, 95

Serer, 171

Serowe, headquarters of District Commissioner of Ngwato Reserve, 54; concentration of Ngwato, 71; population of, 75; population density of, 75

Service, E. R., levels of sociocultural integration, 1, 233n3; concept of chiefdom, 65

Setshele, 64, 65, 68

Settlement, Tswana, pattern, 60; size Tswana, 60, 61; size Ngwato Reserve, 71; shifting of among Tswana, 73; proximity of cattle posts and fields to Tswana settlements, 73, 74; Bemba pattern, 88, 107, 108; Yoruba, 168

Shabani, 186

Shaka, military tactics, 33; trade, 34; rise to power, 34, 35; conquest of Natal, 36, 37; height of Zulu power, 43; assassination of, 49; see also Zulu

Sharpe, estimate of Lunda capital, 113

Shaul, R. J., on densities in Northern Rhodesia, 186

Shepstone, T., 38; estimate of Natal population, 46; on chiefdom formation, 237n4

Shifting cultivation, Bemba, 89

Shila Nkuba, 98

Shire Highlands, density because of European settlers, 186
Shiundu, 140, 145
Shiundus, 140, 142
Shona, 63
Shoshangane, 35, 38
Shoshong, 62, 64
Skinner, E. P., on Tallensi political organization, 119, 124; on caravan tolls, 127
Slater Road, 151, 152
Slave raids, 130, 172, 184, 211; extent of Fulani raids, 219
Slave trade, Bemba, 29, 88, 99, 109; Portuguese, 94, 95; Bemba loss of control, 103; among Tallensi, 128; Guinea Coast, 169; Central Africa zone, 181, 182; Arab slavers, 184, 185; effects of, 185, 186; Ibo, 199; Aro, 205, 206; as middlemen and dictators, 207; Aro use of, 209; influence on population moves, 218
Slavery, among Equatorial Bantu, 181; among Ibo, 200, 201; Aro, 205; for inability to pay debts, 206; influences on supply of slaves, 211; source of supply, 213
Smith, S. R., on location of Aro oracle, 203
Smith-Mackenzie, 141
Sobhuza I, 37
Sobos, 203
Sokoto, density of, 117; 219
Somerville, Dr. W., 59, 60
Songola, 181
Sotho, raids by Kumalo, 35
South Africa, European settlement of, 30; British mastery of, 39; excluded from survey, 165
South Maragoli, density, 132; inaccuracies of boundaries, 132
Southall, A., Alur as segmentary state, 175
Southern Rhodesia, density arc, 186
Spanish Guinea, 180
Stam, N., on state among Wanga, 139
State, as an adaptive institution, 7; Nadel's definition of, 13; condition for expansion of, 16, 17; trade in development of, 25, 26; lacking among nineteenth-century Tswana, 61; Fortes' and Evans-Pritchard's criteria for, 77; analysis of Ngwato as, 82, 83, 84; influence of trade on

Bemba state, 99; influence of stable and dense settlement on, 111; spread of state systems, 111; development of Bemba state, 112; destruction of Bemba state, 114; among Wanga, 147; British, 150; positive relationship with population density, 163; Alur as segmentary state, 175; formation in Central Africa, 181; frequency in Sahara-Sudan fringe, 181; as response to slave trade, 196; Aro state, 207; analysis of, 207, 208; influence of area on emergent state, 208; widespread recognition of Aro sovereignty, 210; reasons for lack of further development in Aro, 212; rise of Dahomey, 216, 217; effects of ecology of Niger Delta on state formation, 217; reciprocal relation to population density and trade, 232
Stateless, Ibo, 188, 193
Steamboats, introduction to Niger, 223; influence on trade, 223
Stenning, D., 72
Sudan, French, migration from, 117
Sudan, Republic of, 180
Sudan-Sahara fringe, 181
Sudan, Western, 161; inventory of states, 170
Sudanese, soldiers in Kavirondo, 140; garrisons, 141, mutiny of 1897, 141
Sukuma, 175; density of districts, 175; Sukumaland, 179
Survey, use of decade 1951–1960 as basis, 166
Swahili traders, 139, 140; armed, 141
Swaziland, 34; borrowing of Zulu military tactics, 37
Synchronic method, criticized, 21, 42, 58, 104, 130

Tait, D., 115, 172
Talbot, P. A., on Aro population, 204; on Aro influence, 205
Taleland, density of, 118; description of, 119, 120; population, 120
Tallensi, density of, 115; district of Zuarungo, 117; antiquity of density, 117; traditional history, 120, 121; political system criticized, 123; political ties Dagomba-Mossi-Mamprusi, 123; chiefship, 123, 124; classes, 125; trade routes and state formation, 126; trade and political organi-

zation, 127; major cleavage, 129; Mamprusi hearth, 131; density excluded, 131

Tamale, 169

Tawana, 54; founding of, 62

Taxation, Aro, 210

Temne, 171

Tendaan, 120, 124, 128

Tete, 95

Theal, G., on estimate of Zulu military strength, 44; on population density of Natal, 46, 47

Thompson, J. Moffat, 105

Thomson, J., 149, 150

Timbuktu, 125

Tiriki, 148

Title societies, Ibo, 199, 201, 225

Tiv, 168, population density, 172; ethnic monopoly of benniseed production, 172; export production, 173; "big men," 173; density, pressure from southeast, 174; 202

Tlhaping, as offshoots of Rolong, 59; visit by Lichenstein, 60, 61

Tlokwa, 54, 66

Togoland, 130

Tolls and fees, Mossi, 127; for safe conduct among Ibo, 199

Tomia, 140

Tongaat River, 45, 49

Tong Hills, 120, 128

Tongo, 119, 120, 125

Tonking Delta, 233n6

Toro, 175; density of, 175; sovereignty over Bwamba, 177, 178

Trade, complicates economic density, 23; in Ibo region and Niger Delta, 24; regional and long-distance trade in state development, 25, 26; trade routes in Africa, 25, 26; Bemba trade with Arabs, 29; Rozvi trade with Orient, 86; trading networks, Bemba and Lunda, 94; trade in Luapula, 98, 99; influence on development of Bemba state, 99; state and trade routes, 100; salt sources and trade, Bemba, 101, Ijaw, 218; slave and ivory, 109; trade routes and state formation, Tallensi, 126; trade routes and political organization, Tallensi, 127; slave and Kolanuts, 128; as catalyst of Wanga polity, 143; regional network, 143; Hobley's description of, 143; cattle, 143;

Wa-Milambo salt trade, 143; Mumia ivory trade, trade through women, 144; Wanga chiefdom stimulated by, 151; Guinea Coast, 169; European contact and trade, 169; relation to state formation and density, 170; Indian Ocean trade, 174; Ibo network, 193; Aro trade and trade routes, 203, 204; facilitation of trade by Aro, 212; loss of monopoly by Aro, 215, 219; dependence of Delta States on British, 221, 222, 223; influence of steamboats, 223; trading empires, 226; relation to population density, 226; reciprocal relation to political organization and density, 232; see also Gold, Ivory, Palm-Oil, Slave trades

Trade, monopoly, by Aro, 207, 215; loss of, 219

Trade routes, state formation and, 126; among Wanga, 140, 151, among Aro, 203, 204; in East Africa, 252n21

Transhumance, 72

Trans-Nzoia, 152

Transport, control of porterage by Aro, 206

Transvaal, 35, 48

Trans-Volta Plateau, 120

Trekking, 29

Trewartha, G., on Tallensi density, 125; 164; on reliability of data, 165; on Ibo density, 191

Tribute, Dagomba to Ashanti, 123; for Mampurugnaba, 127; evidence for, 129

Tri-Dominion, Mussi-Mamprusi-Dagomba, 123, 169, 170

Trüter, P., 59, 60

Tse-tse fly, in Kigezi district, 176

Tshekedi, as Ngwato regent, 56

Tshukudu, 64

Tswana, effect of Zulu on, 27; raiding by Kumulo, 35; large concentrated settlements, 53; settlement patterns, 60, 73, 74; defense requirements, 60; water sources, 60, 73; estimates of settlement size, 60, 61; powers of chief, 61, 76; lacked state in nineteenth-century, 61; traditional history, 62; fissioning among, 62, 73, 81, 86; stratification, 66; cash crops, influence on, 74; historical estimate of density, 75, 76; aboriginal political

Tswana (*Continued*)
  organization, 76, 77; social stratification, 77, 78; serfs, 78, 79; symbiosis of
  Tswana-Bushman, 80; Fried's primary and secondary functions of the
  state as applied to, 81; fissioning of
  support structure, feature of, 82;
  Easton's criteria of political development as applied to, 82, 83; managerial role of chief, 84; western Tswana,
  density of, 162
Tugela River, 40
Tukela River, 49; *see also* Tugela
Tumbuka, 181
Turkana, density, 175
Turnbull, C., on Pygmy-Bantu symbiosis, 80

Uasin-gishu Masai, 140; Plateau, 152
Uburu, 204
Udo, R., on high density and dispersed
  settlements of Ibo, 213, 214
Uganda, 152
Uganda, Kigezi District, 176, 177
Uganda Railway, 152
Umtali, 186
Uyo, 192

Varozvi, *see* Rozvi
Vili, 181
Voortrekkers, 36
Vugusu, 137

Wachero, 145, 146
Wagner, G., on Kavirondo political
  structure, 134, 135, 136, 137; on
  Wanga, 138; on organization above
  the clan, 147; on ancestor sacrifices,
  148; on colonial influences in Kavirondo, 153; on rated growth, 157
Wahkitsetse Clan, 140, 142
Wahola, 140
Wakefield, T., on map of trade routes,
  142
Wakhalivu, 145, 146
Wa-Milambo, salt trade, 143
Wanga, 136, 138, 139; boundaries at
  peak, 139; anti-Wanga agitation, 141;
  persistence of power, 142; traditional
  geneologies, 143; trade as catalyst of
  polity, 143; regional trade network,
  143; political organization, 144, 145;
  interregnum clashes, 146; law and
  penalties, 147; European influence
  on, 147; state, 147, 175

Warfare, Zulu, 32; Zulu tactics, 33, 34,
  35; effect on density, 39; Bemba, 99;
  tribal, 184; Ibo, 194; means to, 199;
  control by Aro oracle, 205; as source
  of slaves, 213; in Delta, 221
Warrant Chiefs, 198
Warren, Sir Charles, 69
Washikava, 145
Whydah, 169, 216
Wiedner, D, cited, 30, 31, 40
Wolof, 171

Xosa, conflict with Boers, 30, 31; population pressure, 31; land scarcity, 31;
  effects of Shaka's conquests, 36

Yaka, 181
Yala River, 139
Yamaha, bombardment by British, 223
Yao, 98
Yendi, 123
Yoruba, state organization, concentrated
  settlements, 168; high density of dis-
  tricts, 169

Zambezi, Portuguese on, 95; Valley, 185
Zaria, density of, 117
Zelinsky, W., 164; on Ibo density, 191
Zimbabwe, 84, 85, 86
Zinza, 175
Zuarungu, density of, 117, 118; location, 120
Zulu, product of penetration of Boer
  and British, 27; political centralism
  and militarism, 27; agnatic lineages,
  32; fissioning, 32, 34; warfare, 32, 33,
  tactics of Dingiswayo, 33; tactics of
  Shaka, 33; rise of Shaka, 34, 35; conquests, 36, 37; density and effect of
  warfare, 39; density analyzed, 40;
  depopulation of Northern Zululand,
  41; boundaries, 43; population in
  1816, 43; estimate of military
  strength, 44; regiment composition,
  45; extermination policy, 45; area
  controlled by, 47, 48, 49; destruction,
  direct and indirect, 48; estimate of
  population, 49; modern density, 50;
  rapid expansion and contraction of,
  50; as a special type of state system,
  52; density, 162
Zwangendaba, 35, 38
Zwide, 34, 35, 37

DATE DUE

APR 25'			
FEB 5 '73			
H 3			
MAY 13 '76			
NOV 4 '80			
NOV 6 '80			
APR 1 9 1996			
MAY 07 1996			
MAY 06 1997			
JUL 03 1998			
DE 01 '99			
GAYLORD			PRINTED IN U.S.A.